DIVIDED
FICTIONS

DIVIDED FICTIONS

FANNY BURNEY
AND
FEMININE STRATEGY

KRISTINA STRAUB

THE UNIVERSITY PRESS OF KENTUCKY

Library of Congress Cataloging-in-Publication Data

Straub, Kristina, 1951–
  Divided fictions.

  Bibliography: p.
  Includes index.
    1. Burney, Fanny, 1752-1840—Criticism and
interpretation. 2. Women in literature. 3. Sex role
in literature. 4. Feminism and literature.
I. Title.
PR3316.A4Z79 1987   823'.6   87-21600
ISBN 0-8131-1633-3

CONTENTS

ACKNOWLEDGMENTS

I have looked forward to writing these acknowledgments as a kind of reward to myself for finishing this book. The people I name here not only helped with the production of this work, but also are, in one sense or another, part of the reason for it. Thanking them is naming part of the audience I wrote for—and naming is not, as feminist theory reminds us, without a certain significance.

I thank Paul Hunter, first, for suggesting Burney's fiction as a dissertation topic, for reading and refining my work, and for being the friendly mentor to whose example I constantly turn when I need to figure out how to do something in this profession. I also thank Bill Morgan for so many good readings of my work, for the sharpening of my critical skills against his fine intelligence, and for introducing me to word processing. Carol Neely and Mary Papke read my work on Burney, made valuable suggestions, and generally humored me through some professional tough spots while I was writing this book. Lore Metzger and John Sitter gave early versions of this study their time and made many useful and challenging comments. Margaret Doody's careful and generous reading of the manuscript determined much that seems best to me about its final form. Finally, my colleague at Miami, Dale Bauer, helped me to see what I was trying to say in early drafts of the final chapter.

The American Society for Eighteenth-Century Studies helped me make finishing touches with a grant to work at the Newberry Library; I thank both institutions for their support. The National Endowment for the Humanities may not have known that they

were helping me write a book on Burney when they funded Jane
Gallop's summer seminar on feminist criticism and theory, but I
thank them for helping me learn so much in so short a time and
for introducing me to Jane, to whom I owe the professional
confidence I needed in order to write this book.

Portions of chapters 2 and 3 were first published in *The Eighteenth Century: Theory and Interpretation* 27, no. 3 (1986); an earlier
version of chapter 4 appeared in *Eighteenth Century Life* 19, no.2
(May 1986). I thank the publishers for permission to reprint them
here.

The personal debts give me the most pleasure to name. Nat
Anderson has given me the benefit of her intelligence, humor,
and affection for all the years during which I was writing this
book—and then some. And Danae Clark puts up with me, even
as I write, with patience, affection—and rare grace.

For Nat

ONE

Critical Methods and Historical Contexts

Fanny Burney's *Evelina* gives us, on one hand, a distinctly interior view of eighteenth-century female life that seems to suggest the autonomy of female consciousness—Evelina telling Mr. Villars how strange it is to have her hair dressed, laughing her head off at a fop at her first ball—Cinderella demystified, as Anthea Zeman points out, transformed from feminine object to subjective consciousness. On the other hand, as Patricia Meyer Spacks makes clear, Burney's novel is also a text about female fear, self-doubt, and automatic deference to masculine authority—female subjectivity as almost entirely and, indeed, morbidly reactive to male initiative. Burney's fiction, read in 1986 with the second wave of feminist social reform pushing at our backs, often seems awkwardly strained in opposite directions: the text presents female experience as distinct and separable from the male while at the same time deferring to patriarchal authority as the moral yardstick for judging women's experience. Some of the best recent readings of Burney's first and most frequently read novel, *Evelina,* such as Judith Newton's in *Women, Power and Subversion,* suggest doubleness, a text that tries to go in two directions at once, toward both a "realistic" assessment of female difficulties and the solution to those difficulties in the ideology of romantic love.[1] The dividedness of the text provokes disturbing questions about Burney's reasons—conscious or unconscious—for writing. Such questions, if one cares to entertain them, even as investigations into unconscious impulses rather than attempts to get at clearly defined intentions, lead to problematic judgments about the novel: does this doubleness bespeak ambiguity, duplicity, or mere confusion?

The apparently self-contradictory nature of Burney's novels is potentially embarrassing both in the context of twentieth-century aesthetics and in that of feminist thinking about women's literature. It suggests, in the first place, that Burney's fiction does not satisfy the need for aesthetic coherence, the unity of purpose or design that makes sense out of complexity; in the second, it suggests that Burney is a feminist manqué, and leaves us nervously muttering excuses about the force of historical context and cultural determinism. I hope to suggest an alternative to these unsatisfactory approaches to Burney's fiction. By ceasing to worship "aesthetic" unity in the text, we shed the anxiety of needing to resolve our conflicting readings into a coherent, consistent aesthetic or political statement. Mary Jacobus writes that the writer's "moment of desire (the moment when the writer most clearly installs herself in her writing) becomes a refusal of mastery, an opting for openness and possibility, which can in itself make women's writing a challenge to the literary structures it must necessarily inhabit."[2] In other words, the writer refuses to extend her language to patch over the contradictions often implicit in cultural ideology, contradictions that tend to leave disturbing rifts in the fabric of words. Recent, theroretically sophisticated work on narrative fiction suggests that carefully *reading* these textual disruptions—instead of dismissing them as "flaws"—can result in interpretations that give voice to previously silenced modes of literary and cultural experience. Leslie W. Rabine, following Julia Kristeva's theoretical guidelines for reading, argues for the presence of a "fragmentary" female voice as well as "the unified masculine romantic subject" in romantic texts. Drawing from French feminist theorists such as Kristeva, Hélène Cixous and Luce Irigaray, Rabine suggests psychological and cultural grounds for not ending our reading process with merely affirming "the totalizing effect of representation," the creation of textual readings that celebrate rather than challenge formalist notions of "unity." Jane P. Tompkins' important work on American sentimental fiction grounds textual interpretation in a historically conceived theory of the reader reception of texts that challenges current academic aesthetic assumptions; Tompkins urges critics to stop stumbling over their own culturally bound notions of "timelessness" and "unity," and get on with the business of talking about how literature makes and reflects cultural ideology.[3] This study of Burney attempts to get on with just such a business.

Jacobus points out the subversive possibilities of textual contradictions, but in the case of Fanny Burney, the ideological gaps and contradictions in her texts seem the result of simple honesty about her cultural circumstances as woman and writer rather than a deliberate attempt to subvert: the doubleness I see in *Evelina* cannot be resolved as either a challenge or acquiesence to ideological conformity, however comforting—or disturbing— that resolution might be to our political and aesthetic sensibilities.

Rather, the disrupted and disruptive nature of *Evelina,* and of all of Burney's fiction, results from strategies for surviving some of the psychic and social contradictions that confront any human being in a constantly changing social context but are often especially acute in women's thinking. The ability to sustain and express contradiction is both a response to ideological conflicts in the culture and a strategy for female psychic survival in mid-eighteenth-century life. Whereas the eighteenth-century novel generally imparted to young women readers ideas and expectations about female life that have been summed up by Judith Newton as the ideology of romantic love—the assumption that female life gains value through romantically conceived marriage—much of the nonfiction written for, by, and about women in Burney's day expresses a vision of female life characterized by its low ceiling of expectations: an ideology of female powerlessness. Satire, conduct literature, sermons, periodical essays, and sundry forms of "advice to young ladies" tend to stress a fatalistic view of female life that is marked by loss, increasing powerlessness, and social worthlessness. This dark vision of women's lives would have informed the life expectations of a well-read middle-class woman like Burney, but it would not have completely defined them, to the exclusion of human expectations non-specific to female life. Rather, the ideology of female powerlessness, as it appears in her novels, journals, and diaries, contradicts culturally reinforced desires to assert self-worth, to maintain a continuing sense of personal power and social value—attitudes equally available to the young writer. The novels of Fanny Burney embody their author's struggle to express the conflicting "structures of feeling," to use Raymond Williams' term,[4] that determined, in part, Burney's situation at the time of *Evelina's* writing and publication.

Burney's social circumstances, as a middle-class young woman dependent on her family's limited economic support, shy, but with a significant, though partially vicarious knowledge of the public world of men and books, meant that she grew up with an ideological double standard, a set of assumptions about what the shape and day-to-day texture of *human* life should be—or was—and a somewhat different set of assumptions about what the shape and day-to-day texture of *female* life should be. I do not wish to suggest that young women of Burney's class and family upbringing were presented with "his and hers" ideologies, or that one set of assumptions is always separable from the other, but rather that despite overlapping and many shared assumptions about the course that life should take for men and women and how their time should be respectively occupied, young women such as Burney were likely to be confronted with ideas about their futures and the appropriate expenditure of their time that were not only different from parallel ideas for young men, but were in direct contrast, even contradiction to what was seen as right and satisfying for generic mankind. Whereas middle-class young men are encouraged to look forward to their futures, to conceive of the shape of their lives on the model of progress, young women like Burney are told not to expect too much from their maturing process—indeed, are often told to expect the worst. And while young men are told to see their time as valuable, too valuable to be wasted, middle-class young women are repeatedly told that their pastimes and occupations have little or no value.

As a result of the mixed and contradictory messages about what was good and/or reasonable to expect from human life—depending on whether the life was male or female—Burney's fiction is a mixed and contradictory *bricollage* of ideological assumptions. Few people can remain unconflicted about accepting a blighted future if the possibility of a happy one is held out by the culture; similarly, few would settle, without a thought, for a daily round of occupations that are seen as appropriate only for those without sufficient ability and status to do anything better. But for women in the eighteenth century, sexual and social identity depended on accepting just those roles that make the shape and texture of female life a depressing prospect and a degrading mode of experience to a young woman like Burney. The result in Burney's novels is the constant welling up—and, hence, exposure—of contradiction between the two opposing ideological impulses of Burney's duplicitous desires—to be human and a woman. The text seeks resolution to these contradictions by asserting the value of the heroine in the guise of romantic love object—one of the few conventionally accepted means to female power and self-assertion—but the gaps in this resolution suggest Burney's refusal to gloss over the contradictory messages of eighteenth-century attitudes toward the value of women's lives.

The notion that growing up as a literate middle-class woman was, for many women, an ideologically contradictory experience may suggest some historical grounding for many of feminist criticism's recent formulations for how middle-class women writers tend, as a class, to approach the problem of writing in cultures that do not readily accept the juncture of femininity and authorial power. The idea that women learn to be two-faced, to dissemble, to hide their "true" selves from the world is one of the insights of radical feminism that feminist literary critics have

incorporated into their readings of pre-twentieth-century women's texts. Behind many brilliant feminist readings, especially
of nineteenth-century women's novels, lies the assumption that
the woman writer is really two people, a masking presence
acceptable to male-dominated culture and an inner self that is
essentially female; this feminine duplicity, baldly posed as a
characteristic of women writers and their texts, suggests the
existence of an essential female quality that is ahistorical and
culturally nonspecific because it reifies the female side of the
writer's discourse (assuming that it exists) as being somehow
separable from and more important than the patriarchal aspects
of the text. The duplicity of Burney's fiction is not the female
discourse that Sandra Gilbert and Susan Gubar discuss, the palimpsest in which male-created conventions are subverted by a
"true" female sub-text,[5] but results instead in texts divided
against themselves, embodying the ideological rifts implicit in
female identity as it is created and creates itself in patriarchal
culture.

Burney's desire to write *and* to see the product in print, to hear
her work praised by the London literary circle of Johnson and
Thrale—in short, to see herself as valuable and as doing valuable
work—inevitably came into conflict with her orthodox adherence to what Mary Poovey calls the ideology of the "Proper
Lady," the strictures of female propriety that forbade such ego-
expansion as becoming a professional writer permits.[6] I am
suggesting that much of Burney's failure—or refusal—to resolve
her conflicting aspirations can be attributed to honesty rather
than hypocrisy: the desire to achieve two different kinds of
mutually contradictory value—as woman and artist—led her to
an unresolved doubleness that, in her fiction, reveals instead of
masking its own contradictions. This strategical duplicity is not,
I suspect, the special property of the woman who writes. The
contradictory roles of women within Burney's culture would
have made double vision a probable learned response to feminine
ideology in general as well as a way of seeing "woman" and
"writer" as linked, though contradictory, terms. Romantic love,

for example, gave the heroine power over male characters—at least selectively—while simultaneously placing strict limits on her behavior within the romance paradigm. Women's role in the "domestic sphere" granted influence and control over husbands, children, and even, to an extent, fathers—but also kept women within a narrow range of appropriate behavior and under the social and economic power of men. Women, in fiction and in life, were rendered powerless by feminine roles that were, in turn, their only means to empowerment. One way of sustaining this contradiction, Burney's career suggests, is through a duplicitous logic that seeks to make use of rather than reject socially sanctioned means of empowerment, but to do so from an ideological viewpoint that also recognizes the potential disempowerment implicit in these means. While this kind of doublethink on one hand simply perpetuates the cultural double bind of women's oppression, the strategy of feminine duplicity that Burney employs also serves to empower her—at some cost—in a male-dominated society and literature by allowing her to place herself within traditional ideological limits of femininity while simultaneously distancing herself from the social roles defined by such limits and assuming a measure of control over them.

This study of Burney will examine two ideological faultlines in her fiction—the contradictions that open up around cultural assumptions about the synchronically conceived structure of the female maturing process and around the texture of female life, the daily occupations that give female time its diachronic identity. Burney's first two novels, *Evelina* (1778) and *Cecilia* (1782), reveal much about the process of Burney's growing up as a woman novelist who took herself seriously as both an informed and carefully self-conscious writer and a woman with a commitment to ideologically orthodox femininity: the two novels reveal Burney's struggle to resolve these two sides of her identity, a struggle that successfully reveals the continuing process of its own culturally over-determined failure. I chose to treat *Evelina* in the most detail because it most clearly reveals the genesis of Burney's strategies for gaining "unfeminine" control over self-

identification while retaining the traditional power of femininity—the power of the "other," the romantic "treasure," as
Judith Newton has it—a kind of control that is all too likely to
recoil on its user.[7] The personal events that followed Burney's
considerable success with *Evelina* taught her the limitations of her
strategy, the extent to which she could not sustain the cheerfully
self-revealing contradictions of *Evelina. Cecilia* expresses Bur
ney's growing sense that she can't have it all, cannot sustain contradictory impulses—at least not without a cost in personal pain.
Whereas Burney's first novel probes hopefully at the possibilities
for control that duplicity seems to offer, her second focuses more
on the strains of contradiction. Thus, a close and careful comparison of Burney's two early novels reveals two sides—the *jeu*
and *angst*—of Burney's formulation of a strategy for writing in a
public mode, a mode that was at odds with large parts of her
personal identity. Burney's entrance into the public world of
authorship intensified both her need for and her anxiety about
writerly control over the cultural contradictions of mid-eighteenth-century female life, and *Camilla* (1796) and *The Wanderer;
or, Female Difficulties* (1814) continue to explore, in bolder and
more ambitious terms, the cultural paradoxes implicit in women's socially sanctioned means to personal power. I offer here a
sort of coda on these two novels rather than anything like a close
or complete reading of them, but my decision to focus on
Burney's earlier fiction is by no means meant to suggest that her
later work is a mere continuation of her earlier work. My focus
on Burney's *entrance* into public literary life seeks rather to deline-
ate, as a nondeterministic beginning for the study of Burney's
canon as well as of other works of eighteenth-century women's
fiction, a crucial event in literary history: Burney's fictional
realization, in the form of her first two novels, of the power
paradox implicit in the role of a woman novelist.

When Burney published *Evelina,* she was old enough to have
experienced the personal gratification of writing, not for the

public, but for a small, private, appreciative audience who led her to think well of herself as a writer of journals and letters. She was also just old enough, as a spinster of twenty-six, to begin to doubt her feminine worth. Samuel Johnson, in an expansive and avuncular mood while visiting the Thrales in London, once greeted her with the witticism, " 'Tis a terrible thing that we cannot wish young ladies well, without wishing them to become old women!"[8] The elderly Johnson found no difficulty in categorizing Burney as a "young lady": she was unmarried, fairly good-looking, and had the retiring, submissive manner and underlying warmth of feeling appropriate to a well-behaved and good-hearted schoolgirl. Whether Johnson actually saw and was alluding to the advance of her maturity or whether he merely wanted to tease or amuse her, he seems to assume that her potential, as a "young lady," is a negative one. Age is, indeed, a "terrible" enough fact in the eyes of an ill and aging man, but especially cruel, Johnson's remark implies, for women.

Johnson's witticism implies that a sort of doom lowers over the lives of women, and that twenty-six-year-old novelists are not exempt from feeling its imminence. Aging is an unqualified evil in female life—it makes a woman less attractive, less valuable, far less worthy of Samuel Johnson's approval—and furthermore, there seems to be absolutely nothing that a "young lady" (or a young lady novelist) can do about it. The assumption behind Johnson's remark to Burney is that the course of female life runs, inevitably, downhill, and Johnson was not, on this occasion, singular in his pessimism: the same theme occurs throughout writing for and about women in the eighteenth century. In educational treatises, moral essays, sermons, and the wide array of instructional literature written for women, writers echo again and again Johnson's idea that loss is inherent in the normal development of female life. Male life may or may not progress, ripen, and fulfill itself through the works of minds or hands, but female development seems placed under special strictures from its very outset.

A number of pessimistic cultural perspectives on femininity create the ideological prospect of eighteenth-century women's lives. A fatalistic approach to female life is reinforced by the eighteenth century's general tendency to lament the ephemerality and fragility of those qualities that the culture held most valuable in women: beauty and chastity. The vulnerability of female beauty to disease and age is a cliché of western Christian morality, the antidote to the sin of pride in women and concupiscence in men. This cliché may ask women to concentrate their energy on more lasting intellectual or spiritual qualities, but it also stresses the short period of their social power. Mary Hays replies to George Saville's famous observation, "You have more strength in your *Looks,* then we have in our *Laws,*" by pointing out that women can rule by *"Looks"* only up to a certain age, and there is more than a little insight into female social reality in the retort. Female maturity, as Hays and others knew, diminishes rather than develops female social power. Hence, Maria Edgeworth wryly commends the "wish of a celebrated modern beauty" not to live past twenty-nine as "good sense";[9] a woman who depends on the attractive powers of the flesh for a place in the world will soon find herself in the ridiculous position of an "Old Butterfly," as Halifax calls her. The ostensibly more durable quality of female chastity is often similarly described in terms of its imminent loss: "brittle glass, that may by accident fall and be broken."[10] Women's greatest social strengths rarely appear in didactic literature without accompanying warnings of probable loss and decay; even if virtue should remain intact, it still loses much of its power when its earthly vessel is no longer attractive.[11]

Of course, the fragility of mortal flesh is a part of eighteenth-century consciousness not wholly confined to women, and many of the metaphors expressive of female ephemerality are close to or the same as metaphors for human mortality in general: *"Flies,* that have pretty shining *Wings* for two or three hot *Months."* But when Mary Hays refers to herself as "Insect of a day," she is probably more conscious of her feminine presumption in addressing a male audience than she is of her mortality; metaphors like Thomas Gisborne's "bubbles vanishing, sooner or later, one after another, and leaving no trace of usefulness behind" or a mock-triumphant discovery of clouds as the perfect image for female mutability carry a particular sting for the women to whom they are applied.[12] The metaphors of ephemerality express a social as well as spiritual reality in women's lives: besides the cosmic condition of human insignificance, a condition shared by men, female worth has a special fragility, expressed in the smashed vase of *The Rape of the Lock* and the beautiful but brittle reputation that Burney's Mr. Villars attributes to women in *Evelina*.[13] Metaphors that express female ephemerality are more poignant than general Christian assumptions of human mortality because they suggest a tenuousness specific to moral as well as physical identity. Moreover, they come close to a painfully literal truth about female life: women have a special vulnerability to ephemerality because of the shortness of their time as socially valued beings. Childhood usually affords them the approval and support of parents, and the age of marriageability brings them into the light of public interest and praise, but their lives soon darken in the gathering dusk of female social maturity.

The young Fanny Burney brought to her fiction the assumption that maturity closed the pleasantest time in a woman's life: marriages locked most women into a prisonhouse of duty to husbands who felt justified in their despotism, while spinsterhood carried with it the risks of ostracism and ridicule. This way of looking at female life makes it a tragedy to which Burney gives a place in all her novels, even the Cinderella story of *Evelina*. The assumption that women spend their time in morally and socially useless occupations lends itself, on the other hand, more to comedy in eighteenth-century literature, a comedy that Burney incorporates into her fiction while, paradoxically, refuting the misogynistic implications that it so often carries.

Time is, indeed, troublesome to eighteenth-century women in more than one way. While it uses them ill, they are also commonly charged by their culture with using *it* in trivial, wasteful, morally debilitating ways; "women's work" ranks only slightly higher than the "dissipation" of their amusements and does little to bestow value on lives that are seen, in the first place, as briefly glamorous maiden plunges into the dullness and obscurity of mature life. The abuse showered on women's pastimes, particularly those of London social life and the labors of the toilette, makes the subject of female occupations and amusements a moral minefield through which Burney charts the progress of her heroines' quests for personal happiness and social value. The frivolous pastimes that occupy but do not corrupt the Burney heroine are often seen as representative not only of what women do but also of what they are; the identification of female life with time-wasting is so strong that it implies a superficiality damagingly attributed to the female character itself.

Women's pastimes are common vehicles for satire in the eighteenth century in part because the popular assumption that women have much time to fill and little to fill it with was so readily available to the writer's satiric purposes. Nonsatiric advice on how women should employ themselves is frequently informed by the same belief found in satire, that women too often give their time and lose their integrity to vain and foolish occupations. Even writers who approve of long hours spent on the toilette, social amusements, and fashionable "accomplishments" tend to see little value in such pastimes except as remedies for the ennui and emptiness of female life. Hence, writers like Swift and Pope were probably building on strong cultural associations between women and time-wasting which had only to be made explicit to become satire. In *The Rape of the Lock,* Pope narrates a day in the life of Belinda, from toilette to coffee, as a type of petty, narcissistic human behavior. The pastimes of upper-class women become mock-immortal emblems for the superficiality of their lives—

> Think not, when Woman's transient Breath is fled,
> That all her Vanities at once are dead:
> Succeeding Vanities she still regards,
> And tho' she plays no more, o'erlooks the Cards.[14]

—and Belinda's toilette is a blasphemous ceremony of female self-devotion. Moreover, Belinda's laborings to be beautiful suggest a dangerous artfulness, a false and treacherous ordering of fragments:[15]

> The Tortoise here and Elephant unite,
> Transform'd to *Combs,* the speckled and the white.
> Here Files of Pins extend their shining Rows,
> Puffs, Powders, Patches, Bibles, Billet-doux.[16]

Pope uses the female labor of the toilette to illustrate an art that is futile because it is based on false priorities—perhaps drawing on and certainly reinforcing the assumption that women's work is too trivial, too repetitive and ephemeral to result in true art. Clarissa paints more respectable options for female creativity, but her colors are dingy and her lines are faint: "what Huswife's Cares produce" in the world of the poem is a pair of scissors to cut the lock.[17] What readers feel is the superficially glittering futility and wrongheadedness of Belinda's occupations.

Swift pillories women for the childishness of their employment ("Poor Ladies! though their Bus'ness be to play, / 'Tis hard they must be busy Night and Day"),[18] but his charges against fashionable female occupations are usually too serious to allow this amused, paternalistic tolerance. For Swift, female amusements and vanities are perversions of human nature, a channeling of energy and emotion into dangerously shallow outlets. In "Cadenus and Vanessa," Venus regrets the fact that women of the age are more interested in fashionable playthings than in love:

> A Dog, and Parrot, or an Ape,
> Or some worse Brute in human Shape,
> Engross the Fancies of the Fair,

> The few soft Moments they can spare,
> From visits to receive and pay,
> From Scandal, Politicks, and Play,
> From Fans, and Flounces, and Brocades,
> From Equipage and Park-Parades,
> From all the thousand Female Toys,
> From every Trifle that employs
> The out or inside of their Heads,
> Between their Toylets and their Beds.[19]

The unhealthy sexuality of those "few soft Moments" suggests a particularly ugly tendency in the thoughtlessness and superficiality of women's obsession with "Toys," a suggestion also hinted at by Shock's ubiquitous presence in Belinda's bedroom. Swift insinuates that nastiness, in this case sexual but often scatological as well, lies beneath the glitter of fashion, and his insinuations become overt charges in poems like "A Lady's Dressing Room" and "A Beautiful Young Nymph Going to Bed." Swift, like Pope, uses the employments of the woman of mode as metaphors for what is mindless, nasty, and dangerous in human nature.

The nastiness that the satirist sees in female employments is an explicit form of the ugliness implicit in many milder estimations of women's use of time. Writers about female education, and hence, about the skills and projects appropriate to the feminine life and character, often echo Swift's image of woman as dirt tricked out in tinsel and Pope's insinutions of moral vacuity. James Fordyce's contempt for a "dirty woman" grounds in reality the hyperbole of Swift's outrageous Celia.[20] Similarly, the broad strokes that satirize old maids and paint female life as a hopeless vision of decline draw large the more moderate sketches of moralists and educators. When Swift and Pope image female life and consciousness as the chaotic circularity of a whirlpool, or an "eddy Brain,"[21] they are pointing to the same lack of progress and the wasting away of energy that the sympathetically gloomy Fordyce and John Bennett see as the shape of women's lives.

While it is easy (although reductive) to see Pope and Swift as misogynists, the greater danger to the female self-concept may, in fact, have come from the milder, more sympathetic sermons of Fordyce, the educational treatises of Hannah More, Maria Edgeworth, and Clara Reeve, the courtesy literature of Halifax, or the moral instructions of the periodical essayists. For, although such writings about women often merely imply the negative assumptions about the quality and shape of female life that the satirists openly state, they simultaneously institutionalize such assumptions by assigning the very pastimes they obviously see as dangerous or of doubtful worth to "women's sphere," the domestic or social realm of female action.

The satiric Pope may seem a harsher judge of women's pastimes than the gentle, sometimes gallant James Fordyce; yet the point of the satirist's vision may well be a firm belief in women's inherent and potential worth and a desire, however paternalistic, to broaden and improve the female realm of interests. Wider, brighter prospects are not, on the other hand, generally offered to women in books of practical or moral advice: immortality provides a promised land for women after death, but life must remain conventionally narrow. Writers who wish to improve women's education (and there are many) commonly hedge their suggestions for broadening women's minds with counter-endorsements for keeping their social and domestic behavior within traditional limits—the same ones that cramp action and ambition. Thus, writers such as Fordyce, Bennett, Johnson, Reeve, and Pennington give credibility and force to the assumptions that the quality of female life is vacuous or morally dubious and its shape a declining curve, and hence, they wield a stronger and more dangerous influence over the self-imaging of a writer like Burney (who read voraciously) than the "misogyny" of the satirists.

Perhaps a disclaimer is necessary at this point. I have no intention of deciding the actual shape of eighteenth-century female life (including Burney's), nor of determining whether or not women of Burney's class and above were really excluded from useful, prestigious forms of labor and respectable types of play. Cynthia Pomerleau's dissertation on female autobiography in the eighteenth century suggests that women often saw their lives in terms of loss, and the young Burney's apparent expectations as well as the old woman's retrospection support Pomerleau's findings, but whether Burney and the women whom Pomerleau studies saw accurately or too much through the lens of cultural expectations is another question.[22] Burney's active and respectable old age does not indicate any particular diminishment in her sense of value for her own life beyond the sense of loss that so frequently afflicts people who live long enough to see many of their friends and family to the grave. Similarly, it is hard to know whether or not women's employments and pastimes were really as vacuous as much of the literature makes them sound. Relatively little evidence of women's work and play is recorded, and much, until recently, has been ignored by scholars who did not think it important.

Lawrence Stone outlines changes that, after the turn of the century, gave the middle-class housewife increasingly abundant leisure to spend on dress and ornaments, and suggests that the growing affluence of the middle-class male and the decline of the self-sufficient household as an important unit of production made the middle-class woman more and more of a "status ornament" to her husband, a symbol of his rising social position—a situation not conducive to taking female occupations seriously for themselves.[23] Stone, however, has his critics, and many, such as Lois Schwoerer, have accused him of not paying sufficient attention to evidence about female life in the seventeenth century. In fact, Schwoerer argues, upper-class women managed their own and their husbands' money and participated in the business community as heads or co-heads of their households, and middle-class women were at least encouraged to take part in managing family affairs. Her corrective is a cautious one, based on her sense of the need for more information about female life: "We do not know enough yet to accept the well-worn conclusion that upper and middle class women led lives of leisure or idleness."[24] Women may, in fact, have been engaged in useful and gratifying employments, despite frequently recorded suggestions to the contrary.

Moreover, I must exclude from consideration what working-class women may or may not have been doing with or thinking about their lives. The documents I have used focus primarily on middle- and upper-class women, although I have also read a good many instructions to servants and suggestions for how trades-men's daughters should be educated. This material, despite its importance to women's history, has less bearing on how the thoroughly middle-class Burney saw herself than the enormous amount of material that is, apparently, directed at young women rather like her (and at their mothers). It is often difficult to tell, however, to what class of women particular tracts or plans of education are directed. Stone writes that eighteenth-century class lines did not always determine how women spent their time, and that tradesmen's daughters were encouraged in almost the same domestic and social pursuits as their upper-class sisters.[25] Although his conclusion is probably a reductive and distorting reading of women's social history, I can understand how he reached it; literature on the subject of women's education and employments tends to give readers an impression of uniformity in women's everyday pursuits that obliterates class lines. However, I will not duplicate Stone's claims for knowing what women actually did with their time. Whatever women's occupations were, much literature of the age depicts eighteenth-century female life above the laboring class as a bourgeois holiday, and Stone may be justified if one takes at face value the writings of the time, especially those of male moralists and educators, which reiterate over and over the empty, trivial nature of female pastimes and the hopeless prospect that haunts the beginning of female maturity.

Given the frequently unarticulated, culturally buried nature of woman's reality, it seems entirely possible that women—bourgeois as well as working class—were leading busy and useful lives while educators and polemicists worried over how they could employ themselves; Burney's role as not only manager but provider of her family's income after her marriage certainly suggests that not all middle-class women were at a loss for what to do with themselves. (The less exceptional case of Burney's stepsister, Maria Allen Rishton, suggests that the management of a middle-class household gave women more than enough to do, even when their husbands provided the money.)[26] Similarly, women may have actually found themselves mentally richer and psychologically more comfortable at fifty than at twenty, despite what the literature suggests about the declining worth and increasing sorrow of an aging woman. The pen has been, to use Anne Eliot's metaphor,[27] in other hands and (even when those hands were actually female) has left a record that often depicts women's maturity as dismal and their pastimes as trivial. That many women wrote about their experiences in the eighteenth century does not necessarily mean that their records are not informed by the perceptions learned from their culture—a culture that valued male over female.

Neither does this essay study the economic realities behind women's occupations in the eighteenth century, although a study of that topic would reveal that economic sanctions gave real force to assumptions about the worthlessness of women's employments. The economic danger of women's lack of training or opportunity for useful work is most certainly verifiable among the lower classes,[28] but the problem of the impecunious middle-class woman, brought up only to leisure and socially and psychologically unfit for paid labor, emerges sporadically throughout the century, finally making frequent appearances in the radical writing of the nineties. Clara Reeve, Priscilla Wakefield, Mary Ann Radcliffe, and Mary Hays write of the financial problems of the "unprotected" woman from firsthand experience,[29] and Arnaud Berquin shows an awareness of women's economic help-lessness.[30] This concern for the unmarried or widowed woman without means acknowledges the tragic side of female use-lessness, the side that Burney reveals in *The Wanderer*;[31] common opinion more often focuses, however, on the comedy, or perhaps melodrama, of the woman with economic security but without skill or opportunity to do anything that her society considers important. It is this woman that Burney takes on in *Evelina* and *Cecilia* and that I will primarily deal with here.

Burney's heroines reveal cultural contradictions in middle-class women's means to social and personal empowerment: the ways in which socially acceptable modes of feminine behavior promise the heroine security while simultaneously limiting the extent of her social and economic power. Her heroines' fictional experience with this power-paradox also reveals and comments upon particular awkwardnesses in the ideological position of the woman writer at mid-century. Is writing novels a means to social empowerment for women? Does it give them a public voice, a role in shaping how they are seen and are, in turn, shaped by their society? Or is it a dangerous erosion of women's established, albeit tenuous, means of social empowerment in romantic love and the domestic sphere? Burney was certainly *not* a monad, writing without a knowledge of or connection with the dozens of English women who had written fiction up through mid-century. And while this study must also disclaim a thorough analysis of Burney's fiction in relation to that of other women novelists of the eighteenth century, it assumes the implicit prem-ise that both Burney's urgency and her ability in exploring the contradictions implicit in the cultural position of women and of women writers were largely determined by an emergent tradi-tion of English women's fiction in mid-century.

The ideological place of the woman novelist was far from a settled social question, and the varying roles accorded to the heterogeneous group of women novelists who had gained fame—or notoriety—by the time of *Evelina's* composition would, I suspect, have contributed to rather than satisfied Burney's need to examine the cultural possibilities and liabilities of women writing in a public form. Writing fiction could be associated with a particular, sexualized outlaw brand of feminine otherness to dominant, bourgeois culture—as in the cases of writers like Aphra Behn, Delariviere Manley, and Eliza Haywood—or with a more respectable precedent of the lady instructor who teaches and amuses a genteel community of patronized or patronizing readers—as with writers such as Penelope Aubin, Frances Sheridan, or Charlotte Lennox. The ambiguous social definition of the woman novelist at mid-century constitutes a territory of ambivalent possibilities for female empowerment that Burney explores through her fictional heroines' quests for social control. The focus of this study—on Burney's specific, individual exploration of this territory—is not meant to suggest that she was a solitary female pioneer in a hitherto all-male field; rather, I hope it suggests specific ways in which an eighteenth-century woman novelist might have shaped the writer's role in relation to her culture. I hope, in turn, that these specifics might prove useful in developing broader, multifigural theories of the woman writer's role in eighteenth-century society.

Burney's first novel, *Evelina; or, The History of a Young Lady's Entrance into the World,* published in 1778, shows her partial acceptance of the young woman's iminent danger from her own maturity and occupations as well as her desire to reject it. The novel's fairy-tale resolution turns female decline into fulfillment, and the trivia of female occupations into rich emotional texture, but the text shows both Burney's acknowledgment of the social realities her fairy tale denies and her self-acknowledged dependence on her own powers, as a writer, to move others to affirm the integrity of female experience. Her redemption of female life, through an apotheosis-like happy ending, is not sentimental reliance on her society's ability to acknowledge and reward female virtue but, rather, a tenuous hope for the efficacy of her own writerly powers. Through the affective control of audience, Burney saw a way to find social affirmation for the value of her work, and hence, of herself, and *Evelina* expresses the tenuous sense of power that Burney gained, through her art, over the shape and quality of her experience as a middle-class young woman. Burney's sense of control over how others saw her, and over the unpromising material of her conventional experience as a young woman was shaken, however, by her encounter with a real audience after the publication of *Evelina*. By the time she was writing *Cecilia,* she seems to have felt the strain of exercising her powers as well as the personal imperative of continuing to use them to create emotional and social alternatives to the worthlessness that characterizes female maturity in her culture. In *Cecilia,* female creative power is less focused on preventing the heroine's near-destruction by attitudes and conventions hostile to her self-worth than it is on working to expose the cultural mechanisms that jeopardize the heroine's—and perhaps the author's—well-being. Burney's fiction, early and late, simultaneously expresses the hope and anxiety of the woman writer laboring to create a bright prospect for herself and other young women out of the ideological gloom of conventionally perceived female maturity, but after *Evelina,* Burney's fiction focuses more and more directly on the psychic and social dangers of such labor—and the personal and social need for it.

From *Cecilia* through *The Wanderer,* Burney's fiction bodies forth more and more dramatically the ideological contradictions implicit in *Evelina*. In *Cecilia,* romantic love leads to madness before it ends in the qualified happiness that marks a sharp departure from Evelina's apotheosis into the vaguely conceived perfection of married joy. In each of Burney's novels after *Evelina*—*Cecilia* (1782), *Camilla* (1796) and *The Wanderer* (1814)—a recognition scene leads to the hero's knowledge of the heroine's worth and her subsequent happy ending. This scene dramatizes as an act of temporary self-alienation the heroine's winning of the masculine recognition she needs: madness, in the case of *Cecilia,* delirium in *Camilla,* and a specifically sexual alienation from self in Burney's last novel, in which the heroine gives herself up to a husband she despises. Burney's fiction reveals more and more emphatically the self-division, alienation, and madness that are dangers of facing and sustaining ideological contradictions, contradictions generally implicit in eighteenth-century female life and particularly present in the work of the woman writer. Burney only hints at, as incipient possibility, alternatives to this self-division, but she unflinchingly expresses the ideological tensions inherent in the lives of eighteenth-century middle-class women—and the strain of writing them into consciousness.

TWO

EVELINA
Gulphs, Pits, and Precipices

Fanny Burney published her first novel, *Evelina; or, the History of a Young Lady's Entrance into the World,* when she was twenty-six years old and a spinster. Still young enough to be treated as a "young lady" by her friend and mentor Samuel Johnson, Burney was nonetheless on the brink of becoming an "old maid," one of the most problematic and vulnerable roles for a woman in the eighteenth century, in part because of its marginal economic status, but also because female maturity, especially outside of marriage, compromised women's powers of self-assertion and their claims to public esteem. "Young ladies," as Burney's outspoken "feminist" character, Mrs. Selwyn, suggests, might be "nowhere"—treasures too fine, too ethereal even to take up physical space—but the woman "over thirty" is, the misogynist womanizer Lord Merton retorts, "only in other folks way" (275). The culture in which Fanny Burney grew up and in which *Evelina* was created offered the mature middle-class woman few options for personal power, self-assertion, or social importance outside the "domestic sphere," and Burney's first novel accurately reflects, in its characterization of women "over thirty," the devaluation and powerlessness of women past the age of courtship. Of the older women who look after the young Evelina, Mrs. Mirvan is well-intentioned but ineffectual, while Mrs. Selwyn is more forceful but equally ineffectual; Madame Duval, Evelina's grandmother, is dangerously stupid, Mrs. Beaumont benignly stupid, and even the dignified Lady Howard crumbles, with as much grace as she can, before the will of her boorish son-in-law, Captain Mirvan.

It would be a mistake, however, to read *Evelina*'s mature female characters merely as the inscription of late eighteenth-century cultural assumptions about the powerlessness of wo-men—particularly the powerlessness that comes, in many cultures before and since, with the onset of age—because Burney's novel is not a seamless representation of the patriarchal ideology that Burney learned from her culture; nor is it, I would argue, a "palimpsest" such as Sandra Gilbert and Susan Gubar see as the form of nineteenth-century women's writing, a buried female subtext within a patriarchal cover story.[1] Rather it is a divided text that reveals its own dividedness—if we, as critics, can eschew the neat but perhaps reductive resolutions between dissonant impulses that a too-zealous devotion to aesthetic "unity" can insist on. Pierre Macherey writes that

what begs to be explained in the work is not that false simplicity which derives from the apparent unity of its meaning, but the presence of a relation, or an opposition, between elements of the exposition or levels of the composition, those disparities which point to a conflict of meaning. This conflict is not the sign of an imperfection; it reveals the inscription of an *otherness* in the work, through which it maintains a relationship with that which it is not, that which happens at its margins. To explain the work is to show that, contrary to appearances, it is not independent, but bears in its material substance the imprint of a deter-minate absence which is also the principle of its identity.[2]

The reading I offer here of *Evelina*'s portrayal of female maturity and its relationship to eighteenth-century culture is, then, an attempt to describe an otherness present in Burney's text which is not a feminine essence somehow separable from the ideology of male-dominated culture, but rather the historical immanence of change within ideology, of what Macherey calls "the uncon-scious which is history, the play of history beyond [the work's] edges."[3] Burney's treatment of the culturally problematic mature woman who has eluded direct male control reveals the process by which art uses, transforms, and makes the ideology that determines gender. *Evelina* shows us Burney's personal division in the course of this process, not as weakness or lack of artistic control, but as gaps in the ideological *bricollage* of Burney's text; not in the sense of empty ideological space, but in the sense of barely articulated, incompletely formulated ideological possibilities that the text cannot, at that moment in history, fully sustain.

Writing *Evelina* was, Judith Newton suggests, a kind of covering strategy, a way of envisioning a female destiny—marriage informed by romantic love—more cheerful than the "realistic" expectations for female maturity, while still expressing and acknowledging the painfulness of those expectations.[4] I would alter Newton's implied base/superstructure relationship between "life" and "ideology" to argue that Burney's first novel rather places in opposition two different social formulations for female destiny: the ideology of romantic love as the raison d'être of female life is juxtaposed, in the novel, to another set of cultural expectations about the course of women's lives that is equally ideological, equally embedded in late eighteenth-century ways of thinking about female maturity. While young women like Burney would have found numerous suggestions in their culture (particularly in novels) that youth ended in a love-match, a happy-ever-after ending to courtship, they would also have found a plenitude of suggestions to the contrary: assumptions that powerlessness and loss—not happiness—were the defining features of growing out of the conventional period of youth and sexual attractiveness. The conflict between these two ideologies leaves traces of strain in the novel, a tension that is itself ideological: the contradictions between the novel's ideologies are themselves incipient critiques of both definitions of female maturity. The reader is constantly tossed back and forth between the pain and loss of women "over thirty"—Mrs. Mirvan's genteel hell of a marriage, the effete male brutality of a race forced by unconsciously powerful young rakes between two physically

and socially helpless old women, for examples—and the Cinderella-like promise of Evelina's married happiness with Lord
Orville. Contradiction is a part of the experience of reading
Evelina and, hence, a part of the ideology produced by the novel.
The novel does not subvert social formations that define female
power or its lack in terms of women's relationship to men, but it
does throw these formations into disturbing juxtaposition and
suggests, in the most embryonic and incompletely expressed
terms, that female power would be more reliably grounded in
human relationships that were less lopsided, that gave precedence
to women as well as to men.

The relationships between Evelina and her older female mentors in the novel probably reflect Burney's uneasy feelings about
the apparently flawed, even threatening potential of her own
maturity. For much of the novel, this potential seems dim; the
failures of the mature women in the text to nurture or defend
Evelina parallel Burney's own sense of her weak potential for
growth or power: the older woman at the other end of the young
artist's life prospect is either a slightly worn, slightly sadder
version of herself or a vaguely frightening alter ego who uses
power in unfamiliar or intimidating ways. The "good" mature
women in *Evelina,* Mrs. Mirvan and Lady Howard, function in
reference to male authority: they acknowledge and work around,
under, or through patriarchal domination. Their effectiveness in
helping the young and vulnerable Evelina is, therefore, limited to
the extent that men in particular and social conventions in general
will allow. Evelina discovers that the length of a ballroom can
become a formidable barrier between herself and Mrs. Mirvan,
her mentor in London society, and that Lady Howard, for all her
dignity and social position, must cultivate ignorance of her son-
in-law's plots against Madame Duval, Evelina's grandmother, in
order to "support her dignity." The grown-up woman who
"misbehaves" offers, however, far more complex possibilities.
The self-defeating strategies of Mrs. Selwyn, the novel's mas-
culinized "feminist," and Madame Duval, the heroine's comic

and sometimes appalling grandmother, ultimately support both the dominant ideologies—romantic love and female powerlessness—that the text brings into conflict: Selwyn and Duval represent forms of behavior that Evelina must learn to avoid if she is to make the system of romantic love work for her. But Burney sketches, in a few brief moments of her heroine's consciousness, the potential for an alternative ideology in which women are valuable in terms of their importance to other women, instead of solely in relation to the men who give them value (or deny it) in female maturity.

Mrs. Selwyn, Evelina's guardian at Bristol Wells, is an outspoken, intelligent woman who seems to disregard her "place" as a mature, apparently unattached woman. Her apparent freedom from male control is, however, actually an unconscious, left-handed deference to masculine authority: her desire to entertain, impress, and dominate the male wits of the novel consumes her energies and condemns her to labor for the male approval she can never command. Hence, her effort is spent on an audience such as the wit Sir Clement, who devalues her satiric intelligence because she is a woman: "In a *woman* I think it intolerable" (343). Seen as powerless, she is actually so. Lord Merton, finding her with Evelina at Bristol Wells, surmises that "that queer woman" is the traditional mother or guardian aunt so inconvenient to lovers of beautiful young women. When disappointed of these handy, dismissive labels, he simply tucks her into the general slot of worthless female maturity: "Whoever she is, I wish she would mind her own affairs: I don't know what the devil a woman lives for after thirty: she is only in other folks way" (275). Mrs. Selwyn's characterization confirms both the powerlessness of the mature woman and the need for romantic love—which at least makes women "treasures"—as an escape from the grimmer aspects of that powerlessness.

Mrs. Selwyn's characterization is, however, one of the places in the text where Burney seems to swerve from defining female behavior in terms of a response or reaction to the male. Despite

Burney's premise that female power must operate out of an awareness of male power, Mrs. Selwyn's verbal talents create a gap in the novel's system of conventional moral judgment: Evelina's criticism of Selwyn points out, albeit negatively, the possibility for real power and value—if she were to act in a female context, and hence be judged on grounds of her value to other women instead of men. Mrs. Selwyn does not, Evelina complains to Mr. Villars, recognize the younger, less verbally aggressive woman's discomfort at being snubbed by the rest of the house party at Mrs. Beaumont's: "She is contented with behaving well herself, and does not, with a distinguishing politeness, raise and support me with others....she is herself so much occupied in conversation, when in company, that she has neither leisure nor thought to attend to the silent" (294). In company with women she lapses into "insipid" silence, reserving herself "for the gentlemen" (289). Yet in pointing out where Mrs. Selwyn fails Evelina, Burney seems to suggest potential success, if only the mature woman were less blinded by the attractive light of male power. Selwyn is generally too involved in plays for male approval to see her chance to be of genuine use to Evelina, but the exceptions to this rule in her behavior reinforce the sense of her wasted potential as Evelina's advocate. In this role, she is "quick as lightening in taking a hint" (345) and fierce in pursuing the younger woman's interests. Although she has uneven success as Evelina's protector, her persistence finally wins Evelina her father's recognition and her rightful inheritance. Judged in terms of her usefulenss to Evelina, Selwyn is a flawed but valuable character; her potential could, however, only be fully realized in a social context where masculine power is not the primary, indeed, the sole object of human desire—for women, the only source of economic and psychological security.

If Mrs. Selwyn represents the crippling effects of being hyperconscious of a male audience, Madame Duval possesses a kind of renegade female strength, gained through ignoring the social formations that define mature female power in relationship to masculine authority. The novel pits Duval's intractibility against the conventional, moral discourse of Mr. Villars, Evelina's guardian, a contest in which Villars sometimes finds himself unable to resist Duval's blind self-assertion: "What arguments, what persuasions can I make use of, with any prospect of success, to such a woman as Madame Duval? Her character, and the violence of her disposition, intimidate me from making the attempt: she is too ignorant for instruction, too obstinate for entreaty, and too weak for reason" (127). Villars' "reasonable" speech cannot always control a will that is impervious to conventional moral didactics; Duval does not transcend or even override the language of reason so much as she simply lies outside of its reach. Her intractibility, like Selwyn's aggressiveness, suggests possibilities for female power that the text's dominant ideological structures ultimately defeat, but, as is the case with Selwyn, Duval occasions the briefest of ideological gaps in Evelina's consciousness of what women are in the social formations of eighteenth-century female life. Although Burney, through Evelina, clearly rejects the moral chaos represented by Duval—who is portrayed as stupidly destructive to her daughter, Caroline Evelyn, and to her granddaughter, Evelina—Duval paradoxically achieves her most sympathetic, most fully human moments in relation to the young women whom she either destroys or comes close to destroying. When she hears of her daughter's death, "the agonies of grief and remorse, with which she was seized, occasioned her a severe fit of illness" (15). With her usual arbitrariness, she does not sustain this burst of motherly feeling in her subsequent relations with Evelina, but this note of serious human emotion jars against the broad comedy of her character. Later, when Duval discovers Evelina in London, she seems again endowed with a seriousness that does not fit with her "Ma foi's" and the absurdity of her banter: "Let me not lose my poor daughter a second time!" (53). Evelina herself feels the power of this "unexpected humanity," as she calls it, and is "softened" by her grandmother's remorseful protectiveness. Although this

emotional bond between old woman and young is of brief
duration, ending when Duval angers Evelina by "the ungrateful
mention she made of the best of men, my dear, and most
generous benefactor"—Mr. Villars, of course—it suggests just
the barest possibility, immediately withdrawn, for an alternative
to the ideology that defines women solely in relation to masculine authority.

Of course, Duval's moment of full human status is acted out in
the traditional role of grieving mother. I do not wish to suggest
that her characterization somehow transcends available ideology—female friendships and loving mother/daughter relationships exist in late eighteenth-century literature, although they are
decidedly rarer than romantic heterosexual attachments—but
rather that it is one of the points in the text of *Evelina* where the
ideology that places masculine power in the center of women's
lives is modified, softened by the suggestion of other ideological
possibilities. This brief glimpse of an alternative to the position of
women for or against male authority parallels Evelina's barely
expressed wish that Mrs. Selwyn would renounce her antag-
onistic role toward male society and redirect her energies toward
fulfilling women's social needs. Burney is far from imagining a
world of women in which being is not predicated on masculine
recognition—"he thinks, therefore she is"—but she does seem to
intuit the debilitating effects of male-centered ideology and to
voice a desire for such a world.

The characterizations of Selwyn and Duval hint at a woman-
centered system of social validation for the individual without,
however, subverting the male-dominated rules of eighteenth-
century culture; in doing so, they reveal Burney's duplicitous
relationship to the assumptions that render female maturity the
locus of powerlessness. For although she seems to wish her
heroine out of the male-centered system that humiliates older
women and mocks the younger with the prospect of their own
future loss, Burney makes quite clear, especially through Duval's
characterization, that a refusal to obey the rules of female aging

wins women nothing but additional humiliation. As carefully as Duval follows the rules of Parisian fashion, she breaks so many basic guidelines for female politeness that it seems unnecessary to catalogue them all. Most important, however, is her obtuseness about the rule that governs female aging, the expectation that a woman "over thirty," as Lord Merton says, will suppress her younger, desirable self and play an asexual, low-profile support-ing role in the drama of courtship. Duval seems blind to this rule, and makes herself ridiculous by trying to wield in middle age the social power once given her by youth and beauty. In an incident symptomatic of this self-delusion, Duval insists on dancing at a Hampstead ball, not only wishing to participate in an activity traditionally associated with young people and the rites of courtship, but wanting to display herself in a particularly con-spicuous manner by dancing a minuet. Her age, coupled with her attempts to ignore or efface it, expose her as ridiculous: "She danced in a style so uncommon; her age, her showy dress, and an unusual quantity of *rouge,* drew upon her the eyes, and, I fear, the derision of the whole company" (222). Duval's real pow-erlessness is not only specifically female; it results, at least in part, from her failure to understand the pattern of loss that defines female aging. Her unconsciousness of the standards by which her behavior is judged makes her unconventionality a weakness, not a strength.

Burney juxtaposes, in a conversation on the uses of hats, Duval's self-delusion with Captain Mirvan's deflating view of the older woman who attempts to hold on to the remnants of her former attractions:

"More likely," answered the Captain, "they were invented by some wrinkled old hag, who'd a mind for to keep the young fellows in chace, let them be never so weary."

"I don't know what you may do in England," cried Madame Duval, "but I know in Paris no woman need n't be at such a trouble as that, to be taken very genteel notice of."

"Why, will you pretend for to say," returned the Captain, "that they don't distinguish the old from the young there as well as here?"

"They don't make no distinguishments at all," said she; "they're vastly too polite." [59]

Duval's assertion that age does not matter to how a woman is seen is, of course, patently ridiculous. Duval is not only blind to the male moral authority that Villars represents; she is even incapable of perceiving the crude social truth of Mirvan's misogyny. Ignoring the interpretations that culture places on female aging, in the case of Mrs. Selwyn as well as that of Duval, does not prevent loss of social status: it merely increases female vulnerability.

Finally, Duval's failure to observe the rules of female aging erases the remains of any relationship with Evelina, and indeed effectively removes her from the novel, except as an off-stage disposer of legacies. Her pretensions to sexual options in her relationship with M. Du Bois place her in the traditionally ridiculous position of a Lady Booby and convert the rude power of her refusal of cultural meaning into an all-too-understandable emblem of female folly. When Duval discovers her paramour at Evelina's feet, the inarticulate and chaotic force of her rage turns her reproaches into garbled batches of words that can only serve as emotional hieroglyphs for her vulnerability and disappointment: "Hastily, with marks of guilty confusion in his face, he arose; but the rage of that lady quite amazed me! advancing to the retreating M. Du Bois, she began, in French, an attack which her extreme wrath and wonderful volubility almost rendered unintelligible; yet I understood but too much, since her reproaches convinced me she had herself proposed being the object of his affection" (252). The potential, rebellious strength implicit in Duval's refusal of the interpretations that culture places on female aging is ultimately defeated by the self-destructive and self-humiliating meanings that she unintentionally creates through her lawless and unselfconscious behavior. The obliteration of

Duval from the text (she does not appear on stage again in the novel) parallels and reflects the character's violence: she who lives in defiance of the rules of female maturity is excluded from the denouement by the action of those rules, and the romance plot that rewards Evelina's youth and beauty punishes and/or excludes the sexually ambitious mature women.

It should surprise no one to hear that Burney did not have the political consciousness to bring her intuitions about the debilitating effects of male-centered ideology on women's lives to the point of explicit social critique, that she accepted, if not without reservations, the ideology of romantic love for her heroines and herself; what deserves acknowledgment in Burney's fiction is the honesty with which she wrote ideological contradiction into her texts, exposing the need to change a set of assumptions that defined female maturity in such woman-defeating terms.

In eighteenth-century culture, childhood is the short, golden period of women's lives, generally portrayed, by both feminists and conservative polemicists, as an almost pastoral period of innocent thoughtlessness sponsored by a protective father who is—writers as different as Mary Hays and George Saville, Earl of Halifax, agree—kinder to his daughters than most husbands are to their wives. Hays contends that "Men in the character of father too, are...infinitely more amiable, and do more justice to the sex, than in any other character whatever." The duration of this kind treatment should not, says Hays, be expected to be long, and the reality that follows childhood's idyll is all the more bitterly felt because of the unrealistic, unworldly attitudes that the brief, protected period of childhood breeds. Young women

find themselves enclosed in a kind of magic circle, out of which they cannot move....In this circle, in this prison therefore, during the reign of youth and beauty they gambol and frisk away life as they best can; happily blind and thoughtless as to futurity. But what comes then? Untaught, alas! by education or habit to reflect in that manner, which by exercising the reason, cultivates the mind, and opens up every day new and latent powers: reflection is to them a source of vexation only. They indeed see clearly enough that they have been injured; but as they cannot see a way for redress, they often in despair turn to vanities and follies.

In spite of her analysis of the "PERPETUAL BABYISM" imposed on young women, and her clear sense of its harmful effects, even Hays slips into an all-too-understandable nostalgia for childhood's idyll. This note is also struck by the female persona in William Kendrick's *Whole Duty of Woman:* "O that I could overtake the wings of time! O that I could recall the pleasures of my youth! for the days of my womanhood have been days of many sorrows; the tears of misfortune have bedimm'd the lustre of my eye; the lily is fallen, and the rose-bud is blown and wither'd in my cheek."[5]

Sexual maturity is nearly always the dark cloud on the horizon of childhood's pastoral scene, as John Bennett muses—"If I was called upon to write the history of a *woman's* trials and sorrows, I would date it from the moment when nature has pronounced her *marriageable.*"[6] Although courtship brings women flattery and public attention, it also marks the beginning of flattery's end and leaves women unprepared for the social isolation that commonly comes either with marriage or merely with the loss of youthful charms: the deadeningly quiet life of the "domestic sphere." Samuel Johnson says that although no one benefits from growing old, age is "particularly to be dreaded by fine ladies, who have had no other end or ambition, than to fill up the day and the night, with dress, diversions and flattery.... With these ladies, age begins early, and very often lasts long; it begins when their beauty fades, when their mirth loses its sprightliness, and their motion its ease." Johnson does not confine his gloomy observations to "fine ladies," however; "a kind of conspiracy," he says, excludes happiness "in whatsoever condition" women pass their lives: "whether they embrace marriage, or determine upon a single life, [women] are exposed, in consequence of their choice, to sickness, misery, and death."[7] John Bennett warns women that "the sedentariness of your life, naturally followed with low spirits or *ennui,* whilst we are seeking health and pleasure in the field; the many, lonely hours, which in almost every situation, are likely to be your lot, will expose you to a number of *peculiar* sorrows, which you cannot, like the men, either drown in wine, or divert by dissipation." Maturity brings women—married or not—boredom, melancholia, and the spleen, while childbirth threatens more serious illnesses and early death; Richard Polwhele gloats over Wollstonecraft's death as a providential sign, which "strongly marked the distinction of the sexes, by pointing out the destiny of women, and the diseases to which they are liable."[8]

Much ink is spent—in eighteenth-century literature instructing young women about their future duties—on reconciling them to the loss of youthful pleasures and comforts. Preparing them to accept this loss gracefully is one of Halifax's primary motives, while Hannah More and James Fordyce stress educating women into employments that will allow them legitimate recourse from the boredom and regret that age, it is assumed, inevitably brings.[9] The threat of making oneself ridiculous is held up by Charlotte Smith and Thomas Gisborne to women who are inclined to resist going quietly into the realm of adult pain and ennui. And finally, religion is seen by Hestor Chapone as the best consolation for the mature woman and by John Bennett as "the only true and unfailing recourse, and its hopes and prospects, the only solid basis of consolation" in the gloom of female maturity.[10]

Hence, while the young Burney grew up with the idea that a woman's futurity could gain an aura of transcendent happiness through the magical effects of romantic love, she also grew up with ideological assumptions that gave her much bleaker prospects. It would be neat—but probably grossly reductive—to label the prospect of romantic bliss as "fictional" and the darker expectations as "realistic" assessments of eighteenth-century wo-

men's lives. In the first place, accepting the female courtesy and
educational literature of the century as anything close to accurate
reflections of women's experience would be somewhat like assuming that television commercials give a true picture of the
American middle-class housewife. Furthermore, early eighteenth-century fiction most certainly does not give a uniformly
bright picture of the salutary effects of romantic love on women's
lives. The romances of Eliza Haywood, for instance, with all
their emphasis on heterosexual love as the motive for action most
pervasive among heroines, dwell, in grueling detail, on the
disastrous effects—as well as the bliss—of such romantic attachments. Eighteenth-century novelists prior to Burney were certainly not uniformly selling romantic pipe dreams to their female
clientele. Rather, I am suggesting that both bliss and disaster were
available to Burney in mixed and contradictory proportions
throughout the several literary genres that could have influenced
her expectations. Reading Burney's *Early Diary,* however, gives
one a picture of the young novelist that is rather like an inversion
of the heroine in Charlotte Lennox's *The Female Quixote,* the
woman who believes every romantic convention that she reads.
In Burney's case, at least, the young woman reader may *hope* for
romantic attachment, but she *counts on* much less.

A comparison of Fanny Burney's journals with those of a
young man—James Boswell—is suggestive of how the social
formations of female life may have shaped her sense of her future
differently from a man's. In Burney's journals the future seems a
curiously barren spot in her imagination, and her vision of her
future self is almost invariably the image of a bored, lonely old
woman poring over the journals written by the young Burney:
on one occasion, she ends a debate with herself on the wisdom of
continuing her journal by deciding that "the pleasure which (in
imagination at least) awaits me in the perusal of these sheets
hereafter, pleaded strongly in favour of continuing to encrease
them." Positive expectations are reserved for the retrospective
enjoyment of the happiness currently in her possession: "I doubt
not but I shall hereafter receive great pleasure from *reviewing,* and

almost *renewing* my youth, and my former sentiments, unless, indeed, the latter part of my life is doomed to be as miserable as the beginning is the reverse, and then indeed, every line here will rend my heart!—I sigh from the bottom of it at this dreadful idea, I think I am in a humour to write a funeral sermon—."[11] The young Burney seems to invest her sense of identity in the present, seeing the time to come only as a replay through recollection and nostalgia, and this strategy is understandable in the context of a culture that offers young women such depressing future prospects. The Boswell of *The London Journal,* on the other hand, looks ahead for his "real" self, seeing the present as a more or less satisfactory process of becoming the definitive James Boswell. He enters London with a prospect far more sanguine than Burney's—"my soul bounded forth to a certain prospect of happy futurity"—and his visions of himself in the future almost always are of a happier, wiser, more complete and fulfilled man. Occasionally he is depressed over the contrast between his inconsistent, wildly variable present self, and "what GOD intended me and I myself chose," but his depression, at least in early life, is usually mixed with confidence in becoming the ideal in "happy futurity": "But I hoped by degrees to attain to some degree of propriety. Mr. Addison's character in sentiment, mixed with a little of the gaiety of Sir Richard Steele and the manners of Mr. Digges, were the ideas I aimed to realize."[12]

Just as it seems reasonable to suppose that Burney's ideas of her personal present and future are informed by cultural attitudes toward female life in general, it may be appropriate to attribute some of Boswell's forward-looking to lessons that eighteenth-century society taught its young men. Whereas conduct literature for middle- and upper-class young women stresses resignation and acceptance of a future much less interesting and usually less comfortable than the days of youth, instructional literature for males emphasizes the "task of improvement."[13] Youth, according to Blair's sermons, is a time to prepare for the truly important actions of a man's life—unlike a woman's, in which the important events occur primarily in youth.[14] Goals are the property of the male world; women are taught that any worldly objective beyond self-governance is unattainable and inappropriate. While young men are pushed toward excellence, the Edgeworths warn young women not to become too interested or progress too far in the lessons they are taught, since any strong engagement in an art or intellectual pursuit would make it more difficult for them to conform to a prospective husband's tastes [15] Low-profile mediocrity is safer and more virtuous in young women than working to excel in pursuits that gratify the ego and challenge minds or hands. These different assumptions about male and female life constitute what Raymond Williams calls "structures of feeling": the patterns of expectations in cultural consciousness that determine the generalized shape of life for men and women respectively. [16] The male pattern is progressive, forward-moving, whereas the female is static or regressive.

I do not wish to imply that male life was uniformly imagined to be rosy in comparison to the female; pessimism is certainly not confined to female circumstances in the eighteenth century. Rather, eighteenth-century minds seem to see men's and women's lives as structured differently, and the difference between these structures is apparent even when one is not valued as particularly better than the other. In Pope's "Epistle to Cobham," for example, the image of human life as a moving stream expresses discontinuity and rapid change. (Although Pope's "we" ostensibly includes both men and women, his humanity, I think it is safe to say, is identified with male experience. His terms certainly change when he speaks exclusively of women.) Pope laments that

> Life's stream for Observation will not stay,
> It hurries all too fast to mark their way.
> In vain sedate reflections we would make,
> When half our knowledge we must snatch, not take.

This is hardly a cheerful image, yet it implies a course with beginning, middle, and end; a potential for progress is embedded even in the despair. This potential breaks down, however, when consciousness is overwhelmed by emotion. Pope's imagery here suggests circularity and chaos: "Oft in the Passions' wild rotation tost,/Our spring of action to ourselves is lost." Yet even this momentary loss of orientation to a linear, progressive model must end in forward motion, if only by default: "Tir'd not determin'd, to the last we yield,/And what comes then is master of the field."[17]

Pope's image of female consciousness in "Epistle to a Lady" is, on the other hand, of endless entrapment in circularity, without the ultimate return to progress of "Cobham"—"No Thought advances, but her Eddy Brain / Whisks it about, and down it goes again."[18] Neither "Cobham" nor "To a Lady" gives a particularly optimistic view of human life, but Pope's imagery grows out of two radically different ways of seeing male and female life: male consciousness may churn in circularity for a time, but it finally spends itself in a moving stream, while the female chases itself, whirlpool-like, or shatters into a series of static portraits, each equally vapid and without connection to the other.

Burney did not, I must add, passively accept the "torrent of her fate," and her life, recounted in her diaries and letters, bears out the necessity of choosing carefully and knowledgeably among the admittedly few options presented by female experience. But the point remains that however bravely or intelligently Burney—or any other middle-class young woman, for that matter—arranged her life, it stretched out before her, as a woman in her twenties, as the promise of almost certain loss, not gain. Fatalism about the female prospect haunts, therefore, Burney's life and fiction and seems to gain the greatest influence in areas of her life where she felt herself to have the least legitimate control: most notably, in her attitudes toward her art and herself as artist. Here she seems to have found herself vulnerable in ways that left her without knowing how to choose, how to defend herself from new losses, new attacks against the ego.

Burney approached the socially conspicuous success of *Evelina* in a manner very like the way she approached the social contract of marriage; she saw it as a risky situation, in which a change could only be for the worse. Her sense of purpose and direction, however, which seems to have faltered very little in the matter of marriage, quickly failed her in her literary career. Why Burney published *Evelina* is unclear; she does not seem, in any case, to have expected the fame it would bring her, but once she had crossed this Rubicon her elation is consistently tempered with a fear of what comes next and a sense of helplessness in meeting the future:

What will all this come to?—where will it end? and when, and how, shall I wake from the vision of such splendid success? for I hardly know how to believe it real.

Well, I cannot but rejoice that I published the book, little as I ever imagined how it would fare; for hitherto it has occasioned me no small diversion and *nothing* of the disagreeable sort. I often think a change *will* happen, for I am by no means so sanguine as to suppose such success will be uninterrupted. Indeed, in the midst of the greatest satisfaction that I feel, an inward *something* which I cannot account for, prepares me to expect a reverse; for the more the book is drawn into notice, the more exposed it becomes to criticism and remark.[*DL* 1:34–35]

Burney assumes, perhaps with good reason, that her reputation will necessarily deteriorate: audiences sometimes do become more harshly critical after their first adulation of a best-seller like *Evelina*. This pessimism, however, robs Burney of her desire to go on writing, at least for the public eye:

I am now at the summit of a high hill; my prospects on one side are bright, glowing, and invitingly beautiful; but when I turn around, I perceive, on the other side, sundry caverns, gulphs, pits, and precipices, that, to look at, make my head giddy and my heart sick. I see about me, indeed, many hills of far greater height and sublimity; but I have not the strength to attempt climbing them; if I move, it must be downwards. I have already, I fear, reached the pinnacle of my abilities, and therefore to stand still will be my best policy.[*DL* 1:40–41]

The youthful Pope's image of alps upon alps in "An Essay on Criticism" comes to mind as a similar expression of the frustra-

tion and discouragement that attend progress, but Burney's recourse to stasis and her fear of falling suggest impossibility rather
than mere difficulty in moving ahead. Progress is simply not
available to Burney as a factor in time.[19]

Some of Burney's distrust of her public success could have
been reinforced, if not totally created by the literary atmosphere
of her father's home. As the child of a working writer, Burney
seems to have been brought up with unromantic ideas about the
relationship between writers and audiences. Writing was hard
work that one did for a sometimes unappreciative public. Her
father's work was done at the expense of sleep, and often, Samuel
Crisp's comments suggest, at the expense of his health and his
family's comfort.[20] Dr. Burney's efforts brought him a good deal
of success, but two visitors to the Burney household, John
Hawkesworth and Christopher Smart, gave Burney evidence of
what the reading public could do to health and sanity: her
journals record her awareness that both men had suffered much
unjustly dealt pain at the hands of the popular press.[21] Crisp's
short, bitter dalliance with publication also may have reinforced
her cynicism about audiences,[22] but her friends and family seem
to have taught her caution, not the paralysis, the fear of moving
ahead with her writing, that set in after *Evelina's* success.

While Burney blamed a cruel and wrong headed public for the
sufferings of Crisp, Hawkesworth, and Smart, she seems to
expect her own failure with the public to come as a matter of
course rather than of malice; indeed, she is far from cynical about
the audience that courted her after her identity as the author of
Evelina was revealed. Burney is starry-eyed in her responses to
the praise of Hester Thrale, Joshua Reynolds, Edmund Burke,
and Samuel Johnson, and except for criticisms from personal
acquaintances and family, seems to dwell on no lesser opinions.
Her fear seems focused not on present realities, but on what she
feels is her own inadequacy to live up to such adulation. Hints of
this fear creep into *The Early Diary* soon after her authorship
became known to friends and family; Susan Burney writes about
reading one of Burney's letters aloud to her father, "as I thought

you might wish to have no expectations raised concerning *futurity*
I omitted the passages I have cited above and the same to
Charlotte [Burney]—I know your muse to be so bashful that I am
terribly afraid of alarming her" (*ED* 2:251). Bashful herself,
Burney suffered somewhat under the insensitively expressed
interest the "young lady" writer raised, but her nervous euphoria
at becoming an important person in the eyes of those she admired
is not the same as the dread which overtakes her when she
contemplates the future: "I tremble for what all this will end in. I
verily think I had best stop where I am, and never again attempt
writing: for after so much honour, so much success—how shall I
bear a downfall?" (*DL*1:126-27).

Burney's anxiety about her future as a writer after *Evelina's*
success suggests feelings of powerlessness, of being caught in a
pattern of declining value that will inevitably overrule her powers
as an artist. In 1778, Samuel Crisp, her friend and mentor, gave
Burney advice on making the most of her success that may have
reminded her of the inevitability of declining value for the maturing woman: "You are now young, lively, gay. You please, and the
world smiles upon you—this is your time. Years and wrinkles in
their due season (perhaps attended with want of health and
spirits) will succeed. You will then be no longer the same Fanny
of 1778, feasted, caressed, admired, with all the soothing circumstances of your present situation" (*DL* 1:138). Crisp probably
meant to urge Burney to greater achievements as a writer, but his
manner of doing so expresses the imminent loss of economic and
social power that characterizes eighteenth-century culture's view
of female aging: Burney could not hold her value as the "Fanny of
1778," and the hope of recouping her losses as a writer must have
been feeble next to the grim sense of female destiny evoked by
"years and wrinkles." Hence, after the publication of *Evelina,*
Burney found herself in the ironic position of having written
herself into a new kind of powerlessness; what began as control
over the imaginative materials of fiction became a form of
powerlessness that must have felt depressingly familiar to her.

Evelina escapes from the gloomy destiny of female maturity
into the happy-ever-after of a fairy-tale ending, but despite her
escape, the novel evinces considerable awareness of the rules of
female aging, which limit chances for a life of romantic happiness. Evelina's happy ending repeats the tradition of Cinderella:
the girl who is "nobody" gains the love of a prince—or a lord—
and becomes "somebody." As Louise Bernikow points out, the
story of Cinderella's success at the ball is a story of female
competition for the prize of economic and social security—all
that makes for a happy ending.[23] And, while Evelina has no
apparent rivals, her success depends, like Cinderella's, on winning the loyalty of a powerful man in a social context—or
contest—that pits women against each other to gain the prize.
Burney seems to be of two minds about the social system that
sets women in competition against other women for the prizes
that male power can bestow: on one hand, this social system
rewards Evelina, but, on the other, it victimizes old women and
implicitly threatens the young with a similar prospect. Burney's
novel does not simply aggrandize female youth at the expense of
age: rather, *Evelina* draws parallels between the ill-usage of old
women and the sexual exploitation of the young, suggesting that
the two forms of abuse are related, and that while society would
divide and isolate women in a system of competition against each
other, women, old and young, are inextricably bound together in
a social system that exploits and mistreats both. One of the most
disturbing incidents in the novel is a race run by two old women
to satisfy the betting impulses of the thoughtless but powerful
young rakes who are gathered at Mrs. Beaumont's house at
Bristol Wells. While this race explicitly expresses the power that
wealthy men have over working-class old women, it also illustrates how the evils of victimization and oppression are implicit in
the workings of the whole society. Even those marked out for
marriage to "princes"—and the "princes" themselves—find
themselves complicit in the roles of victim and/or victimizer.

In the Bristol Wells section of the novel, Burney's focus broadens, paradoxically, as the wide social world of London diminishes to the more compact society of the resort community. The gathering at Mrs. Beaumont's house functions as a microcosm for the social context in which women are devalued and even brutalized, and the implicit misogyny that makes life for women within conventional female roles uncomfortable and life outside them untenable takes the guise of conventional attitudes that direct social behavior towards women. Misogyny informs the behavior of men who, like Lord Merton, appear to see women as disposable means to their personal ends, but it is also inherent in the very social forms that make up the polite world. Even women and men who mean women no harm are caught in the mechanisms of a society that is uncomfortable for and even dangerous to women. Burney's house party at Mrs. Beaumont's dramatizes the institutionalized oppression of women implicit in conventional social behavior.

"Gaming" is a central metaphor in the Bristol Wells section, both in the sense of gambling, the means by which men compete with each other for money and power, and in the sense of structured play, a kind of emblem for social interaction. Gaming of both sorts determines how the men and women gathered at Mrs. Beaumont's treat each other, and functions as a paradigm for how social interaction between the sexes so often hurts women, who seem to have little power over how the games are played. The most literal instance of gaming in the novel is, of course, the old women's race, which serves a clear purpose in the narrative: it underscores the powerlessness of women and the insensitivity of Burney's culture to female pain by giving both a rough, physical presence in the novel. The choice of old women as the contestants in the race is not, perhaps, an unprecedented one, but it is also not arbitrary.[24] The weakest and most helpless women are victims of the most overt physical brutality in this part of the novel. The hardship of the old women in this contrived game reflects and emphasizes the less overt violence inflicted on their younger counterparts in the social game-playing that more subtly victimizes young women.

Lord Merton, Jack Coverly, and Mr. Lovel all, of course, promote the scheme as a way of amusing themselves at gambling and competitive bravado. The activity of pedestrianism, the race itself, is perhaps as "unmeaning" as an earlier plan to decide a bet between Merton and Coverly by drawing straws (292). Like their phaeton-driving, the race is a rather puerile form of male competition, seen by Evelina (and by Burney) as the vying of child-men for power over others. These young men are probably not intentionally malicious (probably not intentionally anything), but their sheer willfulness makes decisions for the whole group; powerful without thought or concern for others beyond what fashion and economic necessity dictate, they exemplify the ways in which a privileged segment of society can selectively blind itself to the humanity of those it uses for its amusement or convenience.

Merton and Coverly apparently see the old women they have chosen as contestants no differently from the horses that they would have raced had not Lady Louisa's nervousness about phaetons altered their original scheme. They are highly solicitous of the elderly female racers when good treatment might lead to a victory. Their crude, obviously self-interested rush to assist the women to their feet, to fetch them seats, and bring them wine parodies chivalry and the "privileged" treatment warranted by female "weakness." The game that gives the two elderly, working-class women a temporary importance to their male "trainers" also entails, however, rules that legitimize their neglect and abuse; when Evelina tries to help Coverly's old woman to her feet after a fall, Merton prevents her with "no foul play! no foul play!" Coverly apparently sees no reason to treat his racer with any further humanity after she loses: when she is "too much hurt to move" he becomes "quite brutal," and "swore at her with unmanly rage,... scarce able to refrain from striking her" (312).

The brutal behavior of Merton and Coverly underscores the essential misogyny of many of the novel's male characters: Lovel persecutes Evelina through most of the novel; Coverly vies with Merton for her in drunken competition for "the best *young* woman" (313)—a prize of the moment who is devalued when sobriety returns to him a sense of Lady Louisa's status as a better investment. Lord Merton's behavior toward Evelina and Lady Louisa is more directly exploitative. The unprotected and socially unimportant Evelina is, of course, his sexual prey. But even his apparent subservience to the vapidly fashionable and wealthy Lady Louisa is an increasingly transparent cover for his intentions to use her as ruthlessly as he uses his old woman or attempts to use Evelina. Lady Louisa's despotism as a rich and attractive young woman is undercut by some stage directions from the novelist:

> "Do you know, Ma'm, we have done nothing but quarrel all the morning?—You can't think how I've scolded;—have not I, my Lord?" and she smiled expressively at Lord Merton.
> "You have been, as you always are," said he, twisting his whip with his fingers, "all sweetness." [280]

This Hardyesque bit of symbolic behavior (along the lines of Alec d'Urberville with a pitchfork) foreshadows Merton's more explicit aside concerning Louisa to Evelina: "She gives me a charming foretaste of the pleasures of a wife! however, it won't last long" (311). These men are ruthless opportunists in their behavior toward women, a point that is emphasized by their usage of the race contestants. Unhappily, as instigators of the games involving the manipulation of both old and young women, they make the rules and therefore determine, to a large extent, how the rest of society reacts to the play.

Although most of the company does not share Merton's irresponsible opportunism about women (indeed, many of them are women), he determines to a large extent what the group does, thereby making his cruelty into a small-scale social convention. The race becomes a spectator event, a source of amusement analogous to the entertainment provided by foolish old women throughout eighteenth-century English literature. This scene at the "race course" dramatizes the moral myopia and social helplessness of the women who are drawn along by Merton's plans. Lady Louisa is, of course, Merton's complete dupe. Mrs. Beaumont and Mrs. Selwyn are considerably less taken in, but their resistance to Merton's bullying is a limited defense of their own egos, not a desire to prevent harm to others. They apparently offer no objection to the race itself, but they decline Merton's entreaty to "*bet on his side*". The terms of their respective refusals indicate the solipsism of even this weak resistance: "Mrs. Selwyn said she never laid a wager against her own wishes, and Mrs. Beaumont would not *take sides*" (310). Mrs. Selwyn is motivated by sheer personal willfulness, a determination to do only as she wants, while Beaumont is, typically, more concerned with the mechanics of distributing her patronage in an equitable manner than she is with the actual welfare of those around her. Neither expresses disapproval on grounds of moral and social responsibility, and Evelina does not exempt them from the crowd of laughing spectators at the race's beginning. Their passive acquiescence suggests both an inability to act counter to male wishes and a self-protective focusing of energy on the preservation of what they define as their integrity. Their behavior at the race is a paradigm of their ineffective protection of Evelina; their moral strength and vision are no more adequate to protecting the young woman than they are at shielding the old.

The behavior of Selwyn and Beaumont at the race is a type of their behavior during the sexual games in which Evelina is unwittingly the target. Mrs. Selwyn's verbal barbs are not, as I have said, always at Evelina's service, but when she does employ them to protect her protegée, they tend to glance harmlessly off the complacency shielding male power. When she and Evelina are set upon by "three gentlemen, who were sauntering by the side of the Avon, laughing and talking very loud, and lounging so disagreeably that we knew not how to pass them," Selwyn boldly threatens to "give my servant the trouble of teaching you better manners": "her commanding air struck them, yet they chose to laugh, and one of them wished the fellow would begin his lesson, that he might have the pleasure of rolling him into the Avon" (273). The rakes are merely amused, until Lord Merton, who is one of the three, saves the two women from further gang molestation when he recognizes Evelina, whom he has previously seen in London. His motives are, of course, far from disinterested, and Evelina is liberated from one form of harassment only to be subjected to another. The erratic, whimsical desires of a man like Lord Merton are more likely to determine Evelina's treatment than the "commanding air" of her female protector; Mrs. Selwyn's assurance that Evelina "may depend upon *me* for keeping him at a distance" (276) may be read with some irony. Mrs. Beaumont's rare attempts to discourage male bullying are based on a sense of what, in propriety, is due to her, and they are equally ineffectual. When Lord Merton drunkenly assaults Evelina before his fiancée's face, Mrs. Beaumont "must beg leave to interfere; I know not if Lady Louisa can pardon you, but, as this young lady [Evelina] is at my house, I do not chuse to have her made uneasy" (313). Mrs. Beaumont's wishes have little effect, and it is Orville who must oppose his rights "as a brother" against Merton's predatory will.

Despite the benign intentions of Lord Orville, the old women's race finally makes clear another social/sexual truth: even those who openly despise such games are made complicit in them by the rules for accepted behavior governing their roles. The behavior of Evelina and Lord Orville dramatizes the unwilling complicity of the few who dissent from the games that victimize women. It also suggests, however, an unrealized potential for deviating from the rules of such woman-victimizing games: as in the characterizations of Selwyn and Duval, Burney points to incipient possibilities for a culture that values women, young and old.

Evelina's part as a sentimental young beauty includes the capacity to pity the old women but not the ability to act, and she is literally stopped by the rules of the game: "a foot of one of the poor women slipt, and, with great force, she came again to the ground. Involuntarily, I sprung forward to assist her, but Lord Merton, to whom she did not belong, stopped me, calling out 'No foul play! no foul play!'" (312). Significantly, Evelina's abortive action is involuntary—not a move considered in social consciousness, but an unarticulated and unformulated impulse outside the rules governing social activity. The race illustrates, in almost allegorical fashion, the social dynamics that make female life depressing in prospect and painful in experience. Those who play by the rules of this cruel social game are not aware of or interested in the inhumanities they commit, while those who break the rules do so with an unselfconsciousness that guarantees defeat. In a sense, Evelina's spontaneous kindness is akin to Madame Duval's rude spontaneity: both are female impulses ill calculated to succeed in a social game too bound by its masculine orientation to admit, for either good or ill, flexibility in its rules.

The old women's race suggests both the destructive effect of social games that exploit women and the apparent inevitability of obeying the rules. But, as with Burney's treatment of female maturity in the cases of Duval and Selwyn, the race sequence in the novel also dramatizes the incipient possibility of alternatives to the social system that allows an easy tolerance of abuse towards women. First, the heroine's subjective point of view does not allow readers to accept the events of the race uncritically: "When we were summoned to the *course,* the two poor old women made their appearance. Though they seemed very healthy for their time of life, they yet looked so weak, so infirm, so feeble, that I could feel no sensation but that of pity at the sight" (311). Evelina feels "pity" and finds more to laugh at in the behavior of the observers than in the appearance of the contestants: "The scene was truly ridiculous; the agitation of the parties concerned, and the bets that were laid upon the old women, were absurd beyond measure. *Who are you for?* and *whose side are you of?* was echoed from mouth to mouth by the whole company." Evelina's narration turns the laugh on those who find the exploitation of female helplessness funny; the old women are possibly amusing to

readers in a crude, physical way, but the real comedy and certainly the satire of the novel are directed at the gamesters who act
out a grotesque parody of an eighteenth-century old-maid joke.

Evelina's point of view, however, also emphasizes her helplessness to act—except as writer, recorder of the scene. And even
this access to a means of expression is hedged by uncertainty, the
unanswered question of whether Evelina's pity can be shared and
acted upon by anyone but herself. Lord Orville, who acts in other
cases as Evelina's morally sympathetic social agent, remains
opaque in his responses to the race, a moral cipher who may or
may not enter into Evelina's feelings on this occasion. While
Orville resists the thoughtless schemes of the gamesters, his
motives for doing so seem defined entirely by a morality opposed to gambling, not humanitarian sympathy for another's
suffering. Evelina's attribution of humaneness to Orville's proposal for settling the bet is cryptically laughed off, neither denied
nor confirmed:

> "I should have hoped," said I, "that the humane proposal made
> yesterday by your Lordship, would have had more effect."
> "O," cried he, laughing, "I was so far from expecting any success,
> that I shall think myself very fortunate if I escape the wit of Mr. Coverly
> in a lampoon! yet I spoke openly, because I do not wish to conceal that I
> am no friend to gaming." [295-96]

Orville focuses on the question of gambling, and gambling is the
only issue on which he can influence the players. His powers do
not extend to curtailing the game altogether, but are confined to
controlling money, the currency of male competition, not its
social and psychological impetus (foreshadowing the nature of
his protection of Evelina as his acknowledged future wife—his
financial power insures her safety). "Gaming" is the primary
issue in Orville's moral stance as he explains it; Evelina seems to
assume this priority when she speculates that his gravity during
the race indicates concern over the profligate behavior of Lord
Merton, his prospective brother-in-law: "Doubtless he must be

greatly discontented at the dissipated conduct and extravagance, of a man with whom he is, soon, to be so nearly connected" (311). Lord Orville's real feelings about the race are unknown, except for this observation; Burney also fails to give us any dramatic hints. After the race he is "thoughtful, and walked by himself" (312). Orville's withdrawal, his silence on the moral issues posed by the race's ritualized cruelty to women, leaves a gap, an empty moral space that may be the possibility of sympathy with Evelina's feelings—or merely silent dissociation from her.

The inconclusiveness of Orville's response suggests uncertainty and irresolution in Burney's view of alternatives to the social rules of victimization and domination that govern relations between men and women, young and old, ruling and working classes. Burney's historically determined inability to do more than expose the contradictions in the ideology that shaped her sense of female maturity—the conflict between a happy-ever-after romantic marriage and the depressing "gulphs, pits, and precipices" of futurity—left her vulnerable to debilitating self-doubts from which a more fully conscious critique of received ideology might have protected her. The limits of Burney's political vision, however, should not blind *us* to the clarity with which she saw the limited, contradictory options in female maturity, and the honesty with which she portrayed the need for more choices in women's lives. Burney's characterization of the mature women at the other end of her prospect reveals the point at which ideology strains against itself, almost but not quite giving presence to new ideological possibilities. What might seem to be flaws in the novel, instances of Burney's loss of control over her development of the themes of female powerlessness and the need for romantic love to transcend it, are perhaps more fully analyzed and understood as moments in the process through which art is shaped by and, in turn, shapes ideology—which is never, in this process, either static or entirely new. The socialist feminist re-analysis of texts such as *Evelina,* as I suggest here, yields a vision of our female precursors which is neither entirely reassuring nor alienating to the feminist critic of 1986. Burney is neither with us nor against us, feminist or patriarchal. We can see her work rather as a part of the process of ideological change that we perceive from our own moment in history: a clue to understanding—not validating or denying—our current personal and political desires.

THREE

EVELINA
Marriage as the Dangerous Die

If the vista of a middle-class young woman's future was composed, in Burney's day, of "gulphs, pits, and precipices," a happy
marriage, according to the conventions of sentimental fiction,
might well be expected to take her to another country, a timeless
realm in which her problematic maturity could be subsumed into
the promise of happy-ever-after. And this displacement of loss by
gain, powerlessness by security, is, of course, the psychic and
social change dramatically expressed by Evelina's marriage and
her removal to Berry Hill at the end of the novel, the retreat from
the world to a sort of domestic utopia. *Evelina* is not, however,
committed to the *probability* of happy marriage as a way out,
however convinced it seems of the desirability of such an escape.
Nor, apparently, was Fanny Burney, who wrote in her diaries
prior to *Evelina* that she needed *"particular inducements"* to unite
herself "for life with one who must have full power to make me
miserable, and perhaps none to make me happy—for it is such
chance!" *(ED* 2:88). Marriage was, in Burney's view, a risk with
potentially catastrophic results that was probably better avoided
than taken. Judith Newton reads Evelina's marriage as Burney's
reaction to her own traumatic experience as an unwilling prospective bride on the marriage market just two years before
writing the main portion of *Evelina:* Burney, Newton argues,
sought in the conventions of sentimental fiction ideological alternatives to the degradation she felt in her own experience as a
marriageable young woman.[1] However ambivalent, even pessi-

mistic, Burney's feelings about marriage seem to have been in
life, fictional marriage could give both the author and her readers
the illusion of culturally sanctioned personal empowerment for
women. And Evelina's marriage is, in fact, just such an illusion, a
fairy-tale drawing down of the curtain on the fair prospect of
Evelina's future happiness.

But even in fiction, Burney does not fully endorse the romance of happily-ever-after. *Evelina,* the most happily and
blithely romantic of Burney's novels, exposes the jarring contradictions between Burney's two ideologically determined perspectives on marriage—as both the means of escape from female
maturity's hardships and as an institution that formalizes and
justifies those hardships. The melodramatic story of the Evelyn
family, related in one of Villars' first letters to Lady Howard,
becomes the background against which both readers and characters in the novel see and understand Evelina's circumstances as a
sexually desirable young woman, a history that sets up the
premise that marriage for women means powerlessness and loss
of integrity, perhaps even personal destruction. The Evelyns'
history is distanced by time (it is a fictional "history," not an
event), form (the stuff of romance, the remote doings of un-
defined, undeveloped characters), and placement in the novel
(early—before readers can come to care much about the heroine's
family), but it hints at the danger to female peace of mind posed
by marriage—the primary institution defining the course of
female life. This danger is transposed to the less tragic but more
immediate portrayal of the Mirvans' marriage. Evelina does not
explicitly apply the warnings of this marital portrait to herself,
yet she records, in her letters to Villars, the helplessness and
discomfort of the Mirvan women. And her own experiences as a
young woman with "too much beauty to escape notice," and
"too little wealth to be sought with propriety by men of the
fashionable world" (18) bear out the implications of the Evelyns'
marital history and the unhappy circumstances of the Mirvan
women: whether the young woman marries or remains single,

her well-being, health, and sanity are more probably endangered than redeemed by the social institution of love and marriage, the main business of women's lives. This pessimistic vision of marriage's role in the female maturing process remains in unresolved and, I would argue, significant contradiction to the novel's conventional happy ending.

The novel evidences not only the conventional assumption that marriage is the shortest route to female happiness, but also the equally conventional notion that marriage is one of life's major snares, a trap in which people (especially women) are destroyed or at best given a life sentence of discomfort. The theme of disastrous marital connections opens in Villars' account to Lady Howard of Evelina's family history, starting with her grandfather's "ill-judged marriage" with Madame Duval. In this union, the husband is the victim, but the plot, as Villars relates it, emphasizes that Evelyn made his own marital bed before he died in it:

His unhappy marriage . . . with Madame Duval, then a waiting-girl at a tavern, contrary to the advice and entreaties of all his friends, among whom I was myself the most urgent to dissuade him, induced him to abandon his native land, and fix his abode in France. Thither he was followed by shame and repentance; feelings which his heart was not framed to support: for, notwithstanding he had been too weak to resist the allurements of beauty, which nature, though a niggard to her of every other boon, had with a lavish hand bestowed on his wife; yet he was a young man of excellent character, and, till thus unaccountably infatuated, of unblemished conduct. He survived this ill-judged marriage but two years. [13-14]

Burney makes Evelyn sympathetic—he is, after all, her heroine's grandfather and the charge of the admirable Mr. Villars—but she also makes it clear that Evelyn is responsible for his own destruction through the male privilege of free choice, however misused. His daughter's union with Sir John Belmont is quite a different matter. She wrongly trusts her husband in consenting to an "ill-judged" private marriage, but she does so under the duress of being pressured into another, even worse. "Madame Duval, at the instigation of her husband, earnestly, or rather tyrannically, endeavoured to effect an union between Miss Evelyn and one of his nephews. And, when she found her power inadequate to her attempt, enraged at her non-compliance, she treated her with the grossest unkindness, and threatened her with poverty and ruin" (14-15). Evelyn's tragedy stems from a marriage made in the weakness and misjudgment of a bad choice; Caroline Evelyn's destructive marriage is made through a total lack of options. Her victimization at the hands of her stepfather, husband, and mother results, ironically, from her father's bad choices—first, in his marriage and, second, in trusting to his conventional assumptions about his wife's maternal instincts. He leaves his daughter in her mother's financial power because it "never occurred to him that the mother, on her part, could fail in affection or justice" (14). Evelina's family history is an object lesson on the riskiness of "ill-judged" marriages for both men and women, but it seems to stress women's lack of recourse or control in the matter. Even the actions of Madame Duval suggest that women haven't much power once sexual maturity has ushered them into the institution of marriage. Her tyrannies themselves arise from a chaotic rage against powerlessness, and she initially acts "at the instigation of her husband," not from any choice of her own. Although Evelyn suffers from marriage, such suffering arises from his own choices, however poorly conceived or misled; the suffering that awaits his daughter proceeds from masculine prerogative.

The theme of bad marriages and what they do to women's lives assumes more immediacy in the marriage of Mrs. Mirvan, Evelina's female mentor and protector in the first phase of her "entrance into the world." Evelyn and his daughter suggest melodramatic possibilities for resolving the "chance" of marriage—disgrace, humiliation, and, finally, death. The Mirvan women, eighteenth-century foremothers of the Victorian "Angel in the House," act within another set of ideological assumptions characteristic of nonfiction conceptions of femininity in the eighteenth century, the assumptions of many sermons, essays, and various forms of advice to "young ladies" written in the service of women's education: the domestic courage and strength of women maintaining their respectability—at a considerable personal cost in comfort and ease—in women's "sphere," the institution of marriage. The Evelyns' history belongs to the conventions of the sentimental novel or even the romance—the melodramatic romantic disasters so characteristic of the novels of Delariviere Manley and Eliza Haywood, for instances. But Mrs. Mirvan, her daughter, and her mother seem formed on the conventions of female virtue recommended by writers like James Fordyce, Thomas Gisborne, and George Saville, Earl of Halifax. And although these models for female conduct do not directly challenge the masculinist conventions that inspire them—female obedience and subservience to the male—they read as a double message. The Mirvan women are sympathetic, even, to some extent, animated patterns for how a male-dominated culture would have women behave, but their portrayal reveals what such behavior costs a woman in time, trouble, and peace of mind. They give readers an ambiguous message about the role of women in marriage—as both models of conventional correctness in whom Evelina and, by implication, Burney clearly invest their approval, and as walking wounded, illustrations of the personal cost of being such models. Thus they reflect both Burney's need to define femininity in socially conventional terms and her implicit fears about what those terms mean to the quality of female experience.

Mrs. Mirvan's life, especially, is seen by Evelina and the reader as a respectable hell of pained silences and strained, polite smiles that must have been recognized by married women in an age that offered them few recourses to an unhappy marriage beyond putting a decorous face on the matter. Mrs. Mirvan is one of the novel's few, feeble champions of politeness and social sanity and is Evelina's most determined, though inadequate, protector.

"This dear lady seems eternally studying my happiness and advantage" (103), writes Evelina, telling Villars that Mirvan is "so infinitely kind to me, that one would think she was your daughter" (73). Her sympathetic qualities have not been rewarded, however, as Evelina's may be, and Villars' apparently were, by a happy and fulfilling domestic life. Mrs. Mirvan seems to have made one of the marriages that eighteenth-century sermons and educational treatises warn women about. Matrimony is not, for Mrs. Mirvan, a happy-ever-after reward, but a lifelong trial of her forbearance. Whether or not readers find Captain Mirvan entertaining, few could call him a desirable husband, and most would agree with Evelina that "the kind and sweet-tempered woman . . . deserved a better lot. I am amazed she would marry him." Evelina finds the captain "surly, vulgar, and disagreeable," and "cannot imagine why the family was so rejoiced at his return. If he had spent his whole life abroad, I should have supposed they might rather have been thankful than sorrowful. However, I hope they do not think so ill of him as I do. At least, I am sure they have too much prudence to make it known" (38). Evelina, like the young Burney, has difficulty accepting the idea of marriage "for life with one who must have full power to make me miserable, and perhaps none to make me happy." But Mrs. Mirvan's marriage is testimony to the fact that not all virtuous and sympathetic women feel free to reject dismal offers if they mean economic security and social dignity. Like Charlotte Lucas's marriage in *Pride and Prejudice,* Mrs. Mirvan's suggests that the fairy-tale union of hero and heroine is not necessarily the fate of all good women.

Mrs. Mirvan seems a pattern for how to make the best out of a bad husband, an object lesson in how to survive marital discomfort. As Evelina comments, Mrs. Mirvan's "principal study seems to be healing those wounds which her husband inflicts" (53). Evelina relates, in her letters to Villars, Mirvan's attempts (usually unsuccessful) to subvert her husband's disagreeable quarrelings by "starting new subjects," or proposing walks after tea, conciliatory and diversionary skills that Burney characterizes as exemplary conduct under fire, making Mirvan a fictional embodiment of courtesy-book patience. But Burney also reveals—even stresses—Mirvan's frustration and discomfort:

Mrs. Mirvan endeavoured to divert the Captain's ill-humour, by starting new subjects; but he left to her all the trouble of supporting them, and leant back in his chair in gloomy silence, except when any opportunity offered of uttering some sarcasm upon the French. Finding her efforts to render the evening agreeable were fruitless, Mrs. Mirvan proposed a party to Ranelagh. [56]

Mrs. Mirvan, dreading such violent antagonists [the Captain and Madame Duval], attempted frequently to change the subject. [57]

. . . every dispute in which her undeserving husband engages, is productive of pain, and uneasiness to herself. [73]

Mrs. Mirvan's life with the Captain dramatizes the discomfort and powerlessness that so much literature (courtesy books, sermons, and educational tracts) warns are commonly the lot of women once they submit to the will of a husband. And if she serves as a model of female patience and forbearance worthy of the pages of Dr. Gregory or Thomas Gisborne, she also lives a fictionally realized life of quiet suffering that gives vivid expression to the psychological cost of model female behavior. Burney is not unusual in suggesting that female duty in marriage may be costly to a woman's mental and physical health—many eighteenth-century writers of nonfiction about the female role in marriage suggest this pessimistic view of the wife's lot. But the suggestion darkens in contrast to the novel's sentimental ideology of women's deserved happiness lying in married love. *Evelina,* I would argue, attempts to sustain this contradictory message about marriage: able to see the pain that the institution inflicts on women and unable to see her way to any alternative, Burney honestly presents us with the moral contradiction between the rightness of Mrs. Mirvan's behavior and the wrongness of its return. The contradiction itself creates an ideological disturbance in the novel, an incompletely articulated expression of uneasiness with the terms of women's lives.

The source of Mrs. Mirvan's discomfort is her husband, Captain Mirvan, whose broad comic humor may or may not blind readers to the role he plays as bully and manipulator—especially of women. Mirvan is, of course, a comic type whose most immediate ancestor is found, perhaps, in the works of Tobias Smollett. A prankster and rough "humorist," Mirvan acts as the satiric vehicle familiar enough in English drama and fiction. But he also illustrates, from Evelina's female perspective, the absolute power of the male in marriage, even over a woman who is superior to him in intellect, morals, and social standing. Mrs. Mirvan is not the only victim of his tyranny; it extends over his daughter, mother-in-law, and Evelina as long as she is "under his protection." When the Captain's practical jokes on Madame Duval make life too embarrassing and uncomfortable for his family to remain silent (their usual defensive response to his whims), his reaction is that of a ship's captain to a potentially mutinous crew: "As to all you, I expect obedience and submission to orders; I am now upon a hazardous expedition, having undertaken to convoy a crazy vessel to the shore of Mortification; so, d'ye see, if any of you have any thing to propose, that will forward the enterprize,—why speak and welcome; but if any of you, that are of my chosen crew, capitulate, or enter into any treaty with the enemy,—I shall look upon you as mutinying, and turn you adrift" (139). The analogy between the male head of a household and a ship's captain is strained and made comic by the Captain's sea-jargon (shades of Peregrine Pickle's sea-going uncle), but it accurately expresses the male's economic and social power over the women of his family (who apparently take his threats seriously enough not to cross him in his plans).

Mrs. Mirvan's only recourse in dealing with her husband's displeasure is avoidance and smoothing over the damage he so readily inflicts: "Mrs. Mirvan, who never speaks to the Captain when he is out of humour, was glad to follow me, and, with her

usual sweetness, made a thousand apologies for her husband's ill-
manners" (153). Similarly, Lady Howard (Mrs. Mirvan's mother), despite her title, house, and the personal strength apparent in
her letters to Villars, can only avoid an unpleasant or demeaning
contest with her son-in-law through a pretense of ignorance: "I
believe that Lady Howard, from the beginning of the transaction,
suspected some contrivance of the Captain, and this letter, I am
sure, must confirm her suspicion: however, though she is not at
all pleased with his frolick, yet she would not hazard the consequence of discovering his designs. . . . Indeed there seems to be
a sort of tacit agreement between her and the Captain, that she
should not appear to be acquainted with his schemes; by which
means she at once avoids quarrels, and supports her dignity"
(141-42). Neither Mrs. Mirvan's matronly status nor her mother's matriarchal position in the family is a match for the
willfulness of husband and son-in-law. These women in Evelina's
world are models of female powerlessness in the institution of
marriage, as well as models of what their society defines as "good
conduct"; they embody the everyday, garden-variety pathos of
attempting to defend familial serenity and sanity against a
culturally powerful male's disruptive behavior. Burney insinuates
into her sentimental love plot the suggestion that marriage is not
an automatic escape from female difficulties: marriage delivers
Evelina from unhappiness, but it also determines a life of
powerlessness and discomfort for the deserving Mrs. Mirvan.

Evelina seems to juggle two apparently contradictory ideas of
marriage: the panacea that cures the ills of Evelina's life as opposed to "realistic," even grim notions of marriage. The happier
view follows the expectations raised by comic fiction, of course,
whereas the darker vision of marriage seems to proceed from
implications in didactic and polemical literature about female life,
as well as the melodramatic disasters of early eighteenth-century
romance fiction. *Evelina's* mixed generic heritage determines, to
some extent, its mixed views on marriage.[2] But this apparent
contradiction may also be the result of Burney's need to remain

honest about both her negative impression of marriage and her
conservative endorsement of traditional female roles. Marriage
is, in Burney's words, "such chance," yet it is also women's *only*
chance at what convention defined as a full life, and the novelist
can hardly be blamed for stacking the deck so that her heroine
wins the gamble. Such "fixing" of the marital game is, in a sense,
the fictional correlative of some rather extraordinary exertions of
will to which Burney resorted, in real life, to ensure her own
personal security and happiness. Her fictional resolution of her
heroine's problems is an easy, perhaps wishful version of the
forcefulness of her own insistence on marrying only for reasons
of affection and compatibility. Evelina's match is, of course, a
sentimental convention, but it also represents an ideal of feminine
happiness in married love that Burney used to defend herself
from the "chance" of less-than-likely-looking marriages—without, however, necessarily expecting the ideal to come true.

Marriage, for Burney as for many young middle-class women
in mid-eighteenth-century England, sustained a double and contradictory ideological value in determining female futurity: although its aspect in much sentimental fiction offered them escape
from the "gulphs, pits, and precipices" of maturity, other conceptions of marriage in romantic fiction and, especially, nonfiction didactic and polemical literature for women codified and
institutionalized that maturity's powerlessness. The stasis and/or
regression common to so many literary images of female life may
be a projection of the male-dominated literary mainstream's
fears: what if the linear continuity of consciousness failed? The
worst possibilities are projected as characteristics of women and
are therefore isolated as aspects of consciousness which do not
threaten male personal or social power. Pope can afford to explore the "mystick Mazes" of the sylphs in *The Rape of the Lock*
even though they may imply a chaos too disturbing to include in
the "Mighty Maze" of *Essay on Man:* the regression and circularity of female life and consciousness can be absorbed by the

(ostensible, at least) order of society as part of a reassuring whole. And the institution of marriage is crucial to that absorption.

Cultural assumptions about women's roles in that institution or their relationship to it rationalize the nonprogressive aspect of female life and consciousness as that which contributes to the good of society. As professional or business vocations codify men's lives in terms of progress toward a goal, the vocation of marriage reinforces and justifies the static, nonprogressive vision of female life. Besides serving as ideological packaging for the grimmer aspects of married life, fictional depictions of marriage traditionally signify both personal fulfillment and the social order, as in the endings of dramatic comedies. But late seventeenth- and eighteenth-century conduct literature, educational treatises, and similar forms of advice to "young ladies" anatomize the female role in the institution in a manner poorly calculated to excite anticipation of happiness; the young woman is asked to accept a career that brings early loss of personal gratification and little possibility of worldly reward. These mixed, indeed, contradictory signals created, I will argue, profoundly ambiguous feelings toward marriage in the young Fanny Burney. On the one hand, marriage offered romantic fulfillment, but, on the other, it codified the expectation of almost certain loss as a condition of female maturity by giving the inevitability of loss the importance and form of a cultural institution.

George Saville, Earl of Halifax, for example, in his *Advice to His Daughters,* instructs his young readers "to forget the great *Indulgence* you have found at home.... The tenderness we have had for you, *My Dear,* is of another nature, peculiar to kind Parents, and differing from that which you will meet with first in any Family into which you shall be transplanted." Future in-laws will not be the only source of trouble, however; Halifax warns the young women most emphatically about their future husbands. The *"Causes of Dissatisfaction between Man and Wife"* are composed of hardships borne more or less well by women and perpetuated by men. Adultery, drunkenness, emotional and physical violence, sullenness, avariciousness, and stupidity are defects in husbands with which women must learn to live.[3] Halifax does not rule out the possibility of a happy marriage, but he emphasizes the ways in which marriage inevitably makes life worse for women in order to prepare his daughters for the transition from the privileges and power granted them in the nursery to the relative hardship and powerlessness of marriage. Obviously, this approach to female indoctrination into the conjugal role is not designed to engender a progressive concept of life.

Even when love is admitted into the picture of marriage, the literature often sees it as a significant help to getting through a socially necessary but personally bad business, not as a prize that women can work for: "The state of matrimony is necessary to the support, order, and comfort of society. But it is a state, that subjects the women to a great variety of solicitude and pain. Nothing could carry them through it with any tolerable satisfaction or spirit, but very strong and almost unconquerable attachments." And the chances for this relief are poor, according to writers such as Sarah Pennington: "Happy is her Lot, who in an Husband, finds this invaluable Friend! yet, so great is the Hazard, so disproportioned the Chances, that I could almost wish the dangerous Die was never thrown for any of you!"[4] The unreliability of a husband's love is another constant theme,[5] and writers often follow Halifax's lead in not mincing words about the "conjugal vexations" of the woman subject to the rule of an unloving husband.[6] One has not far to look for Burney's vision of marriage as "chance," a dangerous gamble carrying very bad odds.

Women cannot, however, avoid danger merely by refusing the bet: even if a woman does not marry, the institution of marriage as woman's vocation deforms and embitters her life. As depressingly as marriage is often depicted, it is the organizing principle, the raison d'être of female life. The prospect of failing at this vocation produces anxiety, and the actuality of spinsterhood brings a spiritual degradation grounded in negative social attitudes toward single women and in the real possibility of economic insecurity. Mary Hays describes the young lady groomed for the marriage market: "in dreams [of marriage] her youth passed away; every rising beauty became her rival; and every charm, as it faded, gave a pang to her heart, which was alternatively harrowed by jealousy, by envy, by disappointed hope, and unavailing regret." Finally, disappointed in her life's main goal, the acquisition of a husband, she finds relief in death, deliverance "from the dreadful vacuity of having nothing to do, to hope, or to fear."[7] Hays' condemnation of the role that marriage plays in shaping women's goals and, hence, their lives is hardly mainstream eighteenth-century thought on the subject, but her analysis of marriage's impact on female life, both in and out of the actual state, differs from more conservative ideas mainly in that she rejects the spiritual gratification of doing one's duty and the prospect of postmortem rewards as adequate compensations for the pain of disappointment, maltreatment, and boredom. The importance of religion as a compensatory avocation of women and the strength of social sanction should not be underestimated. Also, many happy marriages, obviously, did exist (Burney's was one), and much literature (especially novels) puffed mutually satisfying marriage as the most significant worldly engagement of human emotion. But the negative prospect of marriage probably shaped female consciousness as much as rosier visions of conjugal bliss. In Burney's case, the nightmare of hardship, disappointment, or vacuity seems as much a part of her marital expectations as dreams of romantic marriage.

In *The Early Diary,* Burney's reflections on a wedding she witnesses focus on what a poor business it is for the bride—"O how short a time does it take to put an eternal end to a woman's liberty!" (*ED,* 1:17)—and in a later passage she returns to the same theme: " 'Tis preparing one to lead a long journey, and to know the path is not altogether strew'd with roses.... she [the bride] may not find the road it leads her to very short; be that as it may, she must trudge on, she can only return with her wishes, be she ever so wearied" (*ED,* 1:49). The *Early Diary's* account of Burney's responses to the proposals of one rather innocuous Mr. Barlowe gives the impression that Burney saw marriage unsweetened by romantic love as psychic self-annihilation. Burney's record of a conversation with her father at the time of Mr. Barlowe's suit suggests that, for Burney, nonromantic bourgeois marriage for economic security was a poor bargain: she would be risking her father's love and protection for an unknown and terrifying state in which she could not fully imagine living, let alone being happy:

> "Oh, Sir," cried I, "*I* wish for nothing! only let me live with you." "My life!" cried he, kissing me kindly, "Thou shalt live with me for ever, if thee wilt! Thou canst not think I meant to get rid of thee?"
> "I could not Sir; I could not!" cried I; "I could not outlive such a thought!"
>
>   . . .
>
> Thus relieved, restored to future hopes, I went to bed, light, happy, and thankful, as if escaped from destruction. (*ED,* II, p. 70)

Marriage without love meant, literally, an end to Burney's "future hopes." It was better for her, she seems to have felt, to cling to the known safety and potential future happiness of remaining a "young lady" without definite prospects than to risk a marriage that she sees in terms of personal dissolution. Burney's desire to remain "for ever" with an indulgent father reflects what seems a likely, though probably unintentional effect of instructional propaganda on the female mind: if childhood and early youth are usually compared favorably with the trials of maturity and marriage, one can hardly wonder at a young woman's desire to extend the pleasanter state as long as possible.

In fact, such a desire seems as much an intelligent choice as Freudian regression, and, it would seem from the evidence of courtesy and educational literature, not an uncommon one. Once women's educators had thoroughly warned their readers of

the difficulties inherent in marriage, they were apparently faced
with the problem of getting young women to marry anyway.
The prevalence of social sanctions against women of marriageable age who dragged their feet to the altar suggests that Burney
may not have been alone in her resistance to the pressure to marry
young enough to insure economic security. The *Spectator* sends
out warnings to the "demurrer"—she who is "for spinning out
the Time of Courtship to an immoderate Length"—on "what a
strange Figure she will make" when her beauty is gone and
marriage is her only economic and social haven.[8] The *Rambler*
approves the parental management of marriage because leaving
women to their own devices allows them to "trifle away youth
and lose their bloom in a succession of diversions" instead of
performing their social duty.[9] Writers frequently warn young
readers about the ridiculousness of the unmarried older woman
who would like to ignore the passage of time—pushing women
toward the very object that they have taught them to dread.[10]

The economic sanctions against women's remaining single are
powerful arguments for marriage of which Burney was certainly
aware. Samuel Richardson, Mary Astell, and Samuel Johnson
discuss the financial vulnerability of the unmarried woman,[11]
and it becomes, of course, a major feminist issue in the nineties.[12]
Burney lived with the reality of a father who could do very little
for her financial security after his death, and in middle age she
took a position at court (much against her own wishes) with this
fact in mind.[13] Economic arguments apparently had little effect
on Burney in the matter of marriage, however. In 1775, Samuel
Crisp urged her to accept Mr. Barlowe in order to avoid "the
situation of an unprotected, unprovided woman" (*ED*, 2:54), but
Burney was unmoved in her determination to refuse a suitor who
did little worse than bore her, but whom she felt she could not
love. Although the economic motive must have been important
enough to Burney's friends and family to make them push the
match, it was not strong enough to carry all before it, and Burney
would not have been without moral reinforcement in refusing to

give in to marriage on the sole grounds of economic necessity. The heroines of romance—from Haywood's disinterested female characters, who fall in love for every reason but monetary gain, to Maria Edgeworth's Helen at the end of the century, who specifically comments on women's foolishness in marrying for money—would have offered Burney fictional precedent for rejecting the primacy of economic motivation in marriage. And in this case, at least, fiction is in accord with ideas pervasive in nonfictional writing for women. Purely mercenary marriages are the object of Johnson's disgust at midcentury, and Hestor Chapone, at about the time of *Evelina*, advises young women not to risk an unhappy marriage for the prospect of financial security. [14] The protestant nunnery scheme formulated by Mary Astell in the late seventeenth century and reiterated in the eighteenth by Richardson and Reeve suggests that Burney was probably not without support in imagining a single life as an option; as strong as the economic argument for marriage was, it was probably less overwhelming than the meanings (almost mythologies) that society built around the spinster.

Although the unmarried woman might choose to trade economic security for a pardon from the hardships of married life, she seems inevitably to have been handed a role that defined her as peevish, unattractive, ridiculous, or in some way an incomplete and sorry speciman of femininity. John Gregory warns his readers about "the chagrin and peevishness which are apt to infect their [spinsters'] tempers," and the "great difficulty of making a transition with dignity and cheerfulness, from the period of youth, beauty, admiration, and respect, into the calm, silent, unnoticed retreat of declining years." John Bennett assumes that married women are "generally more pleasing, than such, as never formed the connection"; Edward Moore sees spinsterhood as a "living death," and William Kendrick says that virginity is "unbecoming" in an old woman. [15] The century is not without awareness that such charges are rather cruelly directed at women whose worst fault was living in a society that provided

them with few useful and productive roles, but its voice is usually
defensive, speaking against a strong and influential opponent:
"Those who believe themselves possessed of wit, use it to turn
them [spinsters] to contempt and ridicule; not because they are
unworthy, but because they are unfortunate. There are few modern Comedies that do not give irrefragable proofs of this—The
Aunt Deborah's, and Mrs. Malprop's, are the standing jest of the
Modern writers; and even Mr. Cumberland, though a chaste and
refined writer, has lent his hand to throw a stone at sisters and
aunts who are unmarried, whatever merit they may have, or
whatever misfortunes they may have endured." The "stone" so
commonly thrown at mature and aged spinsters in eighteenth-
century comedy struck sparks from Clara Reeve's normally
sedate pen. Society denies the mature, unmarried woman a
dignified or even worthy part to play, and then adds to the injury
by assuming that the moral deficiency lies with its victim. Reeve
writes testily, "Every woman in this situation must be an old
maid; or she must be something worse. What then; do you think
the latter state the most honorable?"[16]

Thus, if marriage threatened to end a young woman's period
of social pleasure and power, it at least saved her from becoming a
pariah without even the consolation of her own self-respect.
Spinsterhood brings an even more poignant loss of social value
than marriage; Samuel Crisp urged the young Burney to accept
the lesser deprivation before age left her without the power to do
so: "The opportunity [of marriage] is never to be recover'd; the
tide is lost, and you are left in shallows, fast a-ground, and
struggling in vain for the remainder of your life to get on,—
doom'd to pass it in obscurity and regret. Look round you Fan;
look at your aunts! *Fanny Burney* won't always be what she is
now!" (*ED* 2:54). Yet if spinsterhood threatened "obscurity and
regret," marriage without romantic love apparently did not seem
a significantly better "opportunity" to Burney: her pessimism
about women's role in the institution must have been validated
later in her life by her sister Susan's grim marriage and early

death, brought on, in Burney's view, by her husband's cruelty.[17]
Burney's stepsister, Maria Allen Rishton, was also married unhappily, and Burney was her sometimes unwilling confidante
during the long process of alienation that ended in separation—
against Burney's advice.[18] Once a woman had placed her neck
within the noose, Burney seems to have felt that she owed an
absolute duty to her husband, whoever he was or whatever he
did. Burney's ambiguous attitude toward her stepsister's increasingly unbearable marriage may seem distastefully priggish
to us today: her sympathy with Rishton's plight is always mixed
with admonitions to duty, and at times Burney almost seems to
be hiding from her stepsister, as if she could not bear the combination of emotional empathy and conventional strictness herself.
Burney could not see past the conventional limits for acceptable
female behavior in the institution of marriage, although she
could see quite clearly the suffering that took place within these
limits. I suspect that she avoided confronting the implied contradiction in these two perspectives on marriage by holding as
firmly as she could to what power she had in minimizing the
unpleasanter of the two in her own personal life-prospect. She
was, in fact, remarkably strong-minded—and careful—about
making her own choice, finally marrying, at forty, the penniless
French immigrant, Alexandre d'Arblay—to her own personal
satisfaction and against both the wishes of her beloved father and
all economic sanity.

One of d'Arblay's attractions for Burney seems to have been
his personal and moral dependability; if marriage was, in her
words, "such chance," then the only way to guarantee one's
safety in the institution was to trust one's self to the right despot,
as Burney reflects in a letter to her sister, Susan, just before her
marriage to d'Arblay: "if it should, indeed, be my lot to fall into
the hands of one so scrupulous in integrity, how thankfully shall I
hail my Fate!" (*JL* 2:117). While Burney seems to have accepted
the institutions and attitudes that darkened her prospects as a
young woman, her response to them was to make as intelligently

as possible the choices left open to her. Although she might dread
the future, she did not passively accept the hardships and personal
degradation implied in contemporary discussions of marriage,
and her life, as well as her fiction, bears out the necessity of
choosing carefully and knowledgeably among the options presented by female experience.

Burney controls her heroine's destiny as she controlled her
own matrimonial course, guiding her through danger to a marriage that enables her to resist the destructive potential inherent in
the institution. In her personal life, Burney resisted not only
admonitions of writers on female duty, but probably a great deal
of pressure, diffused through many areas of eighteenth-century
life and letters, to avoid becoming an old maid, a social pariah and
an economic burden. Her novel gave her more choices than her
life, or at least gave them to her sooner, and she resolves Evelina's
problems more quickly and easily than she did her own; but
Burney's fiction and her autobiographical writings seem to agree
on a desire to reject the sacrifice of life and happiness to the
institutions she both accepted and feared. Fiction could cheerfully and easily uphold Burney's desire not to go gentle into a bad
marriage, but it also anticipates her refusal to do so in real life
under circumstances often neither cheerful nor easy. Writing
allowed her to manipulate the conventional stuff of fictional
wish-fulfillment in a way that must have satisfied an understandable desire to escape the difficulty of avoiding real institutionalized dangers to her life and happiness. Yet her novel does
not totally deny the dangers: it maintains the integrity of her
personal life-choices by placing Evelina's extraordinary marriage
in a social context that suggests just how extraordinary it really is.
Survival, for Burney, meant sustaining the clarity of her double
vision, for giving in to resolution meant either blinding herself to
real, present dangers or encountering the new terrors of un-
charted regions outside the conventional boundaries of feminine
possibility.

While *Evelina* gratifies the desire for a happy ending, to see the

heroine one has come to care about richly and happily settled, it
may also have gratified eighteenth-century female readers on a
different level, that which confirmed their experience of coming
to terms with how society defined their lives. Evelina's "entrance
into the world" is an entrance into sexual maturity and an
introduction to the rituals and institutions that will define the
quality of her experiences as a woman. Burney intertwines the
discourse of Evelina's innocence and her sexual unselfconsciousness—the story of a passive Cinderella who will be duly rewarded with the prince—with an implied discourse that charts
her transition from a protected, idyllic girlhood into the exposed
and treacherous territory of young womanhood. Evelina's full
consciousness of the dangers she faces, the "gulphs, pits, and
precipices" of her future, comes late in the novel with Villars'
warning to fly the disappointment and regret that an unrequited
love for Orville threatens; the reader who lived with the social
realities of eighteenth-century female life, however, may see, as
Evelina does not, the deadly serious initiation into female sexual
adulthood that places her unselfconscious narration in a socially
determined context of imminent pain and loss. The text cues the
reader's thoughts to the cultural pattern of marriage and spinsterhood as the forked path of young women's future expectations. Evelina's unselfconsciously experienced initiation into the
social institution of female sexual maturity ultimately expresses
hope for escape from the unpleasant prospects it implies, but her
narrative also unselfconsciously dramatizes the imminence of
such sinister prospects.

Villars' second letter to Lady Howard raises the theme of
Evelina's "expectations." Villars fears that a trip from Berry Hill
into London will cause her to hope for more from life than her
social and economic position can offer: "Destined, in all probability, to possess a very moderate fortune, I wished to contract
her views to something within it." Evelina's "views" are, Villars
goes on to hint, inextricably connected to her expectations from
marriage; her economic and social future is indivisible from her

sexual future. His concern is specifically for the effects of Evelina's initiation into sexual consciousness and the cruelty and
disappointment she must experience in discovering how little the
world values her except as a sexual commodity: "The town-
acquaintance of Mrs. Mirvan are all in the circle of high life; this
artless young creature, with too much beauty to escape notice,
has too much sensibility to be indifferent to it; but she has too
little wealth to be sought with propriety by men of the fashionable world." Evelina's departure from Berry Hill is, in a sense,
leaving behind sexual unconsciousness and the relative security
of childhood's idyll; Villars, like the writers of sermons and
courtesy literature he so resembles, envisions the probability of
pain and loss in that transition. Also like such writers, he sees a
season in town as inflammatory to the young's innate tendency to
expect too much: "A youthful mind is seldom totally free from
ambition; to curb that, is the first step to contentment, since to
diminish expectation, is to increase enjoyment" (18). He fears
that she will come to hope for more than life will probably give
her. Whatever Evelina's expectations may be, the reader is cued to
the low ceiling of possibility and the probable disappointments
that characterize her specifically feminine future prospects.

When Evelina takes over the narration, Burney continues to
remind readers of the social circumstances that narrow her heroine's chances of a peaceful, happy life through the running account of her relations with Lord Orville. Although she is not, of
course, aware of her love for him until Villars' warning letter, her
response to Orville expresses the vulnerability of the woman in
courtship from the first moment of their meeting, appropriately,
at a ball. Evelina's experience in dancing with Lord Orville is a
nearly perfect analogue for the terrifying helplessness of a woman faced with the prospect of marriage. She "colours" when
asked to dance (which she does not do when Lovel asks her
earlier), and is frightened at being isolated among strangers,
paired, even "worse, *with* a stranger" (29). Her terror turns to
chagrin and disappointment, however, when she discovers Lord

Orville's first impression of her as "*A poor weak girl*": "I would
not live here for the world. I don't care how soon we leave town"
(36). Evelina unselfconsciously wishes to reject the society in
which she seems devalued: Orville's dismissive words reflect
what little consequence she has in the eyes of a single, attractive
male and, by implication, in the eyes of the social world that
empowers him. Without being conscious of the fact, she is
proving, so far, the truth of Villars' prediction that she cannot "be
sought with propriety by men of the fashionable world." The
first assembly is curiously emblematic of a young woman's
entrapment in the assumption that marriage is her "career."
Being paired off with a virtual stranger is frightening, but being
rejected by that stranger increases her vulnerability by spitting
her out of the system that is her best means of protection and
social acceptance. Although Evelina apparently remains unconscious of any such implications, the reader is reminded of the
dependency and precariousness of her social position as a marriageable young woman of no great means.

Similarly, although Evelina never evinces a conscious wish to
marry Orville, her generalized admiration of him begins to offer
her an important, though unfocused sense of hope for her future
happiness. The qualities that attract her to Orville are precisely
those that make Villars such a satisfactory protector, thus bridg-
ing the gap between the security and happiness of her childhood
at Berry Hill and her undetermined future:

I sometimes imagine, that, when [Orville's] youth is flown, his vivacity
abated, and his life is devoted to retirement, he will, perhaps, resemble
him whom I love and honour. His present sweetness, politeness, and
diffidence, seem to promise *in future* the same benevolence, dignity, and
goodness. [72, my emphasis]

I thought there existed another,—who, when *time had wintered o'er his
locks*, would have shone forth among his fellow-creatures, with the
same brightness of worth which dignifies my honoured Mr. Villars; a
brightness, how superior in value to that which results from mere

quickness of parts, wit, or imagination! a brightness, which, not contented with merely diffusing smiles, and gaining admiration from the
sallies of the spirits, reflects a real and glorious lustre upon all mankind!
[261, Burney's emphasis]

Orville seems to offer Evelina the hope that there exists among
"mankind" a protector as dependable as Mr. Villars. Instead of
labeling her feelings as Oedipal and having done with them as
tell-tale indications of Burney's repressed desire for her own vital
and attractive father, it seems reasonable that Evelina is drawn to
Lord Orville—as Burney was to her husband M. d'Arblay—out
of an instinct for survival.[19] Villars and Orville are the only two
men who seem likely to extend Evelina's personal consequence
beyond the courtship stage of her worth as sexual commodity; if
Villars gives comfort and order to Evelina's youth, Lord Orville
holds out the hope that a man exists who can do the same for her
maturity and old age.

Evelina suggests, however, how fragile this hope may be.
When Sir Clement's forgery causes Evelina a temporary disillusionment with Orville, her hope and expectation are converted
to a pointed unwillingness to look ahead, a sense that happiness
lies behind, not ahead of her: "I cannot express the reluctance
with which I parted from my revered Mr. Villars: it was not like
that parting which, last April, preceded my journey to Howard
Grove, when, all expectation and hope, tho' I wept, I rejoiced,
and though I sincerely grieved to leave him, I yet wished to be
gone: the sorrow I now felt was unmixed with any livelier sensation; expectation was vanished, and hope I had none!"
(268). Even if one is tempted to interpret Evelina's physical illness
at this time as green-sickness, the eighteenth century's medical
formulation for the ailment supposedly caused in virgins by
frustrated sexual desire,[20] the heroine's sexual frustration encom-
passes a dimension beyond the disappointment of mere lust.
Evelina's present sense of her future has come, not coincidentally,
I would argue, to depend on her relations with Orville, the

means of her romantic escape from a maturity culturally defined in terms of loss. Her letters to Maria Mirvan after her return from London to Berry Hill express confusion over her present circumstances and depression over her future prospects, a state that she attributes to disappointment in Orville and her own mortification. Her pain is, of course, what a heroine of "sensibility" should feel, but it also suggests her physical and emotional vulnerability to what Villars later calls "secret repining, and concealed, yet consuming regret" (309)—a future of lost hopes. The impertinent letter that Evelina thinks is from Lord Orville ostensibly dissolves her confidence in disinterested male behavior—one buffer against the hopelessness of female expectations. But beyond the limits of Evelina's consciousness, it also implies a damning flaw in the "prince" who is so necessary to the traditional protection afforded to women by romantic love.

Tellingly, Evelina's renewed confidence in Orville after meeting him at Bristol Wells restores her present complaisance and her expectation for the future: "Oh, Sir, Lord Orville is still himself! still, what from the moment I beheld, I believed him to be, all that is amiable in man! and your happy Evelina, restored at once to spirits and tranquillity, is no longer sunk in her own opinion, nor discontented with the world;—no longer with dejected eyes, sees the prospect of passing her future days in sadness, doubt, and suspicion!—with revived courage she now looks forward, and expects to meet with goodness, even among mankind" (278). Obviously, Evelina is in love, but her words reveal more than a seventeen-year-old's crush. To build one's expectations of happiness on the sensitivity and kindness of one man may indeed be love, but it also implies that the young woman's ability to look forward to her life depends on the narrow chance of her future worth's validation by a single representative of masculine social power. Evelina's unselfconscious effusions express starry-eyed infatuation, of course, but they also imply a sense of the power men have over women, the "chance" of finding the lover who will justify female faith in "goodness, even among mankind."

Orville is Evelina's one possibility for lifting the darkness that seems to cover her prospect. The one eligible male in the novel who, in Villars' words, "may be sensible of her worth" (15), he makes it possible for the future to mirror the happiness and security she has known at Berry Hill. Therefore, when Mr. Villars awakens Evelina to her dependency on Orville, and the tenuousness of his protection, Evelina realizes the grim potential of her "friendship" with Orville, the probability that he will not be willing or able to become her friend in the only way that can insure his protection converts her pleasure in his company to dread of the future: "Oh, Lord Orville! could I have believed that a friendship so grateful to my heart, so soothing to my distresses,—...would only serve to embitter all my future moments!" Terrified, Evelina re-entrusts her hopes to Villars: "To you alone do I trust,—in you alone confide for every future hope I may form" (322). She is rather in the position of a trapeze artist who lets go of one pair of hands only to realize in midair that no one waits to catch her—and there is no net.

Evelina's happy ending should not blind us to the implied, though ultimately incomplete, plot of the heroine's negative progress toward emotional deprivation, the barren realms of institutionalized failure. Marriage, or at least the expectation of it, shapes the course of Evelina's coming to maturity, and it is, in Burney's words, "such chance"; the institutions of marriage as woman's vocation and spinsterhood as woman's failure in that vocation form the course of female life into a gloomy prospect, which can be redeemed only by chance or by the woman writer's ability to create better alternatives through conventional sentimentality. The heroine's courtship, although ultimately successful, suggests the pattern that often ends in failure, "secret repining, and concealed, yet consuming regret"—a suggestion that contradicts and disturbs the resolution of Evelina's fears in the fairy-tale-like marriage that guarantees the happiness of her "futurity."

FOUR

EVELINA
Trivial Pursuits

Consciousness that the human mind and body are shaped by what they do, not always with pleasant results, informs social and economic theory since the eighteenth century, and although such theory tends to focus on men, especially of the working class, feminist social theorists, beginning with Mary Astell, have pointed out the particular dangers that this truism suggests about the process of female self-identification. If Marx's industrial-age worker is in danger of fulfilling the fable of Menenius Agrippa—in which one part of man becomes the whole through repeated selective usage of the body—then women are in danger of fulfilling Swift's fantasy of the female body and mind artificialized through constant obsession with the toilette:

> Dorinda dreams of Dress a bed
> 'Tis all her Thought and Art,
> Her Lace hath got within her Head,
> Her Stays stick to her Heart.[1]

Although middle-class women in the eighteenth century probably had more to do in managing their households, raising their children, practising their various arts, and even sharpening their intellectual skills than Dorinda, Pope's Belinda, or other examples of fashionable ladies of leisure suggest, much of the ideology of female occupations—the formulation of the feather-brained walking art object, who thought of little other than her appearance and her "diversions"—was, I will argue, both an internal and an external threat to middle-class women's sense of identity: as the feminists of the nineties were quick to point out, women who are told that they are best fitted for only trivial occupations soon become just that.[2]

The relationship between eighteenth-century, middle-class women and their work is, however, complicated and made difficult to define because the lines drawn between tasks we would be inclined to see as recreational—mere hobbies or amusements—and tasks performed out of a sense of obligation or duty—"work," in short—are often blurred in eighteenth-century writing. Do we consider needlework of a nonutilitarian nature a hobby or a feminine responsibility? Are the labors of the toilette self-indulgence or the necessary occupation of a socially dutiful woman? The very ambiguity of the term "work" when applied to what kept middle-class women's hands busy while sitting and visiting in polite company gives one pause. The sewing and mending of clothing and linens, supervising of domestic tasks, cooking, and the care and education of children fall unambiguously into the category of women's work; going to the theater, socializing, music, and concerts are clearly play. But most writing on the subject of middle-class women's employments focuses on occupations that either fall in the latter category or are hard to define. Middle-class women's occupations often seem, therefore, as they did to Lawrence Stone, symptomatic of a leisured female class growing concurrently with the rising social star of the middle-class male.[3] I wish to stress my skepticism about the implied portrait of the middle-class woman of leisure, but I would also suggest that whatever women actually did, the conclusions that Stone draws may well derive from the overwhelming impression given by much eighteenth-century writing about women's occupations, and I would argue that the very blurring of lines between work and play is symptomatic of a general and pervasive tendency to devalue the ways in which women spend their time. The permeable boundaries between work and play, duty and pleasure account in part for the specific form of women's vulnerability in the ways that their identity is generally seen as shaped by what they do: the very ambiguity of many women's pastimes contributes to the shadiness that they cast on women's characters.

My analysis of the ideological value of women's occupations focuses, therefore, on this ambiguity and its effects on how Fanny Burney came to know herself in relation to those occupations. And as desirable as a strictly materialist analysis of this subject might be, the economic grounding (in so far as we can know it) of the cultural meanings implicit in women's occupations seems to compound rather than resolve their ambiguity: are the occupations of middle-class women valuable as "work" remunerated only by the vague (and often tenuous) return of "support"? Or are they valuable as the outward manifestations of the middle-class male's economic status? Burney's—and Evelina's—situation is made even cloudier, more resistant to material analysis by the elusive economic role of the young woman before she has entered the institution of marriage. Part of and yet not part of domestic labor, the single, young, middle-class woman's employments are particularly hard to define as "work" or "play" on either economic or ideological grounds; when Evelina shops and has her hair dressed are her occupations economically useless and morally trivial or are they an important part of both her economic role and her social duty as a marriageable young woman? Burney herself seems ambivalent about the answers to these questions, and it is this ambivalence that I hope to explore and explain.

As Mary Wollstonecraft and Mary Hays, among other feminists of the nineties, well knew, overt criticism of the ideology defining women's occupations placed the critic in conflict with society, and perhaps with herself.[4] To criticize the social system that characterized middle-class women's work in ambiguous, often trivializing terms, as opposed to criticizing women for being so shallow, hinted at a subversion of traditional institutions of femininity that could, if detected, become dangerous, at least psychologically, to the writer. More cautious writers such as Hannah More and Clara Reeve carefully avoid the subversive potential in their critiques of female education and employments by fervently espousing traditional feminine values while they pick away at what they see as the more problematic of women's occupations. Whereas Mary Wollstonecraft was able, not without personal difficulty, to criticize such values with a direct, unambiguous social logic, Fanny Burney seems ambivalent about what middle-class women conventionally do. But Burney's responses to the ideology of female occupations, as evidenced in her journals and novels, are different from Wollstonecraft's in degree and not in kind. The "lady" novelist who was a dresser to Queen Charlotte and the outspoken free-thinker who decried women's trivialization through mind-dulling labor or play both see the problematic impact of middle-class women's occupations on the female character; and both, by the turn of the century, see middle-class women's lack of utilitarian occupations in terms of the pain or, at least, the threat of economic and spiritual deprivation. Burney's *The Wanderer; or, Female Difficulties,* published in 1814, dramatizes the lack of economic options available to middle-class women outside of marriage—a theme common in the feminist writing of the 1790s—although romantic love, not revolution (even in its milder forms) is the solution to which Burney finally turns in this novel. For much of her career as a novelist, and certainly during the period of *Evelina* and *Cecilia,* it seems likely that Burney felt something more like discomfort than open anger at the ways in which middle-class women are conventionally told to use their time, an uneasiness with the sphere of female employments that falls short of radical critique.

Evelina gives evidence of this discomfort and also reveals Burney's strategies for allaying it. Burney does not challenge common assumptions about what women do and, hence, what they are; she does not take on the position of radical "other" necessary to revisionist social—or literary—strategies. She seeks, however, to break with the determinism implicit in assumptions about women's pastimes. *Evelina* attempts to sever female identity from female occupations, to free the woman writer's ego, at least by fictional proxy, from the social constraints of her trivial pursuits, without directly challenging the social system. Burney situates Evelina in two places at once—inside the conventional social roles that shape what women do, but outside their power to define her. Fanny Burney, the writer and the woman, sought the freedom of self-definition *and* the security of ideological orthodoxy, and these contradictory impulses create in both Burney and *Evelina* a sort of guileless duplicity, a double and contradictory stance toward the pastimes of the "young lady" that is not motivated by the intention to deceive but rather results from a contradiction inherent in the ideological terms of eighteenth-century, middle-class female self-identification. Like other women of her class, she learns to see herself in part through the performance of ritual social occupations that she is, in turn, discouraged from seeing as valuable. She seeks to extricate herself from this potentially damaging contradiction by separating female self-definition from the problematic roles in which middle-class women's pastimes cast her—without, however, challenging conventional attitudes about either the propriety or the triviality of a "young lady's" duties and pleasures during her first season in town. The result is an ambiguous formulation of Evelina as both conventional and outside of convention, a practitioner in the fashionable rites of town life who is, nonetheless, not morally defined by the role that she plays in them.

Occupations for middle-class women, from the relatively harmless vocation of the needle to a morally and socially dangerous addiction to "diversions," are tainted with suggestions that women are dim-witted or corrupt or, at best, in the process of becoming one or the other through constant exposure to tedium or triviality. But while women are encouraged, at least to an extent, to cultivate an intellectual and spiritual refinement that might place them above the dangers of female pastimes, they are seldom encouraged to break with traditional definitions of womanly work or play. The middle-class girl was taught the rightness of her work role at the same time that she also seems to have been implicitly tutored in a quiet contempt for it. Fanny Burney writes in her diary of July, 1768, "I make a kind of rule, never to indulge myself in my two *most* favorite pursuits, reading and writing, in the morning—no, like a very good girl I give that up wholly, accidental occasions and preventions excepted, to needle work, by which means my reading and writing in the afternoon is a pleasure I cannot be blamed for by my mother, as it does not take up the time I ought to spend otherwise" (*ED* 1:15). This passage suggests more than a young woman's self-submission to social convention (although it certainly suggests that): it expresses, of course, Burney's fear of blame for venturing outside the traditional work role, but it also implies her desire to place herself and her energies outside that role. Like the modern bumper stickers that announce "I'd rather be running," or "I'd rather be reading Jane Austen"—attempts to deny the uninspiring anonymity of the expressway or city intersection at rush hour—Burney's statement says what she would really rather be doing, and, by implication, being. But her fear of blame is too great to allow her to disclose this desire directly, and she presents her self-identification as one who would rather read and write than sew in the moral context of her duty to the traditional work role. In other words, Burney is ambivalent toward the occupations that define her, on one hand, as a "very good girl" and, on the other hand, as a rather boring, trivial person. She cannot be comfortable without the conventional role, but she is left unsatisfied, incomplete if she invests herself entirely in it. Burney's attempt to define herself in this passage from *The Early Diary* is not hypocritical, therefore, so much as it is duplicitous by necessity—a double-dealing forced by her own irreconcilable desires—the need to take herself seriously as a thinking (and writing) human being opposed to the need to see herself as conventionally feminine in her employments.

While some of Burney's dissatisfaction with orthodox middle-class women's occupations might be attributed to the simple need for greater complexity and challenge in what she did, much of it could have been caused by being cast in the social and

psychological roles that women's pastimes often imply in eighteenth-century writing on the subject. A nagging uneasiness
about the effect of women's employments and pastimes on
female personality infects a wide range of literature on women's
education and employments throughout the century. Mary Astell, writing at the end of the seventeenth century, calls for more
focused and disciplined studies in women's education, observing
that women's interests and occupations often tend to leave the
mind dangerously unstable, the will unsteady. The time given to
"external objects . . . disposes them to Inconstancy, for she who
is continually supply'd with variety knows not where to fix; a
Vice which some Women seem to be proud of, and yet nothing in
the World is so reproachful and degrading, because nothing is a
stronger indication of a weak and injudicious mind."[5] Approx-
imately one hundred years after Astell's comments were made,
Hannah More decries the occupations that a fashionable education brings to a young woman's personal resources: *"That their
daughters shall learn everything…* at once weakens the general
powers of the mind, by drawing off its strength into too great
variety of directions; and cuts up time into such an endless
multiplicity of employments."[6] Abuses in female education lead
to a fragmentation of the energy that women give to their
employments, a fragmentation that, in turn, reflects a fragmented and enervated female intelligence.

Wollstonecraft, for instance, blames the "soullessness" of women on their trivial pastimes and mindless employments,[7] an
analysis of the psychological effects of women's work and play
that resembles, in content if not in tone and intention, Pope's
brief but remarkable passage in "Epistle to a Lady" in which he
observes that women lack integrity because of their limited social
and professional options. After anatomizing Cloe's moral cen-
terlessness, Pope reasons,

> But grant, in Public Men sometimes are shown,
>   A Woman's seen in Private life alone:
> Our bolder Talents in full light display'd;

Your Virtues open Fairest in the shade.
There, none distinguish 'twixt your Shame or Pride,
Weakness, or Delicacy, all so nice,
That each may seem a Virtue or a Vice.[8]

Pope's analysis prefigures Wollstonecraft's in that both blame women's moral weakness on their confinement to the domestic and personal. Wollstonecraft is more explicit than Pope about the connection between women's characters and employments, however; a paucity of employments renders women unable to calculate beyond immediate and superficial concerns: "Men have various employments and pursuits which engage their attention, and give a character to the opening mind; but women, confined to one, and having their thoughts constantly directed to the most insignificant part of themselves, seldom extend their views beyond the triumph of the hour." Female thought is bound by the tiny scope of women's occupations. Thomas Gisborne similarly observes that a young woman is more likely to have her character formed by her amusements—the lighter side of her employments—than a young man because her "time is not absorbed, nor her turn of mind formed and steadied, by professional habits and occupations," and Catherine Macaulay Graham generalizes that the "situation and education of women" is "precisely that which must necessarily tend to corrupt and debilitate both the powers of mind and body."[9]

Young women require self-discipline and careful self-regulation in order to circumvent the dangers posed by unfocused, "shady" occupations in the private sphere, but the ambiguous nature of women's domestic employments makes even the performance of female duties into troublingly double messages about women's worth and the quality of their experience. On one hand, domestic chores and responsibilities comprise some of the most respectable possibilities for middle-class female occupations; on the other, the sphere of domestic duty constitutes a cultural ghetto that limits female dignity and self-worth. Domestic administration is, for example, recommended by the Earl of

Halifax and Priscilla Wakefield, writing at opposite ends of the century, as among the most useful and respectable of female roles,[10] but this aspect of women's work is also stereotyped as responsible for the vacuousness that is so integral a part of eighteenth-century cultural mythology about women. Hestor Chapone waffles between a belief in the value and dignity of housewifery and her concern that too much attention to the "common things of life" narrows women's minds and makes them petty and peevish.[11] Chapone's dual attitude toward domestic chores, like Burney's ambivalence about her sewing duties, may well derive from the pervasive assumption that domestic labor trivializes the laborer, however dutiful she may be in attending to her conventionally "right" occupations. Samuel Johnson pokes fun at the country housewife's perpetual bustle over domestic trivialities, and satirizes "Mrs. Busy," the good manager whose obsession with the repetitive detail of housewifery blinds her to the personal and social needs of even her own family and guests.[12] Mary Hays anatomizes the housewife's degradation into "hands without a head," prefiguring Marx's warnings about the effects of the division of labor in the sphere of manufacture.[13] Nearly a century before Hays' critique of women's domestic concerns, Swift warns a lady of his acquaintance of the mind-stunting effects of domestic dutifulness:

> Tho' you lead a blameless Life,
> Live an humble, prudent Wife;
> Answer all domestick Ends,
> What is this to us your Friends?
> Tho' your Children by a Nod
> Stand in Awe without the Rod:
> Tho' by your obliging Sway
> Servants love you, and obey:
> Tho' you treat us with a Smile,
> Clear Your Looks, and smooth your Stile:
> Load our Plates from ev'ry Dish:
> This is not the Thing we wish.

> Col'nel _____ may be your Debtor,
> We expect employment better.
> You must learn, if you would gain us,
> With good sense to entertain us.[14]

Both Hays and Swift warn that intelligence and social value can be lost in over-attention to everyday tasks; both the early feminist and the satirist offer a critique of women's domestic obligations that conflicts with assumptions that women's "Virtues open Fairest in the shade" of domestic duty. Most confusing to young women like the Burney of *The Early Diary*, however, might be the double messages of writers such as James Fordyce, who condones women's involvement in trivial domestic chores even as he belittles it: "Little things belong to little mortals."[15]

Perhaps even more laden with mixed messages about the value of female occupations are attitudes toward the more "genteel" female employments: needlework and "the accomplishments." Seen as respectable and appropriate to women's social and moral identity, such employments are nonetheless not valued for themselves but rather as work-play therapy programs for a gender and class-defined group—middle-class women—seen as having little really useful work to do. Needlework is viewed as a duty or diversion according to the degree of its utility, but in the last half of the century the pervasive view in educational treatises and instructions to "young ladies" is that its main value lies in keeping women at home and occupied in doing something that is, at least, harmless. Richard Lovell Edgeworth and Maria Edgeworth stress that young women "should rather be encouraged, by all means to cultivate those tastes which can attach them to their home, and which can preserve them from the miseries of dissipation," but their attitude toward what such young women actually produce with their needles is contemptuous: "pictures of Solomon and the queen of Sheba" will soon be consigned to the attic, they warn women who might be inclined to take their art seriously. Like the Edgeworths, John Bennett sees needlework as a more respectable pastime than "play, public pleasures, or a *perpetual* round of *visits*"; it is also, in his view, relief from the "langour and *ennui*, which are the most unpleasant feelings of human life," and from which he apparently thinks that women have little other recourse. His comments on the subject read rather as if he were discussing finger painting as an amusement for children on rainy afternoons. John Gregory is, however, the most blunt about the worthlessness of needlework: "The intention of your being taught needlework, knitting, and such like, is not on account of the intrinsic value of all you can do with your hands, which is trifling, but to enable you to fill up in a tolerably agreeable way, some of the many solitary hours you must necessarily pass at home."[16]

These negative signals to women about the value of their handiwork are, however, mixed with assurances that skill with a needle is an important part of the middle-class housewife's domestic responsibilities *if* it is employed in what Priscilla Wakefield calls "family needlework" as opposed to "embroidery and fine works." Any pride or interest in the art for its own sake is ridiculed or condemned in ways that leave little room for an investment of ego in the occupation. Johnson pokes fun at the redundant quantities of firescreens, garters, and slippers that women turn out, and Sarah Pennington admonishes her daughters not to invest money or their servants' time (apparently more valuable than their mistresses') on decorative needlework. Yet while the art is itself degraded and trivialized, it is also closely bound to what middle-class women do and are: Catherine Macaulay Graham says that the "great priviledge of female life" is to "amuse ourselves with trifles"—and to some extent, women in the eighteenth century are seen in terms of what they do.[17]

The female "accomplishments" of polite society—the skills of music and drawing, in particular—are just as rarely valued in and for themselves. Like needlework, they are acceptable as a recourse to ennui and public pleasures, but they are generally not seen as having any other value to the mature woman or her family. The Edgeworths warn mothers against giving their daughters skills that can have only such ephemeral value as is given by window dressing on a highly competitive marriage market. Indeed, they point out, too great a commitment to an art form such as music or painting may become an incumbrance if a young woman's husband turns out to have no particular liking for his wife's art.[18]

In sum, young women like Burney were encouraged to engage in daily occupations that were, in turn, held in such low esteem as to make ego-investment in them foolish or perverse. This cultural ambivalence towards women's employments situates femininity awkwardly in occupational roles that women, themselves, are not supposed to care about or take seriously. Women are seen as curiously both "in" and "out" of what they do, performers with little investment in their performance. This potentially debilitating or, at least, demoralizing psychological positioning of the female subject in relation to its employments is transformed by Burney, I will argue, into a social and psychological strategy for retaining both her femininity and her self-respect. Her fiction and her journals establish the female subject within the conventional territory of feminine employments and pastimes while disassociating the subject's worth from that territory. The result is a duplicity that has more to do with social adjustment than with dishonesty: Burney and her heroines are always in the contradictory position of conforming to conventional modes of female employment while remaining somehow separate from the stereotypical roles those modes imply.

While the ambiguity with which many female employments are seen in the eighteeth century may well have taught Burney this socially respectable duplicity toward women's private occupations, women's *public* amusements are generally seen, unambiguously, as corrupting. Feminine consciousness generally assumes a sinister aspect in association with the public life of London; in *Spectator* 499, for instance, Will Honeycomb dreams that the survival of London's men depends on its women, who are allowed to leave the city before it is destroyed, carrying with them whatever they consider the most valuable—their husbands, as Will assumes. The women of London show their false priorities, however, by carting off clothing, china, lap dogs, household goods, and their foppish beaus.[19] The uneasiness with which many women's domestic occupations are viewed in the eighteenth century ripens into mistrust and fear in the public realm: is femininity too unstable an ideological construction to be depended upon outside the containing boundaries of the domestic?

Much of Burney's culture, as Will Honeycomb's dream suggests, is uneasy to downright frightened by the threat of feminine social irresponsibility outside the domestic realm; the Burney who wrote *Evelina* differed, I will argue, from the *Spectator* on this issue. Using the social strategy of detachment from feminine employments as a means of morally separating herself and her heroines from the contaminating influence of public amusements, Burney turned the odd dislocation of women from what they do into a means of establishing female integrity as morally *outside* while still participating in activities that her culture was inclined to see as contaminating to the female personality. In *Evelina*, Burney disassociates female consciousness from the satiric vision of women as corrupted by their fashionable pastimes (evidenced in Will Honeycomb's dream) by establishing the female subject's experience as wholly separate from, indeed, in sharp contrast to conventional satiric formulations of female identity as a moral vacuum, fashionably packaged. In general, Burney's response to literary—especially satirical—characterizations of feminine instability was strongly dismissive. Burney's diaries, journals, and letters indicate that she often found herself impatient with the age's misogynistic satire. While she is perfectly capable, in *The Early Diary*, of laughing at women she considers silly, blanket condemnations of female behavior annoy her intensely. She makes particular note of Homer's portrayal of women as unstable and flighty, and dismisses it with a terse, "I don't in fact believe it" (*ED*, 1: 30). When Samuel Crisp remarks on female "inconstancy," Burney replies with an uncharacteristic testiness that "though I readily allow you a *general* superiority over us in most other particulars, yet in constancy, gratitude, and virtue, I regard you as unworthy all competition or comparison" (*ED*, 1: 282). (Annie Raine Ellis points out that Burney's reply anticipates Anne Elliot's "We certainly do not forget you, so soon as you forget us" in Austen's *Persuasion*.) Thoughtless, knee-jerk satire on women seems to have particularly disgusted her. In 1774, she writes of John Shebbeare, "the most morose, rude, gross, and ill-mannered man I was ever in company with": "He did, to the utmost of his power, *cut up* every body on their most favourite subject, though what most excited his spleen was *Woman,* to whom he professes a fixed aversion; and next to her his greatest disgust is against the *Scotch*; and these two subjects he wore thread-bare; though indeed they were pretty much fatigued, before he attacked them; and all the *satire* which he levelled at them, consisted of trite and hackneyed abuse" (*ED* 1:285).

Burney, like most of her household, was a fan of Swift, and she plays the satirist of feminine weaknesses herself in both her novels and journals; her impatience is with the kind of mockery that refuses rather than makes fine distinctions, that reduces humanity—including women—to monolithic moral categories that allow for little complexity of feeling and no ambiguity of moral position. Her personal attitudes toward the female character in general suggest a need for more complicated assessments of women and their pastimes, assessments that allow for ambiguous or even contradictory experience. And *Evelina* suggests that room for this complexity could be obtained through the heroine's detachment, her separateness from a satiric vision of femininity in the realm of public "diversions."

Hence, in *Evelina,* Burney complicates the issue of how women's characters are formed by their pastimes by creating in her heroine a sort of innocent ambivalence toward the public diversions of London that bespeaks detachment and a controlling judgment rather than blind complicity in her own corruption. The early chapters of the novel introduce Evelina, in the company of her friends, Mrs. Mirvan and her daughter Maria, to the fashionable pastimes of the town—among the most tainted of women's trivial amusements. At the same time, Evelina is introduced to Captain Mirvan, a Smollettian prankster and rude satirist whose chief enjoyment seems to be baiting the novel's other characters—especially the women, most pointedly—for their interest in fashionable "diversions." Hence, Evelina discovers simultaneously the public pleasures of "high life" and the taint of disrepute that they carry for women. Evelina is herself ambivalent about London and its pleasures, neither condemning them, as Mirvan does, nor unreservedly enjoying them; the novel shows us both how far short of accuracy falls the satiric formulation of feamle consciousness as the sum of its trivial pursuits and how such inaccurate formulations can nonetheless be oppressive. Burney insists on the separateness of her heroine's integrity from the falsifying roles in which society places her. But her unwillingness to break with ideological orthodoxy on the subject of women's trivial pastimes—to criticize openly a social system that defines feminity and feminine occupations as rightly and properly trivial—means that she can only save Evelina's moral integrity by abstracting her from the ideology of women's occupations and giving her a measure of distance on them. This solution leaves Burney writing with a firm belief in female integrity but without resolving her own ambivalence about the occupations associated with women's ideological devaluation.

Captain Mirvan's satiric remarks on the shallowness of women's fashionable pastimes operate as a kind of false consciousness in the novel, a set of unconsidered responses to the social reality of female experience that show little real awareness of it. A young lady who is obviously enjoying her first visit to town must, in Mirvan's view, be the pleasure-seeking, useless creature typically connected with such enjoyments. Like John Shebbeare in Burney's diary, Mirvan reduces women and their experience to reductive categories; indeed, to the Captain, women have a simple material value which is measurable by certain fixed, conventional standards. Greeting his daughter after a seven-year absence, he "began some rude jests upon the bad shape of her nose, and called her a tall, ill-formed thing"[38] Similarly, Mirvan sees Evelina as an inconvenience, an excuse to do battle with Madame Duval, or as a piece of meat, good only as long as she "keeps": "why she's good white and red, to be sure, but what of that?—I'll warrant she'll moulder away as fast as her neighbours" (112). These moments in Evelina's narrative when one is invited to share her embarrassed silence suggest that both "tall, ill-formed" things and "good white and red" are more complex than is allowed by their status as objects in Mirvan's view of feminity. In a sort of mechanical operation of the satirist, he fires hackneyed charges at the innocent and bewildered Evelina and Maria Mirvan when they seek to reply to Lord Orville's request for their opinion on London's "public places": "Ask 'em after any thing that's called diversion, and you're sure they'll say it's vastly fine;—they are a set of parrots, and speak by rote, for they all say the same thing: but ask 'em how they like making puddings and pies, and I'll warrant you'll pose 'em" (109). Mirvan's bullying silences the two young women "for the rest of the evening"; while many of those present (including, of course, the readers of the novel) certainly do not accept Mirvan's interpretation of the girls' feelings, this scene demonstrates the dominance, the un-answerability, of such pronouncements about the mindless en-thusiasm with which young women supposedly value their occupations. Mirvan succeeds in silencing not only the young women, but "for some minutes," "every body else" as well, and Evelina discovers that she cannot prevent Mirvan from acting out his knee-jerk misogyny without endangering herself. When she protests Mirvan's physical assault upon her grandmother, Ma-dame Duval, in the course of a "practical joke" aimed at the vain, overdressed older woman's obsession with fashion and personal appearance, Mirvan issues a threat to herself: "A sullen gloominess instantly clouded his face, and, turning short from me, he said, I might do as I pleased, but that I should much sooner repent than repair my officiousness" (153). Evelina's experience with Mirvan demonstrates the inflexibility of an ideology that defines women too narrowly to allow them autonomy in self-definition and shows us this inflexibility's danger to the women who depend on male support; as Mirvan says, "if any of you, that are of my chosen crew, capitulate, or enter into any treaty with the enemy [Madame Duval],—I shall look upon you as mutinying, and turn you adrift" (139). There is little room for honest ambivalence toward fashionable pastimes in the world within Mirvan's control.

However trapped Evalina might be, the clear inadequacy of Mirvan's rigid categories marks him as the object, mechanical and unthinking, while Evelina and the Mirvan women become complex, feeling, sympathetic human beings, subjects rather than objects. Burney shows us the gross misinterpretation of women's thoughts and feelings that comes of assuming that women are as mindless as their pastimes are trivial, but her case for female integrity does not take on the task of reevaluating the relationship between what women are and what they do. She rather suggests that one should not assume too quickly or easily that fashionable pastimes do, indeed, form the female character. Even Mr. Villars errs on this point, in fearing the effects of a trip to London on the mind of his ward: "The mind is but too naturally prone to pleasure, but too easily yielded to dissipation" (81). Evelina's actual responses to the "dissipation" of London do not bear out Mr. Villars' dark expectations; they rather complicate an issue that her guardian tends to see according to unambiguous moral formulae. Evelina's feelings are more mixed and her judgment more detached than Villars—let alone Mirvan—apparently expects. She is enraptured by the opera but disappointed in the Mall at St. James (26); Garrick's performances transport her, but other theatrical presentations are simply pleasing. In fact, Evelina is far from corrupted by London diversions, but neither is she untouched by enthusiasm for them. Her request to be allowed to accompany the Mirvans to London suggests neither indifference nor unselfconscious desire:

> They tell me that London is now in full splendour. Two Playhouses are open,—the Opera-House,—Ranelagh,—the Pantheon.—You see I have learned all their names. However, pray don't suppose that I make any point of going, for I shall hardly sigh to see them depart without me; though I shall probably never meet with such another opportunity. And, indeed, their domestic happiness will be so great,—it is natural to wish to partake of it.
>
> I believe I am bewitched! I made a resolution when I began, that I would not be urgent; but my pen—or rather my thoughts, will not suffer me to keep it—for I acknowledge, I must acknowledge, I cannot help wishing for your permission. [24]

Experience quickly tempers Evelina's enthusiasm, but this initial outburst of eagerness reveals a characteristic duality in her desire, to be safe within the realm of domesticity and still to explore new areas of experience, to be both inside and outside the eighteenth-century definition of female "goodness." In turn, this ambivalence places the heroine both inside and outside stereotypical notions about a young lady's enjoyment of "diversions," allowing her to relish the prospect of town pleasure without completely losing moral self-consciousness.

Despite Burney's complication of the issue of women's pastimes, she leaves their problematic nature intact, neither refuting nor affirming their conventional place in women's experience. Her heroine's ambivalence, probably like her own, remains unresolved, her feelings about what she does mixed. Evelina ends a vivid and enthusiastic description of shopping for clothes and having her hair dressed with an apology to her guardian for "the wretched stuff I write," and then, as if unrepentant of her taste for triviality, adds, "Poor Miss Mirvan cannot wear one of the caps she made, because they dress her hair too large for them" (28). This complex mixture of interest and embarrassment allows

Evelina both engagement in feminine pastimes and the detachment of an intelligent observer. Burney ensures her heroine's
integrity by changing the ideological terms of female self-definition: that is, Evelina is a valuable human being neither because of
nor in spite of what she does, but rather because her ambivalence
complicates and breaks down a too-simple binary opposition of
either condemning or embracing the propriety of the young
woman's amusements as they are conventionally defined. She
achieves value as one whose ambivalence places her both morally
outside and socially within the ideology that defines women as
what they do.

Evelina's ambiguous detachment is illustrated almost di-
agrammatically in a visit to Cox's Museum in the company of
the Captain and Madame Duval. As is often the case in Evelina's
reactions to the pleasures of the town, her feelings are a mixture
of amusement and detached criticism: the Museum is "very
astonishing, and very superb," but gives "but little pleasure, for it
is a mere show, though a wonderful one" (76). Captain Mirvan
and Madame Duval, on the other hand, exhibit opposing reactions, unselfconsciously playing out the roles of knee-jerk satirist
and mindless devotee of empty, fashionable pastimes. While
Evelina finds the effect of a mechanical concert "pleasing," Duval
is sent into "extacies," which lay her open yet again to a malicious
attack from the Captain, who sees the displays at Cox's as "*jem
cracks*...only fit, in my mind, for monkeys,—though for aught I
know, they too might turn up their noses at it" (110). Evelina's
barely acknowledged sanity in a society of mechanical shows and
equally mindless and mechanical reactions to them suggests how
an intelligent, conventional woman like Burney might have seen
herself in the context of discussions on women's pastimes: she
can neither ignore nor thoughtfully participate in disputes that
tend to polarize at equally untenable extremes. Hence, she assumes the marginal status of observer, the only role that seems to
allow the ambivalence she feels.

Evelina's innocence, her lack of complicity in mindless pas-

times and equally mindless responses to them is an answer—
perhaps somewhat wishfully thought out—to Burney's own
desire to be seen as both thoroughly conventional and as someone who is really more complicated, fuller, and richer than what
conventionality permits women of her class. The role of observer
is, however, difficult to reconcile with that of participant, and
Evelina's ambivalence, however innocently posed, must inevitably seem, at times, like either complicity in or a critique of the
ideology that defines her as the product of what she does. The
task of remaining separate from the ordinary life of a middle-class
young woman in London for a season while still being a part of it
is, perhaps, most difficult when the occupation is not a spectator
sport, but rather one which intimately affects the heroine, touch-
ing her body as well as engaging her eyes and ears: the toilette, the
middle-class female obligation to prepare and don elaborate
costume and hairdress, meant that a young woman like Evelina
could spend a large part of her day in sartorial and cosmetic
preparations: shopping, sewing, and, of course, the ceremony of
dressing itself.

Until the emergence of a fashion for simplified female dress in
the 1790s, a woman had to arrange some combination of a
complicated collection of clothes: a robe, gown, or bodice and
overskirt, petticoats, stomacher, corset, underbodice, false front,
handkerchief, tucker, modesty piece or tippet, ribbon necklace,
apron, hoop or false rump, and a bewildering array of caps.
Hairdress went through varying degrees of complexity, from the
relatively simple head of close curls and *tete de mouton* of the early
eighteenth century to the astonishing structures of Evelina's day,
involving cushions, pads, wire supports, masses of false hair,
pomatum, and powder. Feathers, plumes, jewels, knots, ribbons, and pompoms required careful placement, and patches, lip
rouge, nail polish, lead combs, red and white paint, and plump-
ers (cork balls to round out the cheeks) were some of the cosmetic
aids on a lady's dressing table.[20] Eighteenth-century middle-class
women made themselves into walking art objects only vaguely

resembling the female body, and aside from the "Anguish, Toil and Pain," of assuming the age's stylized beauty, the more respectable sisters of Swift's nymph must have spent hours sewing and shopping.

Anyone who had read *The Rape of the Lock* has had a lesson in the moral dangers of spending such a large amount of time in a vain, potentially narcissistic occupation. Belinda's absorption in the toilette satirizes the building of identity on weak and ephemeral foundations by a whole leisured class, not just by women, but Pope's portrait of Belinda nicely sums up the anxieties expressed by many more specific discussions of the female toilette in the eighteenth century. Belinda's behavior dramatizes Mary Astell's observation that women are taught to see their self-worth in the value and arrangement of their clothes—her explanation of why her female contemporaries spend so much time worshipping at the toilette. A hundred years later, Wollstonecraft repeats Astell's criticism: women have little else to do besides attending to personal adornment, and hence they become, through habit, so to speak, vain and superficial narcissists.[21]

Eighteenth-century attitudes toward female self-adornment are not simply and clearly pejorative, however, and even Pope's loving attention to the details of Belinda's toilette (despite or, perhaps, because of "gray hairs") suggests the same mixed and contradictory attitude toward dress that much eighteenth-century writing manifests on the subject of other female employments. The toilette is potentially a morally dangerous territory, but it is also among a middle-class woman's expected duties and interests. Rousseau is somewhat extreme in giving his Sophie only a few occupations beyond caring for "her person, her clothing . . . her toilet," but his belief that women are best suited to the labors of the needle and dressing table is not uncommon. Fordyce, for all his urging women to adorn their souls as well as their bodies, accepts and even condones personal vanity as a part of women's character that is specifically designed to please men by "external graces and decorations: we pretend not to deny, that the love of dress, and an habitual study of personal attractions, are closely interwoven with the female character."[22]

Women are frequently exhorted, nonetheless, to distance themselves morally from the pleasure and duty of personal adornment, however "closely interwoven with the female character." This particular female occupation seems to have been problematic to a wide variety of writers on the subject of women's moral character and proper conduct. Sermons and educational literature written in the later half of the century express uneasiness over the possibility of women becoming too absorbed in this particular occupation. Thomas Gisborne, Catherine Macaulay Graham, and James Fordyce all warn against taking the toilette too seriously, despite their sense of its propriety in female life. William Kendrick's more rigorous religious views on female duty allow women only one session at the dressing table a day, while Charlotte Smith and Sarah Pennington anticipate, in milder forms, Wollstonecraft's outright rage at the engrossment of female energy in the dressing table's rites.[23] Female self-adornment is not, however, usually seen as evil in itself. Rather, satirists and moralists see the possibility of a love of dress becoming false self-definition, a type of human perversity that is threatening to traditionally valid ways of defining human identity.

Perhaps no occupation of eighteenth-century, middle-class female life engendered more objectifications of women as artifact or animal than the toilette. Belinda's perverse self-creation as a walking art object in *The Rape of the Lock* stands at one extreme from the earthy stench of Celia's excrement in "A Lady's Dressing Room," but both portray the toilette in terms of moral decay. Felicity Nussbaum identifies a satiric tradition of the lady's dressing room as emblem for what is nasty in human nature, and one can see a cultural logic in such metaphorical use of the toilette—Belinda's crime is a form of what Paul Fussell calls "over-symbolizing"—and the Augustan satirists are, on this issue, in good feminist company; both Mary Astell and Mary Wollstonecraft, writing at opposite ends of the century, would agree with Swift

that women are trained to see themselves in terms of their value
as partially artificial decorations.[24] Like Swift's "Dorinda," who
literally becomes her clothes, the coquette dissected by the *Spectator* has a heart made up of "innumerable sort of trifles," the
most outstanding of which proves to be a "flame-coloured
hood." *Spectator* essays also rail at women's obsessions with
headdresses, patches, transparent handkerchiefs, fans, and, most
pointedly, hoops, a fashion that seems a particularly inevitable
focus for charges of female "over-symbolizing": it creates a
falsely expansive female "self" which gives little evidence of what
is within, and the Spectator muses that he "cannot but think of
the old philosopher, who after having entered an Aegyptian
temple, and looked about for the idol of the place, at length
discovered a little black monkey enshrined in the middle of it."[25]
Analysis of the overdressed, inflated female seems to end, for
many writers, in the discovery of a small-scale heart of darkness,
the animal lurking within the artifact.

The fragmented, sadly mortal nature of Swift's "Beautiful
Young Nymph," and the sartorial and excremental litter of "A
Lady's Dressing Room" find echoes in the strictures of moral
essayists and educators later in the century, and the association of
fashionable women with filth seems to suggest some prevalent
fears about what women are really like inside their fine clothes.
Johnson's "Nitella" in *Rambler* 115 privately lounges in nasty
dishabille between public appearances in the most elaborate finery. John Bennett and James Fordyce are both "shocked" at the
idea of a dirty woman, and Fordyce, like Johnson, focuses
specifically on the Swiftian contrast between the fashionable lady
in all her splendor, and the same lady seen outside of visiting
hours—"slovenly, I might have said squalid and nasty." Fordyce
turns from this idea with a shudder—"I cannot express the
contempt and disgust I feel, when I think of it. I will not think of
it"—and like Swift's Strephon, closes the door of the lady's
dressing room, having seen enough to make him anxious to
know no more about the secrets of the female closet.[26]

The activities of the lady's closet—the toilette and various preparations of dress—are widely associated with dangerous and unsavory aspects of female identity, if they are not simply dismissed as boring. Burney may or may not have had these associations—or the boredom—in mind when, as an old woman, she crossed out in her diaries and letters many allusions to dress, but her impatience with Samuel Crisp's ignorance of the time that clothes took from her life, in a letter dated 1780, indicates the same mixture of dutifulness and impatience that characterizes her attitudes toward needlework in general: " 'Fact! Fact!' I assure you—however paltry, ridiculous, or inconceivable it may sound. Caps, hats, and ribbons make, indeed, no venerable appearance upon paper;—no more do eating and drinking;—yet the one can no more be worn without being made, than the other can be swallowed without being cooked; and those who can neither pay milliners nor keep scullions, must either toil for themselves, or go capless and dinnerless." The demands of dress during her stay with the Thrales in London impinge on her writing time, she explains to Crisp, and she must put "Furbelows and gew-gaws" before "duodecimos, octavos or quartos" (*DL* 1: 314). Burney's obvious irritation with the time consumed by such conventional tasks (her fingers, unlike those of Rousseau's Sophie, were not formed more for the needle than the pen) suggests that she sees her obligations to dress both as Crisp would see them—as "paltry, ridiculous" wastes of human energy—and as a necessary part of her life as a middle-class lady in town.[27] Evelina evinces a similar perspective—both accepting and contemptuous—on the role that the toilette and its attendant tasks, shopping and sewing, play in her experience of "high life." She writes, with apologetic zest, of "making caps" (23) and going to the shops; the women of Evelina's party see their first priority upon arrival in the city as "Londonizing" themselves, refurbishing their dress according to current fashion. Mrs. Mirvan, one of the few pleasant people in the novel, objects to going to the theater before this task is complete, and, when "teized" into compliance, stipulates that they "sit in some obscure place, that she may not be seen" (25). Evelina reports, with an air of neutrality, all this effort spent on keeping up sartorial decorum, simply accepting her part in the customs of public life for the well-off young lady. Evelina's polite neutrality is taxed, however, by the merchant-class, urban chic of her cousins, the Branghton sisters, and the vanity and super-ficiality of her grandmother's obsession with the toilette; Eve-lina's distaste for these women's disregard for politeness, kind-ness, decency—almost, indeed, their own identities—in their devotion to fashion places her in danger of a complicity with satiric attitudes toward women and dress. Anger at misspent female energy upsets the delicate balance of Evelina's am-bivalence, her detached engagement in (or engaged detachment from) the morally problematic duties of the female toilette. Evelina's point of view on the Branghtons and Madame Duval approaches alignment with a critical perspective on the toilette too easily tainted by a contempt for women—too similar, in fact, to Captain Mirvan's misogynistic perspective. Evelina runs dan-gerously close to seeing and, hence, portraying Madame Duval, her grandmother, in many of the same terms that Mirvan as-sumes in his condemnation of the fashion-conscious, "French-ified" old woman. In Evelina's account of her to Mr. Villars, Duval fulfills the stereotype of the woman who invests her self-image in her clothes ("did you ever see a wash-woman in such a gown as this?" [51]), almost as if Evelina were, against her will, giving evidence to confirm Mirvan's material approach to female identity. Evelina is embarrassed by her grandmother's obsession with the toilette (perhaps because it hints strongly at the moral chaos and "dirty" sexuality so often associated with women of her age who are, as Evelina says, so particular as to dress), and Evelina's role of observer in recording Mirvan's physical and verbal assaults on Duval is tainted by her awareness of her grandmother's guilt on many counts commonly associated with women's obsession with dress; she is certainly not on Mirvan's side, and would stop him if she could, but she also sees too clearly how her grandmother plays into the Captain's hands, and a laugh of complicity in Mirvan's pranks often hovers just above the surface of Evelina's discomfort with them.

Burney, however, evades the implication of Evelina's complicity—and, as a result, of her own—in Mirvan's behavior by also giving us, through Evelina's dual point of view both as a woman conventionally implicated in the feminine duties of dress and as a detached observer on them, a critical perspective on Mirvan the satirist as well as on the feminine occupations he satirizes. Evelina recounts Mirvan's assaults on Duval as crude, physical dramatizations, far from clever and unlikely to establish the moral superiority of their perpetrator. On one occasion Mirvan literally covers the hapless Duval with more-than-metaphoric mud, an over-literalization of the filth that is so commonly associated with women of more fashion than sense. Another of his physical attacks on her results in a Swiftian dismantling of the bits and pieces of artificial feminine splendor—like Celia's "White, Black, and Red / Which Though still in Sight, had changed their Ground":[28] "Her head-dress had fallen off; her linen was torn; her negligee had not a pin left in it; her petticoats she was obliged to hold on; and her shoes were perpetually slipping off. She was covered with dirt, weeds, and filth, and her face was really horrible, for the pomatum and powder from her head, and the dust from the road, were quite *pasted* on her skin by her tears, which, with her *rouge*, made so frightful a mixture, that she hardly looked human" (148).

In the context of Duval's role in the novel as the stereotypic clothes horse who invests her identity in what she wears, Mirvan's attack on her is a debased, mechanical dismantling of female artificiality that reveals the sadism of the prankster more effectively than the filth and fragmentation of his victim. Evelina's description deconstructs the satirist while he takes apart the satirized: although Duval is reduced to the object who "hardly looked human," a symbol of fragmented, tainted femininity lurking beneath fine clothes, the satirical objectification of the woman is qualified by Evelina's insight into the crude, mechanical nature of this particular satirist's actions. Evelina also gives us a victim's-eye view of the effects of such debased satire through her awareness of her grandmother's "real suffering." Burney—through Evelina—seems to be seeing double, looking at the unreflecting satirist from the point of view of the satirized, while granting some justice to the criticisms made by the attack.

Similarly, while Evelina portrays the Branghton sisters after the manner of Swift's Celia, she also sets up their brother as an embarrassingly sophomoric Strephon: "But the best fun is, when they've got all their dirty things on, and all their hair about their ears, sometimes I send young Brown up stairs to them; and then there's such a fuss!—there they hide themselves, and run away, and squeal and squall like any thing mad, and so then I puts the two cats into the room, and I gives 'em a good whipping, and so that sets them a squalling too: so there's such a noise, and such an uproar!—Lord, you can't think, Miss, what fun it is!" (175). Evelina responds with disgust to both the vain, superficial women and their mindless, superficial critics in the novel; but while she softens occasionally toward her grandmother, and even speaks a favorable word or two about the obnoxious Branghton sisters—at least one of them—her dislike of Mirvan and Tom Branghton remains unqualified. Although Burney clearly wants to detach her heroine from a blind obsession with the toilette, she seems just as eager to distinguish Evelina's critical stance toward obsessions with dress from stupid, misogynistic equations of the female character with filth and superficiality.

Instead of taking the unambivalent position of either questioning the extent to which women's roles are shaped by their obligations to the toilette—as Wollstonecraft does—or affirming the inherent value of conventional female sartorial duties, Burney seeks an ambivalent detachment within the problematic role of animate decoration. The rites that the Branghtons turn into squalor and chaos are orderly and decorous for Evelina but also remote, as if just on the margins of her consciousness; unlike the woman who merges her identity with her dress, Evelina is quietly detached from what she does at the dressing table, while still firmly within the physical confines of the traditional role: "I have just had my hair dressed. You can't think how oddly my head feels; full of powder and black pins, and a great cushion on the top of it. I believe you would hardly know me, for my face looks quite different to what it did before my hair was dressed. When I shall be able to make use of a comb for myself I cannot tell, for my hair is so much entangled, *frizled* they call it, that I fear it will be very difficult" (27-28). Evelina's mind is so far from being merged with the external, that she feels almost alienated from her own body, as if its new complexities placed it beyond her control. This passage turns inside out material objectifications of female consciousness as the sum of its external trappings and suggests that however women's bodies may be transformed by trivial pursuits, their minds may remain curiously separate within the conventions that define them, and, hence, may be unknowable from a masculine perspective: "*You can't think* how oddly my head feels."* (My emphasis, of course.) This "oddness" is, however, not a transcendence of Burney's ambivalence, but rather a highly problematic emotional and intellectual freedom that is gained at the cost of Evelina's alienation from the physical reality of self: the female body becomes a strange and uncontrollable terrain rather than a manifestation of identity, toward which the female mind assumes a weirdly dispassionate attitude of separateness.

But if the strains of ambivalence lead to a vision of entrapment—detached female intelligence in the cage of the socialized woman's body—Evelina's sense of separateness from the artificiality of women's self-creation at the toilette also results, at moments in the text, in what Hélène Cixous has called "the laugh of the Medusa," a fully woman-centered response to patriarchal conventions and power.[29] The observer status that protects Evelina from complicity can also lead to an incipient critique of ideology—instead of mere evasion. Evelina expresses her sense

of the experience of a woman psychologically outside the patriarchal institutions of feminine life; the shops, she coolly reports, are "really very entertaining, especially the mercers," but
her response to them is more analytical than gushing. She remains an amused and detached spectator, tempted to laugh at the
masculine proponents of sartorial vanity, a vanity so often seen as
the special weakness of young women:

> There seem to be six or seven men belonging to each shop, and every
> one took care, by bowing and smirking, to be noticed; we were
> conducted from one to another, and carried from room to room, with
> so much ceremony, that at first I was almost afraid to follow....But
> what most diverted me was, that we were more frequently served by
> men than by women; and such men! so finical, so affected! they seemed
> to understand every part of a woman's dress better than we do ourselves;
> and they recommended caps and ribbands with an air of so much
> importance, that I wished to ask them how long they had left off
> wearing them! [27]

This passage locates sartorial vanity outside female consciousness, in one of the economic institutions of eighteenth-century
culture. The joke in this passage is that Evelina stands apart from
institutionalized triviality—as country girl come to the city—
while men enthusiastically promote the economic enterprise of
women's trivial pursuits. Instead of emphasizing women's love
for dress—the stereotype assumed by *Evelina's* male clerks (as
well as by many of its readers)—this incident in the novel suggests that female vanity may be a product of society—more
important to patriarchal economic institutions than to female
self-identification—and proposes, however tentatively, that women are morally and politically outside—not inside—the social
formations that promote their triviality.

Evelina's response to the male shopkeepers has, perhaps, a
more serious side to it. Around the turn of the eighteenth century, Clara Reeve, Priscilla Wakefield, and Mary Ann Radcliffe
protest against "male usurpation" of employments traditionally

suitable for impecunious, middle-class women. Shops constitute a large area of potential jobs for women where men were taking an ever-increasing share of available employment. When Evelina ridicules men who were encroaching on women's few paid occupations in the eighteenth century, Burney may be alluding to the grim economic side of female employments, the side that she develops in her novel at the turn of the century, *The Wanderer; or, Female Difficulties.*[30]

While Burney rarely takes the position that Wollstonecraft takes in the *Vindication* or in her unfinished novel, *Maria; or, the Wrongs of Women*—the step into radical revision of the institutions that shape women's lives—she is acutely sensitive to the difficulty of finding self-worth within those institutions. Her novels most frequently show her seeking conventional, not revisionary, solutions to this difficulty.[31] Her creative energy did not run to criticizing the informing assumptions of female life, but to revealing, without resolving, basic contradictions within ideology. At what point does the keen observer become the social critic? At what point does *Evelina's* separation of female identity from ideologically conventional roles become a critique of them? I suspect that the line between observer and critic is less distinct than we might wish to assume and that many more rebellions against the means of women's oppression are incipient rather than actual in eighteenth-century women's texts—though nonetheless real, and nonetheless akin to rebellions more easily recognizable to the feminist critic of 1986.

Evelina and Wollstonecraft's *Maria* approach the dissonances of middle-class women's lives in ways that are obviously different, but they are not texts alien to each other: they both seek ways of living with contradictions that arise from women's ghettoized position within—and yet separate from—their culture. Ambivalence and the need to resolve—or evade—contradiction are, logically, products of living in roles that one is told are both necessary and, in the larger sense, without much value. Wollstonecraft's *Vindication* and Burney's *Evelina* manifest different

strategies for coping with the contradictory and potentially debilitating ideology of femininity: Wollstonecraft by countering
the contradiction with a revisionary stance, Burney by making
the very terms of contradiction into an enabling duplicity. While
we may be more comfortable discussing Wollstonecraft's "feminism" than we are in making claims for Burney's, we lose a great
deal that is important to feminist, revisionary views of literary
history if we, like Captain Mirvan, place eighteenth-century
women writers such as Burney in reductive categories, making
ghettos within the ghetto.

FIVE

CECILIA
Love and Work

Cecilia (1782) was Burney's follow-up after *Evelina*'s success brought her out of anonymity and into the public notice of literary London. Besides bringing her public attention, the acclaim given to Burney's first novel also, ironically, brought her under the controlling influence of family and friends she wished to please: her father, Charles Burney, her longtime friend and mentor, Samuel Crisp, her new mentor, Samuel Johnson, and Hester Thrale, with whom she spent much of her time after the authorship of *Evelina* was discovered. While writing *Evelina* had been a private, unsupervised activity, *Cecilia* was created in a relatively public context, under the surveillance of a primarily male group of mentors. Initially during the period after *Evelina*'s publication, Burney turned to writing a play at the urging of her friends and mentors, but this enterprise—a satirical piece that touched on many of Burney's literary acquaintances—appeared too risky to Charles Burney and to Crisp, who firmly advised her to suppress the play and return to work in the genre of her first success. Burney followed this advice, but not without resentment; characteristically, her response to this critical direction of her creativity is mixed and contradictory. She apparently never questioned the right of her male mentors to direct her, but she was clearly annoyed at their interference. The psychological conditions under which Burney wrote *Cecilia* were, then, conditions of conflict between love and work; her feminine sense of subservient relationship with masculine authority made her genuinely, sincerely obedient—a socially defined form of love—but this love was at odds with her desire to direct and control her own writing projects—a desire to be empowered by and in her own work. The contradiction implicit in the very term "woman writer" takes the specific biographical form of Burney's struggle, after *Evelina*'s success, to control both her self-image as a woman defined in terms of class and gender ideology and her own artistic career. Her firsthand experience as a successful novelist who was also a young, dependent woman suggests the formidable odds against the successful outcome of such a struggle.

Cecilia, I will argue, reflects the contradiction between love and work in a double plot structure that exposes women's over-determined social powerlessness through the use of two conventional concerns of eighteenth-century English fiction: romantic love and the search for "a course in life." Cecilia, the heroine, is involved in the working out of two plots, which could be characterized as different plans for achieving happiness. First, a romantic love story (parallelling Evelina's progress toward marital joy) places female happiness in the ideological context of married love as women's greatest earthly success; second, a *Rasselas*-like search for a plan of life appropriate for the middle-class, affluent young woman, the occupations and employments best suited to genteel female happiness, places the heroine's story in the context of concern for what women can or should safely and virtuously do with themselves besides falling in love or being loved. I am not suggesting that *Cecilia* should be read, however, as a radically new mix of romantic fiction and Johnsonian philosophical narrative. Cecilia's attempts to arrange and control her life are certainly reminiscent of Rasselas' search for a course in life, and Burney's use of a romantic love plot recalls hundreds of earlier sentimental novels, but the conjunction of the heroine's progress in romance with lessons in proper occupations for young women is not, in itself, an innovative one. Many eighteenth-century fictional heroines had prepared the way for Burney's juxtaposition of a quest for romantic fulfillment with experiments in feminine employments and amusements. Richardson's Harriet Byron, for example, learns not to go to mas-

querades in the process of falling in love with the hero, Sir
Charles Grandison. Eliza Haywood's Betsey Thoughtless finds
out how careless indulgence in the pleasures and pastimes available to fashionable young women can misrepresent her to the
man she wishes to marry. (Indeed, Burney may well have learned
much from Haywood about the plotting and thematic uses of
female blundering into the suspicious-minded hero's tendency to
see his intended in as unfavorable a light as possible. *Cecilia* and
the 1796 *Camilla* both make use of this paradigm, so effectively
deployed by Haywood to chart some of the dangers implicit in
middle-class women's ideological position.) While Burney's debt
to other novelists—particularly women—is a given that could
bear considerably more analysis than it has received, my focus
here is on Burney's deployment of such fictional paradigms and
how that deployment changed over the course of her shift from
anonymity to fame.

Whereas in *Evelina* the love plot easily subsumes the far less
striking and less visible allusive suggestions about female occupations and pastimes into its fairy-tale resolution of a young
lady's entrance into the world, in *Cecilia* the course of the heroine's true love, although ultimately successful, is made rougher
by a complicated series of misunderstandings and misap-
pearances in which the heroine's "course of life" plot entangles
her. The social relations in which the heroine's course of life
involve her are defined by gender in ways that militate against her
achieving happiness through either love or work because they
mask her real character in damagingly superficial—and wrong—
assumptions: they prevent her being romantically loved as she
deserves, and this thwarting of affection, in turn, taints her
attempts at happiness outside the sphere of romantic love. The
plot of love and the plot of searching for a course of life interfere
with and frustrate each other in Burney's second novel because of
the specific social conditions of femininity in mid-eighteenth-
century culture.

The production of *Cecilia* was strikingly public, compared to

the secrecy and quiet that attended *Evelina* into print: the novel
was written at the urging of Burney's father and her mentor,
Samuel Crisp; it was read in manuscript by a fair number of
Burney's literary acquaintances and was generally talked about
and commented on as the five volumes came out in the summer
of 1782.[1] Burney's July, 1782 preface acknowledges the "far more
encouragement" with which she "sends *Cecilia* into the world,"
and denies, at the same time, "all vanity of confidence," asserting, instead, "the precariousness of any power to give pleasure."[2]
As I have argued, public recognition did not dispel her pessimism
about being treated well herself as a woman writer entering the
world, however happy an ending she had arranged for Evelina,
and the evident reluctance with which she sends her second novel
"into the world" is reflected in her new heroine's forced entrance
into a society governed by rules not personal and familial. Twice
orphaned—first by the deaths of her parents, then by her uncle's—Cecilia must, by the terms of the latter's will, leave the
"quietness of the country" and the "bosom of an aged and
maternal counsellor, whom she loved as her mother, and to
whom she had been known from her childhood" (I, 2) in order to
live with one of three town-dwelling guardians, men appointed
by the will, for the rest of her minority. Reluctantly leaving the
locus of the personal and maternal for that of the legal and
masculine, Cecilia solaces herself "by plans of future happiness"
in the renewal of friendship with one of her guardians' wives, a
childhood friend; in other words, she makes her entrance into the
world by seeking to retain the social terms of female bonding that
inform the personal and domestic realm that she is leaving.

The originating events of *Cecilia*'s plot both recall and significantly depart from Evelina's entrance into the world. Evelina
leaves the secure domain of a male parent substitute—Mr. Villars—to encounter a series of social and psychological dangers
and eventually gain renewed security under the male protection
of her real father and her husband. Cecilia's exit from "the abode
of her youth, and residence of her forefathers" locates parental

protection in the past—Cecilia's parents are four years dead—and portrays her more recently deceased uncle in legalistic terms that contrast sharply with the emotionally charged language used to describe both Evelina's Villars and the maternal "bosom" of the female counsellor that the uncle's death forces Cecilia to leave (I, 1–2). Male protectors are consistently portrayed, from the novel's beginning, as outside the realm of secure domesticity or as somehow antithetical to it. Cecilia's uncle is primarily important for making legal arrangements that militate against her regaining the domestic security that she loses by his death: First, his will hands her over to three male guardians who, it seems, could not be less inclined to afford her domestic comfort and emotional security, and, second, he stipulates a "name clause" requiring her future husband to take her family name of Beverley—a stipulation that later frustrates her marriage and reentry into domestic security. While Cecilia finally achieves emotional and social equilibrium through marriage, the male mentors who secure that equilibrium for Evelina generally bungle the management of Cecilia's domestic arrangements and emotional comfort.[3]

While Evelina certainly encounters some bad male "protectors" after leaving Mr. Villars—Captain Mirvan being a case in point—Cecilia's male guardians are virtual parodies of the patriarchal social authority that theoretically should protect her. Mr. Harrel, the young and fashionable husband of Cecilia's childhood friend, tangles Cecilia up in his own dissipated life, forces her to go into debt in futile attempts to recoup his gambling losses, and tries to manipulate her into a marriage with an aristocratic creditor, the opportunistic and exploitative Sir Robert Floyer. Eventually, unable even to save himself, let alone protect Cecilia, Harrel kills himself. The aristocratic and pathologically proud Mr. Delvile humiliates, rejects, and refuses to protect her when she is most in need of his aid; Mr. Briggs, appointed guardian for his business sense in managing Cecilia's fortune, subjects her to a veritable travesty of domestic comfort when she attempts, against her better judgment, to make her home with him: Briggs'

idea of making his ward comfortable involves coarse comments
on her marital possibilities, the ordering of poverty-level furnish-
ings for her chamber, and the procurement of a lobster, which he
frugally refuses to discard even after it begins to stink. Male
protection pointedly fails to give—even militates against—the
domestic security and comfort it is supposed to afford.

Female companionship assumes an emotional centrality in
Cecilia, not as a truly viable alternative to the protection of men,
but as an underscoring of its inadequacy. Cecilia, not surprisingly
given the quality of her masculine "friends," tends to depend on
women for emotional security. When she leaves home, she regrets leaving her older female companion, Mrs. Charlton, but
hopes to compensate for her loss in the companionship of Mrs.
Harrel, a childhood friend, now married and living a fashionable
life in London. Mrs. Harrel, however, is the first indication that
female friendship is not entirely separable from the social relations determined by male authority; women's companionship
fails as a reliable haven when the male protection that should
nurture domesticity fails. When Cecilia goes to make her home
with her old friend, she finds that Mrs. Harrel has lost all capacity
for intimacy in her fascination with public pleasures and superficial society, a fascination created in her otherwise "innocent"
heart by her marriage to a man with little interest in encouraging
domestic pleasures: "married very young, she had made an
immediate transition from living in a private family and a country town, to becoming mistress of one of the most elegant houses
in Portman-square . . . and wife to a man whose own pursuits
soon showed her the little value he himself set upon domestic
happiness" (I, 30). Cecilia's first evening of the much-anticipated
reunion with her friend is spent with a large company of visitors,
and she soon finds herself pushed into a way of life that is
antithetical to the ideal of secure, domestic intimacy she pursues:
"the mornings were all spent in gossipping, shopping, and dressing, and the evenings were regularly appropriated to public
places, or large parties of company" (I, 48). Female friendship in

Evelina leaves much to be desired in its practical efficacy in protecting the heroine, but it provides significant emotional support for Evelina in the first stage of her entrance into the world. In *Cecilia*, the fashionable life in which women engage and which men control militates against such emotional solace. Instead of the comforting—if practically ineffectual—intimacy of Evelina's relationship with Mrs. and Miss Mirvan in the midst of London pleasures, Cecilia meets women who act out of mindless adherence to social custom rather than real social concern. The meaningless volubility of Miss Larolles and the near catatonic nonresponsiveness of Miss Leeson are both, as the novel's social satirist Mr. Gosport points out, fashions of the "TON misses": "the SUPERCILIOUS . . . and the VOLUBLE" (I, 37). Outside the space of domesticity, female companionship is a matter of form rather than intimacy, and the domesticity that nurtures real connection between women is betrayed by the male protectors who should, in eighteenth-century gender ideology, ensure its survival.

Emotional intimacy suffers and dies in the fashionable wasteland of Burney's second novel. I suspect that this darkening of Burney's view of being in the world (once the young lady has entered it) is at least partially the effect of Burney's acute sense of insecurity outside of relationships defined in personal, familial terms, her feelings of disempowerment in social relations that are not informed by intimacy. After *Evelina*'s success, the problem of power in nonpersonal, nonfamilial relations was clearly on her mind: she writes of Elizabeth Montague's precarious position as head bluestocking, "many as are the causes by which respect can be lessened, there are very few by which it can be afterwards restored to its first dignity. But where there is real affection, the case is exactly reversed; few things can weaken and every trifle can revive it." And the social life of London was the antithesis of the personal intercourse that Burney saw as the most reliable means to empowerment; she writes, in winter of 1782, "I begin to grow most heartily sick of this continual round of visiting, and these eternal new acquaintances" (*DL* 1:462; 2:210). Cecilia's experience in town parallels Burney's personal sense of being exposed and vulnerable in the midst of an emotional wasteland. The failure of domesticity and the unreliability of male protection in *Cecilia* also suggest that Burney's entry into the public realm of literary fame may have reinforced an already strong distrust of women's powers outside the limited range of personal influence over the male authority that, through cultural sanctions, structured so much of her life.

Outside the realm of domestic intimacy, social life assumes, for Cecilia, a multiplicity of emotionally meaningless forms. Whereas the fashionable life of dissipation is laughed at in *Evelina* as sometimes entertaining, sometimes silly, *Cecilia* treats it with narratorial distrust: its emphasis on superficial forms of social behavior interferes with—indeed, almost prevents—any emotionally gratifying or intellectually useful interaction. Cecilia finds that the life of dissipation leads to social alienation and personal loneliness:

She saw nobody she wished to see, as she had met with nobody for whom she could care;...upon every first meeting, the civilities which were shown her, flattered her into believing she had excited a partiality that a very little time would ripen into affection; the next meeting commonly confirmed the expectation; but the third, and every future one, regularly destroyed it. She found that time added nothing to their fondness, nor intimacy to their sincerity; that the interest in her welfare which appeared to be taken at first sight, seldom with whatever reason, increased, and often without any abated. [I, 50]

Social interaction continually excites and disappoints Cecilia's desire for affection, in a repeating pattern of form promising a content it fails to deliver. Cecilia's experience in town sets forth the paradox between a set of rigid social forms that *should* render meaning reassuringly stable—if somewhat predictable—and an emotional content, a psychological and personal meaning that continually eludes Cecilia as a reader of social forms.

Burney expresses this paradox most forcefully in the masquerade scene set early in the novel, while Cecilia is still new to the system of social relations associated with town life. Terry Castle brilliantly reads this scene as a "set piece" encoding the potentially subversive energy of the "carnivalesque" into predictable social forms.[4] Indeed, the narrator's world-weary tone in describing the event undercuts the heroine's naive amusement and asks the reader to read the carnivalesque representation as predictable, as set in codes formed by social—and literary—expectation. The narrator's ennui is not the only attitude toward the scene that the text makes available to the reader, however, and the set piece of masquerade also affords the pleasure of watching a social ritual, known but still rich enough to amuse. In fact, the narrator's superior distance on the scene may enhance the enjoyment of form for familiarity's sake, of the predictability of the show. There is yet another vantage point on this scene, however: Castle argues that Cecilia is herself totally objectified during this scene, that the reader is completely excluded from her point of view;[5] I would argue that while readers do not view the scene from inside Cecilia's mind, they are certainly given access to both her pleasure and her discomfort in what is, to her, a novel phenomenon that both entertains and confuses. Indeed, what Cecilia does not know, what she does not understand about events, inserts unknowability into predictability, the puzzling and unrepresented into the over-familiarized forms of the masquerade. Even the narrator's world-weary tone in describing the masks suggests the elusiveness of meaning in the scene, the point at which the over-familiarity and predictability of form blur into meaningless social gesture. The narrator stresses the conventionality of the scene, but also points to a lack of emotional or intellectual content, glossing the quality of Cecilia's "real" social interactions:

Her expectations of entertainment were not only fulfilled but surpassed; the variety of dresses, the medley of characters, the quick succession of figures, and the ludicrous mixture of groups, kept her

attention unwearied: while the conceited efforts at wit, the total
thoughtlessness of consistency, and the ridiculous incongruity of the
language with the appearance, were incitements to surprise and diversion without end. Even the local cant of, *Do You know me? Who are you?*
and *I know you*; with the sly pointing of the finger, the arch nod of the
head, and the pert squeak of the voice, though wearisome to those who
frequent such assemblies, were, to her unhackneyed observation, additional subjects of amusement. (II, 102)

The dearth of personal referents for human social identity in
Cecilia's social life is parodied by the nonreferentiality of the
masqueraders' familiar costumes and behavior—"Dominos of
no character, and fancy-dresses of no meaning, made, as is usual
at such meetings, the general herd of the company: for the rest,
the men were Spaniards, chimney-sweepers, Turks, watchmen,
conjurers, and old women; and the ladies, shepherdesses, orange
girls, Circassians, gipseys, haymakers, and sultanas" (II, 102-
103)—a lack that the narrator emphasizes, however entertaining
Cecilia at first finds the show. This distance between the heroine
and the narrator of her story destroys, for the reader, any possibility of an innocent ambivalence—such as Evelina's—toward the
first mode of living Cecilia encounters after leaving the Happy
Valley of her youth, and it underlines the need to resist actively
the slippage of social form away from emotional and intellectual
content. Spectatorship is amusing for a while, but Cecilia soon
finds that even passive observation can embroil her in social
relations that bewilder and oppress. The masquerade scene illustrates that meaning is not firmly encoded in the predictability of
social form; neither, however, is it evaded or erased by the
arbitrary referentiality of social behavior and appearance. Rather,
it is released into an uncontrolled and dangerous slide through a
confusing series of social signifiers. Cecilia finds herself caught in
a living social text that is as dangerously obtrusive as it is hard to
read. A passive acceptance of the human show, however entertaining, is untenable for Cecilia. The very predictability of the
masquerade itself hides a subterranean system of social relations
unknowable and, hence, threatening to the heroine.

Cecilia is the only guest at the Harrels' masquerade to remain in her usual dress, a fact that renders her conspicuous and an easy target for the various masqueraders who have designs of one kind or another on her. A clear, direct correspondence between dress and identity makes Cecilia vulnerable, a paradigm that parallels and underscores the vulnerability of the heroine's personal integrity in a society where the appearance of social relation is so often unrelated to actual human feeling. The text of the masquerade is not arbitrary in its relation between appearance and reality, signifier and signified; rather, the form that represents meaning communicates incompletely and imperfectly to Cecilia by leaving out some essential piece of information. Castle tells us of the eighteenth-century habit of masquerading as the opposite of one's real class or personal nature, and the masks at the Harrels' masquerade follow this custom with some predictability.[6] The flighty, foolish Miss Larolles, for instance, is dressed as Minerva—in contradiction to her character. As Castle also points out, however, many characters come dressed allegorically as themselves, only more so. Mr. Briggs, for instance, comes in the dirty, foul-smelling clothes of a real chimney sweep—an over-literalization of his earthy materialism. Belfield, an unrealistic but well-intentioned young man of great moral courage and little practical sense, comes as Don Quixote, an appropriate fictional signifier for his character. In one sense, the dress of these masks is an indicator of real identity, but the fact that costume may be directly or inversely related to character underscores the arbitrary logic of the code. More important, while the relation between form and meaning may be clear to the reader and narrator, Cecilia's ignorance of real agendas—psychological and economic—suggests the dangerously unknowable within the over-familiar relations between mask and character, appearance and emotional content.

For example, Cecilia is beset at the masquerade by a man in a devil's costume who most oppressively and obsequiously hovers about her—in the manner of a submissive, courtly lover—while aggressively keeping at bay everyone else who might wish to

speak to her. Initially slightly irritating, the devil's attentions
becomes increasingly difficult to bear as he isolates her with his
oppressive "devotion." Cecilia mistakes him, at first, for Sir
Robert Floyer, a dissipated nobleman who, indeed, rather devil-
ishly seeks to repair his family fortunes by marrying her. Sir
Robert is, however, too imperiously indolent to go to any such
trouble to capture Cecilia, a fact that is relayed by his actual
costume—that of a Turk. The reader is informed that the devil is,
in fact, Mr. Monckton, a man considered an old family friend by
Cecilia. Monckton is married—for economic reasons—to an
aging and irascible wife, Lady Margaret; throughout the novel,
he plots to keep Cecilia unwed until Lady Margaret dies and then
to marry her himself—not solely for money, but also for the
intellectual and sexual companionship he covets and is denied in
his current wife. The relation between Monckton's real agenda
and the appearance and behavior he takes on at the ball is not,
therefore, illogical or inappropriate—quite the reverse. But it is
predicated on a factor—Monckton's desire for Cecilia—that the
heroine cannot know. The correspondence between social form
and personal reality is not, as I have said, arbitrary, but it is often
based on factors that are hidden from the heroine. Similarly,
Cecilia meets and likes the hero, Delvile, her guardian's son and
her future love interest, in the guise of a "white domino," a
costume, as the narrator says, of "no character" that gives Cecilia
little indication of the emotional agenda beneath his pleasing
behavior. Castle documents the ambiguity of this costume in
eighteenth-century masquerade, the impenetrable nature of its
appearance.[7] The narrative of the novel bears out the logic and
appropriateness of Delvile's costume: the subsequent ambiguity
of his feelings for Cecilia while she, in turn, falls increasingly in
love with him, makes him, like the white domino, a fair but
unwritten page for much of the novel. But this logic is initially
unavailable to Cecilia, and must be revealed through the painful
working out of the narrative. Even the obvious logic of Delvile's
costume gestures toward what Cecilia cannot know, the arbitrary
and unpredictable nature of personal circumstances. There is a

logic to social appearance's relation to psychological and economic reality, but this logic is often based on arbitrary, personally
specific circumstances. Cecilia has no way of knowing that the
eccentric pride of her guardian prevents his son, the white domino, from declaring and acting on his feelings for her. The masquerade scene in *Cecilia* calls our attention to the complexity and
particularity of meaning's relation to social form and underscores
the vulnerability of the heroine's integrity in such an unpredictable social context.

The fashionable life that living with the Harrels offers Cecilia
is not merely boring; it is dangerous in both psychic and material
terms. Harrel ruins both himself and his wife with gambling and
dissipation, while also seriously damaging the finances of both
Arnott, his brother-in-law, and Cecilia herself. His plots to marry
Cecilia to Sir Robert Floyer, in payment for a gambling debt,
embroil her in gossip and a series of misunderstandings with her
other guardians and with Delvile, the man she would actually
like to marry. Harrel's suicide releases Cecilia from the persecu-
tions that constitute his "protection." Mrs. Harrel is, on the other
hand, emotionally and intellectually dead, to all intents and
purposes, before Cecilia even meets her in town. Cecilia "found
her insensible to friendship, indifferent to her husband, and negli-
gent of all social felicity. Dress, company, parties of pleasure, and
public places, seemed not merely to occupy all her time, but to
gratify her wishes" (I, 29). Like Swift's Dorinda or the *Spectator*'s
coquette, Mrs. Harrel has practically ceased to exist except by,
through, and in her fashionable enthusiasms. The fashionable life
that Cecilia encounters in her entrance into the world is one that
drains human personal and social identity of any emotional
content beyond its own trivial enthusiasms and the anxiety of
fending off ruin and exhaustion. The Harrels' ruinous course of
life carries Cecilia along against her desires and exertions to stop
it, and Cecilia finds herself in a social state devoid of the personally empowering emotions of friendship and replete with those
that disable and enervate.

Cecilia is quick, however, to see the dangers of passively accepting the life offered her by the Harrels, and she soon begins forming new plans to replace the expectations of a happiness based on an intimacy that barely exists. After visitors have left the Harrels on Cecilia's first night in town, she finds the evening "much more to her satisfaction; it was devoted to friendship, to mutual enquiries, to kind congratulations, and endearing re- collections" (I, 24). The next morning, however, she discovers that she is alone in her expectations of renewing "a conversation which has afforded her so much pleasure," as the fashionably late hours of the town keep the family upstairs and apart until visiting hours bring more company. Cecilia learns quickly not to depend on the pleasures of "friendship." "The next morning, Cecilia took care to fill up her time more advantageously, than in wan- dering about the house in search of a companion she now ex- pected not to find: she got together her books, arranged them to her fancy, and secured to herself, for the future occupation of her leisure hours, the exhaustless fund of entertainment which read- ing, that richest, highest, and noblest source of intellectual enjoy- ment, perpetually affords" (I, 27). Cecilia, disappointed of the domestic intimacy she sees as central to a full and happy life, begins her search for pastimes and entertainments that will instill her time with meaning and a sense of control. The narrator's panegyric on the intellectual pleasures of reading does not at- tempt to mask their status as a substitute for the emotionally gratifying, conversational pleasures that are Cecilia's first choice—a choice denied to her. And apart from the real esteem in which the narrator—and Burney—hold literary pastimes, this passage stresses one of their main advantages: they allow Cecilia control over her time, empowering her in ways that social inter- course does not. Books, unlike people, can be "arranged to her fancy" and give a pleasure that is "secured to herself." And, I might add, literary texts, however complex, are less bewil- deringly diverse and seemingly arbitrary in their systems of signification than the social text that Cecilia tries, with difficulty, to decipher.

Cecilia's planned alternatives to real human intimacy are attempts to achieve the autonomy that her wealth and single status
would seem to offer her. Her revulsion against trivial pursuits
leads her to seek a "plan of conduct, better suited to her taste and
feelings than the frivolous insipidity of her present life, to make at
once a more spirited and more worthy use of the affluence,
freedom and power which she possessed. A scheme of happiness
at once rational and refined soon presented itself to her imagination. She purposed, for the basis of her plan, to become mistress
of her own time, and with this view, to drop all idle and uninteresting acquaintance, . . . she could then show some taste and
discernment in her choice of friends." Admitting acquaintance
only on the basis of "piety" or "accomplishments and manners"
would soon, she wryly reasons, leave her with plenty of time left
over for "music and reading"; her private life arranged in a
manner that conduces to control over her own time, Cecilia then
plans for "what was due from her to the world," her "strong
sense of DUTY, a fervent desire to ACT RIGHT." As with the
allocation of her private time, Cecilia's plans for social responsibility are attempts at self-empowerment, schemes to enable
herself to act and initiate rather than being acted upon: "now she
supported an orphan, now softened the sorrows of a widow, now
snatched from iniquity the feeble trembler at poverty, and now
rescued from shame the proud struggler with disgrace" (I,
51-52). But these fantasies of doing good run head on into the
problems of achieving personal power in a social context that
limits her actions; in fact, Cecilia cannot act on her plans as long
as she remains a dependent minor: "She felt the impracticability
of beginning at present the alteration in her way of life she had
projected, and therefore thought it most expedient to assume no
singularity, till her independency should enable her to support it
with consistency" (I, 68).

The plan for benevolent action that empowers her in fantasy is
ironically reversed in reality, either forwarded or thwarted by the
impetus of others, as it turns out. Cecilia is induced to charitable

action prior to her majority by the emotional blackmail of Albany, a half-crazy moralist and philanthropist whom she meets at the beginning of her "entrance into the world"—her impulse to "ACT RIGHT" serving as the means to her manipulation rather than her empowerment. Albany's role in relation to Cecilia—an ambiguous combination of moral guide and persecutor—illustrates the vulnerability of the middle-class woman whose actions, however morally laudable on the grounds of charity, involve her in a role more conspicuous, more public than is socially proper or comfortable for her. His repeated public sermons urging her to charitable action expose and discomfort Cecilia by placing her in a situation of public notice damaging to her feminine respectability; Albany's reproaches to her during a party of pleasure "raised such a general alarm, that all the ladies hastily quitted the room, and all the gentlemen endeavoured to enter it, equally curious to see the man who made the oration, and the lady to whom it was addressed. Cecilia, therefore, found her situation insupportable" and pleads with him to approach her with his philanthropic projects in private—since "lessons and notice thus public can do me nothing but injury." For middle-class young women like Cecilia—or Fanny Burney—the "virtues open fairest in the shade," and even virtuous occupations imperil when they draw such public notice. Albany replies to Cecilia's reproach, "spotless were then the hour of thy danger!" (IV, 285)—but danger is danger, however spotless, and thus made public, Cecilia's plan renders her less, not more in control of her actions and how they are perceived.

Cecilia's alarm at public exposure—even of her philanthropy—is akin to the keen, almost morbid alarm that Burney herself felt after the publication of *Evelina* brought her before the public eye. While Burney enjoyed being praised by her father and his illustrious friends, she viewed public exposure of her name with a horror that occasionally wore on the patience even of a then-sympathetic Hester Thrale. When Burney's name came up in a satire, she was physically sick with concern and vowed she

would never be able to reconcile herself to the "horror irrecoverable, of personal abuse" (*DL* 1:127). Cecilia's allergy to publicity,
constantly aggravated throughout the novel by the linkage of her
name with one or another real or imagined suitor, may well be a
fictional corollary of Burney's fear of public exposure. In any
case, *Cecilia* dramatizes the social fact that a middle-class young
lady's course of life must be shaded by the private and domestic,
however virtuous it may be.

Another problem with Cecilia's plan for a life of charitable
works is that even when it does not expose her to the public gaze,
and even when she manages to perform her social duty with a
degree of autonomy, it fails to satisfy the need for human intimacy, the locus, for Burney, of female enpowerment. Cecilia's
scheme for happiness through active charity and quiet study
leaves her emotional nature unsatisfied: "And thus, in acts of
goodness and charity, passed undisturbed another week of the life
of Cecilia: but when the fervour of self-approbation lost its
novelty, the pleasure with which her new plan was begun first
subsided into tranquillity, and then sunk into langour. To a heart
formed for friendship and affection the charms of solitude are
very short-lived; and though she was sickened of the turbulence
of perpetual company, she now wearied of passing all her time by
herself, and sighed for the comfort of society, and the relief of
communication" (II, 126). She longs for "private meetings and
friendly intercourse," but "the endless succession of diversions,
the continual rotation of assemblies, the numerousness of splendid engagements" preclude such supposedly common human
contacts. Since what will satisfy is unavailable, Cecilia seeks to
mingle "amusement with benevolence, to try, at least, to approach that golden mean, which, like the philosopher's stone,
always eludes our grasp, yet always invites our wishes" (II, 127).

This Johnsonian view of human plans for happiness as productive of endlessly deferred satisfaction, an on-going process of
seeking an ever-elusive rule for living, takes on, through plot
developments, a form grounded specifically in Burney's sense of

women's socially defined experience in her culture—an experience informed by the primacy of romantic love. Cecilia, attracted
to Delvile, the son of her pathologically proud, class- and name-
obsessed guardian, finds her growing love for him alternately
frustrated and encouraged by the young Delvile's ambiguous
behavior. Delvile, though attracted to Cecilia, is, for his part,
intimidated by (correct) anticipations of his father's resistance to
the match as socially beneath him, and, partially as a result of that
discouragement, he is ready to grasp at any opportunity to think
Cecilia already "taken" by another man so that he can nobly give
over thoughts of marrying her—and get himself off the hook
with his father. Despite Cecilia's efforts at clarification, Delvile
bows out of her life, with repetitious grace, at every drop of a
rumour: Mr. Harrel's publicity to promote the marriage between
Cecilia and Sir Robert, Cecilia's purely altruistic relationship with
the family of the impractical but deserving Belfield, even the
scanty accumulation of circumstantial evidence linking Cecilia
with these and other men. Cecilia finds herself unable to get on
with her course of life because every action—however uncon-
nected with either Delvile or romance—seems to turn into romantic evidence against her.

Deciding that going with Mrs. Harrel to the opera would be a
good first step toward the "golden mean," Cecilia, after being
frustrated by foolish young ladies' chatter on dress and romantic
conquests, carried on at such a volume as to drown out the voice
of her favorite singer (Burney's real-life favorite at the time,
Pacchierotti), finds herself caught in a misunderstanding that illustrates how a young woman's disinterested feelings of concern
for others—her genuine humanity—will necessarily be confused
with romantic, sexual impulses. This confusion brings the love
plot into conflict with the plot of finding a course in life and
makes the search for any nongender-specific "golden mean"
totally irrelevant to Cecilia's circumstances—which, in turn,
again render the heroine powerless. The ever-elusive "golden
mean" is deferred, for Cecilia, not by fate or the inexorability of

the *human* condition but by the particular vulnerabilities of her femininity as defined by the ideology of romance. Having found some solace in the few minutes of music she was able to hear, Cecilia and the other women of her party seek to make their way into the coffee room; the impetuous Belfield seeks to escort her— out of a spirit of gallantry toward any pretty and amiable young woman, not from a romantic interest in Cecilia—but is pre-empted by Sir Robert Floyer, who, though no more in love with Cecilia than Belfield, is, as usual, obtrusive and rude in his claims to her attention. Belfield's temper flares at this affront, the incident escalates in violence, and swords are drawn. Cecilia, "in an agony of fright," calls out, "Good heaven! will nobody interfere?" (II, 133), and when a duel is later talked of, is quick to propose their friends' interference (II, 136). Cecilia's concern that a human life might be lost over such a trivial matter is widely misconstrued as preference for one man or the other, and she has a great deal of difficulty convincing Delvile that she is not nor does she intend to be engaged to Sir Robert *or* Belfield. Her generalized human feelings are both personalized and sexualized by being forced into a nonexistent love plot, and these misconstructions contribute to a long, complicated series of misunderstandings with her guardians and friends—who are remarkably thick about mentally marrying her off to whatever vaguely eligible male happens to appear connected with her.

Evelina, like *Cecilia*, suggests that social expectations about the moral and social nature of femininity often mean that the heroine is misunderstood by characters too unthinking to perceive her actual integrity and intelligence; but Evelina's pain at being misread is considerably allayed by the reliably appreciative Lord Orville, who, while he does not always understand the heroine, is, at least, disposed to see her favorably. Even when Orville is jealous, with some cause, of Evelina's meetings with her half-brother Macartney, he restrains himself from immediately assuming that she has been duplicitously enjoying his company while already self-disposed to another man. Delvile's tendency to place the worst construction on Cecilia's behavior escalates rather than abates over the course of the novel, culminating in a climactic misreading that literally drives the heroine mad. His first, expedient tendency to see her as romantically involved with someone else becomes a compulsive jealousy—even though he has been given ample assurances of the heroine's affection for him. Indeed, he and Cecilia are secretly wed, but marriage itself does not prevent Delvile from thinking that Cecilia is in love with Belfield when her disinterested liking for him and her concern for his sister, Henrietta, places her in a relation to the Belfield family that looks like intimacy. Delvile refuses explanations and runs after Belfield in a jealous rage, leaving Cecilia hysterical with fear at the encounter between two such hot-headed young men. The romance plot erodes Cecilia's control over circumstances as quickly as she is able to exert it, finally robbing her of control over even her own mind. Femininity, in Burney's second novel, carries specific vulnerabilities inadequately accounted for by rational schemes for happiness, vulnerabilities that derive from the association between femininity and romantic love.

The search-for-a-course-in-life plot of *Cecilia* bears out the good sense of Cecilia's original hopes for the happiness of domestic intimacy, however disappointed these hopes during her stay with the Harrels. Personal friendship is hard to find but nonetheless necessary for making what Cecilia does with her time into a meaningful business. Cecilia's few moments of satisfaction with her London life derive primarily from the visits of Mr. Monckton, on whom she depends as a friend prior to the discovery of his duplicity; later, she enjoys the friendship of Mrs. Delvile, the much more amiable wife of her most unamiable guardian, and the mother of the "white domino," young Delvile. These satisfactions are, however, rare and not necessarily Cecilia's to command. She is able to control and structure, to an extent, what she does outside of the personal and relational—choosing books, music, and charitable causes with which to employ herself—but the social satisfaction of real intimacy remains only marginally

within her power. Her circumstances do not easily yield the
emotional and intellectual satisfaction of an intense engagement
with others' feelings and ideas. As she tells Mr. Monckton about
her dissatisfaction with her life in town, "the disappointment...comes nearer home, and springs not from London, but
from my own situation." What Cecilia means by her "situation"
is evidently the group of people with whom she spends her time:
"from the time of my quitting your house," she tells Monckton,
"till this very moment, when I have again the happiness of
talking with you, I have never once had any conversation, society
or intercourse, in which friendship or affection have had any
share, or my mind has had the least interest" (II, 158). Since she
ranks "friendship the first of human blessings," and the only
reliable inducement to a real interest in others, the diversions that
she thinks might have pleased merely tire her (II, 158). Friendship, when she finds it, invests Cecilia's daily employments with
a worth that diversions, study, and even charity fail to give:
Cecilia, "charmed with having spent the morning with her new
acquaintance [Mrs. Delvile], and the evening with her old friend
[Monckton], retired to rest better pleased with the disposal of her
time than she had yet been since her journey from Suffolk" (II,
162).

Friendship, in *Cecilia*, seems the only consistent and dependable means of investing the heroine's daily employments with
personal gratification and moral value. Cecilia finds in the society
of Delvile and his mother a refuge from the tedium of London
social life with the Harrels: "Easy, gay, and airy, she only rose to
happiness, and only retired to rest; and not merely heightened
was her present enjoyment by her past disappointment, but,
carrying her retrospection to her earliest remembrance, she still
found her actual situation more peculiarly adapted to her taste
and temper, than any she had hitherto at any time experienced."
Mrs. Delvile's company gives her "sources inexhaustible of entertainment" and "every look" from her son is a "reciprocation of
intelligence" (III, 234). Unlike reading, however, this agreeable

form of amusement is not wholly Cecilia's to "secure to herself,"
and other people's agendas—the mercenary needs of the Harrels,
the familial pride of the Delviles—frequently separate her from
these "sources inexhaustible of entertainment."

Cecilia's search for a way of life that includes the satisfaction of
personal intimacy reveals how the ideology of romance poisons
the promise of incorporating this satisfaction into a nonromantic
course of life. Cecilia's devotion to books and music, her first
recourse after being disappointed in the possibilities for domestic
intimacy with the Harrels, leaves her lonely, and she seeks more
active occupations in pursuing the course of charitable work
recommended by the philanthropic, half-mad Albany. Through
his efforts, Cecilia becomes acquainted with the plight of
Belfield's mother and sister, Henrietta. Cecilia discovers these
women, the widow and daughter of a once-prosperous merchant, living in uncomfortable, almost squalid lodgings, without
adequate housekeeping funds or even enough to eat. They have
been reduced to these circumstances by the inability of Belfield to
manage his father's business with even bare success, let alone
profit. In the course of seeking to help the two women—fit-
tingly, to compensate for the inadequacies of male protection, a
form of social security that Cecilia herself has not found particularly reliable—she discovers an interest in developing a personal relationship with Henrietta, who offers the possibility of
good-natured, well-bred companionship. The friendship com-
bines, for Cecilia, some of the charms of charity with the attractions of personal intimacy, and friendship in this case is facilitated
by patronage. The search for meaningful occupations is infused
with the interest of emotional intimacy. Cecilia's friendly power
over Henrietta gives her an emotional as well as altruistic means
of redeeming her own time from the sorrow and tedium of her
relations—or nonrelations—with her guardians and the London
society to which they introduce her. Cecilia finds emotional
balance, if not happiness, in Henrietta's society: "in friendly
conversation and virtuous forbearance, passed gravely, but not

unhappily, the time of Cecilia" (IV, 337). In other words, friendship at least allows Cecilia to make a calm spot in the emotional
storm that is brewing around her as the Harrels pick up their
already frenetic pace toward economic disaster and Harrel's suicide, the end of his guardianship.

Even this measure of control, afforded by the combination of
friendship with charity, is subverted, however, by Cecilia's position as a marriageable young woman. The insensitive Mrs.
Belfield, whose view of human relations is reminiscent of the
Branghtons' of *Evelina*, is incapable of believing that Cecilia's
interest in her daughter is not motivated by a secret passion for
her son, and Cecilia often finds that she is forced to avoid the
friendship of the sister in order to avoid being linked romantically
with the brother. Even more dangerous is young Delvile's tendency to attribute Cecilia's interest in Henrietta to love for her
brother; already disposed to think Belfield an admirable if impractical young man, Delvile has little trouble seeing him as his
rival for Cecilia's affections, however she tries to dispel this false
impression. Cecilia, the beautiful, amiable heiress with warm
feelings and strong desires for affection, is inevitably implicated
in the very notion of romantic love as it occurs to other characters
in the novel—and, of course, to readers of the novel—and romance, real and imagined, continually edges out any other possibilities for Cecilia's empowerment. The hopes and vulnerabilities of romantic love supplant friendship and employments
at the center of Cecilia's concerns in life; the love plot gradually
decenters the course-in-life plot of the novel. This displacement
or decentering results from both real and imputed love on
Cecilia's part: for Delvile, the son of one of her guardians, and, as
false report and ill-informed assumptions would have it, for
Belfield. Whether real or false, romantic love is the snake in the
garden of friendship. The illusion of Cecilia's love for Belfield
blocks her empowering friendship with Henrietta, and when
Henrietta, in a plot twist that anticipates Harriet's love for
Knightley in Austen's *Emma*, conceives a passion for young

Delvile, her brother's friend and patron, Cecilia's intimacy with the young woman is seriously constrained. Cecilia's love for Delvile, in turn, complicates and spoils her friendship with his mother, the amiable and intelligent Mrs. Delvile, who, though she loves Cecilia as a friend, is initially opposed to Cecilia's match with her son on grounds of family pride. Most insidiously, perhaps, sexual desire and greed lurk beneath the surface of Monckton's friendship for Cecilia, so that what Cecilia thinks is his disinterested concern for her welfare is actually a series of poisonous attempts to manipulate her into marriage with himself after the death of Monckton's despised wife. Love—true or false, virtuous or corrupt—reacts on friendship like lemon on cream, leaving Cecilia's course in life outside of romantic love a curdled mess before the novel's ending resolves tensions between the two opposed plots.

Aside from romantic love's disastrous effects on friendships, the feelings that are commonly associated with being in love— both pleasant and unpleasant—consistently and persistently disrupt Cecilia's attempts at a *Rasselas*-like resignation to life's imperfections, made tolerable through employment and social intercourse; Burney's novel at times becomes almost allegorical in illustrating this conflict. The suicide of Harrel allows Cecilia to leave London with the Delviles to stay at their country estate; the time she spends there, between her apparently unrequited love for the son, her affection for the mother, and her hurt and anxiety over their apparent rejection of her as a prospective wife and daughter-in-law, is both emotionally rich and psychologically painful. Much of Cecilia's energies are spent in keeping emotional chaos at bay through conversation and the employments appropriate for a young lady in the country: walking, music, books, and fancy work. In one scene, Cecilia's and Mrs. Delvile's combined efforts at conversation succeed in transforming a potentially strained and dreary atmosphere into "gaiety, and tolerable ease"; Cecilia, not coincidentally, I suspect, is engaged, as the two women work and talk, in "embroidering a screen" (VI,

479-80). Lady Honoria, a young relation of the Delviles who delights in upsetting any form of social complacency, disrupts the calm by voicing her partially facetious suspicion that young Delvile is keeping a mistress in a nearby cottage. This suggestion dispels the atmosphere of ease that the other two women have woven between them and exposes Cecilia's real feelings, turning her screen quite literally into the means of that exposure: "Cecilia, to whom Henrietta Belfield was instantly present, changed colour repeatedly, and turned so extremely sick, she could with difficulty keep her seat. She forced herself, however, to continue her work, though she knew so little what she was about, that she put her needle in and out of the same place without ceasing" (VI, 480). Cecilia's attempts not to react to Lady Honoria's "news" in any way that would call attention to herself are frustrated by the very screen—the work she is doing—that had previously masked emotion: "Lady Honoria then, turning to Cecilia, exclaimed, 'Bless me, Miss Beverley, what are you about! why that flower is the most ridiculous thing I ever saw! you have spoilt your whole work' " (VI, 480-81).

The irony of this scene as I have read it is that the employment intended to divert attention from the troubling emotions of unsanctioned romantic love betrays the heroine, leaving her even less in control of the awkward social situation that the occupation was intended to mask or, at least, contain. Cecilia repeatedly seeks to subdue the feelings created in her by the inconsistent and puzzling behavior of young Delvile through the means of rational employment—"She amused herself with walking and reading, she commissioned Mr. Monckton to send her a Piano Forte of Merlin's, she was fond of fine work, and she found in the conversation of Mrs. Delvile a never-failing resource against langour and sadness. Leaving therefore to himself her mysterious son, she wisely resolved to find other employment for her thoughts, than conjectures with which she could not be satisfied, and doubts that might never be explained" (VI, 450). But however "wisely" she acts, the romance plot will not leave such resignation alone, and the very employments designed to give Cecilia control often betray her into helplessness. Control shifts into powerlessness all the more readily as romance begins to taint the nature of Cecilia's daily occupations. One of Cecilia's favorite pastimes in the country is walking with Fidel, Delvile's dog; this pleasure, however innocently begun by Cecilia, finally betrays her love to young Delvile and introduces Cecilia to the social helplessness of a woman in love with a man who is absolutely sure of her. Lady Honoria, who is fond of teasing Cecilia about her affection for Fidel, sends the dog to her after Cecilia has separated herself from the pleasures and pains of living under the same roof with Delvile: "Her tenderness and her sorrow found here a romantic consolation, complaining to [Fidel] of the absence of his master, his voluntary exile, and her fears for his health" (VI, 534). Young Delvile unexpectedly walks in on her during one of these soliloquies: Cecilia's attempts to conceal her love are ended, and Delvile avows his determination to bring about their union. But whereas the mutual revelations of lovers empower Evelina, Cecilia is left exposed and helpless:

Delvile, upon whom so long, though secretly, her dearest hopes of happiness had rested, was now become acquainted with his power, and knew himself the master of her destiny; he had quitted her avowedly to decide what it should be, since his present subject of deliberation included her fate in his own; the next morning he was to call and acquaint her with his decree, not doubting her concurrence whichever way he resolved.

A subjection so undue, and which she could not but consider as disgraceful, both shocked and afflicted her; and the reflection that the man who of all men she preferred, was acquainted with her preference, yet hesitated whether to accept or abandon her, mortified or provoked her alternately, occupied her thoughts the whole night, and kept her from peace and rest. [VI, 539–40]

The dependency and relative helplessness of Cecilia formulating her schemes of happiness in the course-of-life plot are doubled by the subjection of Cecilia in love. Neither work nor love empower the heroine; rather, love frustrates gratification through work or friendship, and the two sides of Cecilia's life combine to disempower her in both spheres.

Indeed, romantic love steals from Cecilia what solace she does gain from her plans of life. The narrative establishes a repetitive pattern in which Cecilia banishes romantic love and adheres to her charitable enterprises—closing her Byron and picking up her Goethe—only to have romantic love forcibly intrude upon her carefully cultivated serenity in a life of good works. Her initial plan to work under the philanthropic tutelage of Albany is disrupted by her hope and bewilderment over the ambiguous behavior of Delvile. When she first realizes how far her feelings for Delvile have progressed—from liking to love—her employments immediately lose importance: "neither the exertion of the most active benevolence, nor the steady course of the most virtuous conduct, sufficed any longer to wholly engage her thoughts, or constitute her felicity" (III, 245). Much later in the troubled course of her relations with Delvile, she is forced by the desires of his mother to give up prospects of their marriage, and she returns to a life of benevolence and the quiet intimacy of old and new female friends, Henrietta and the "maternal bosom" of her earliest companion, Mrs. Charlton; Cecilia's newly rewon, calm autonomy is broken, however, by Delvile's reassertion of their marriage plans: "And thus, again, was wholly broken the tranquillity of Cecilia; new hopes, however faint, awakened all her affections, and strong fears, but too reasonable interrupted her repose. Her destiny, once more, was as undecided as ever, and the expectations she had crushed, retook possession of her heart" (IX, 793). The love plot does not allow Cecilia any power to pursue her plans, however well conceived, for a course of life off the roller coaster of romantic love's hopes and disappointments.

Burney, I would argue, ties this particular helplessness specifically to the social and psychic position of women as it is defined by the ideology of romantic love. She interpolates into Cecilia's

story the tale of Albany and the innocent young girl whom his
love betrays; this tale parallels Cecilia's story and illustrates the
relative inability of women to counter a disabling love with
enabling work. In his student days, Albany falls in love with a
pretty and innocent villager's daughter, seduces her, and then
thoughtlessly leaves her to the supervision of a "bosom friend"
who seduces her in turn. While Albany is away, he falls ill,
repents, and returns to marry the young woman who "instantly
acknowledged the tale of her undoing." Albany, infuriated, beats
and leaves her, repents again in a cooler moment and returns once
more to find her a prostitute. Filled with guilt, Albany attempts
to save her, but she starves herself to death, having made a vow
"to live speechless and motionless, as a penance for her offences!"
(VIII, 693). Albany goes mad for three years, but once he recovers his senses (more or less), he begins his lifelong penance of
active philanthropy. What seems significant about this story are
the different modes of penance for sexual sin on the parts of
Albany and the young woman: charitable works give him a way
of living with guilt, however it may taint his life, but she chooses
a bizarre death by standing still. Albany's history illustrates the
sexual politics of love and work and their relation to each other in
the lives of men and women, respectively. And it is in the context
of this politic that we are asked to read the gender-linked resolutions of Cecilia's story of love and work.

    While Cecilia's "sin" is not the blatant sexual error of Albany's
mistress, her love is, from its inception, tainted by perceptions of
its impropriety: she is continually seen by someone as in the
wrong, whether or not she actually is. First, even when she is not
in love she is perceived as being so (with Sir Robert and with
Belfield), a perception which continually places her on the defensive; when she really is in love, her feelings, like Evelina's, are
clear to her before she is sure of a return, but unlike Evelina's,
Cecilia's feelings are clear to her long before matters are clear
between her and her lover. As a result, Cecilia is more open to
shame when those feelings appear to be inappropriate. Guilt dogs

the course of her love, and it intensifies when she finds that the marriage she desires is not approved by Mrs. Delvile, whose friendship and esteem she needs. After being hard pressed by Delvile and finally approved by Mrs. Delvile, though not by her husband, Cecilia consents to a secret marriage, a step she had hitherto seen as immoral and underhanded, an act which compounds her sense of real guilt. Finally, after this marriage, Delvile suspects her, yet again, of an intrigue with Belfield: real and imagined offenses drive Cecilia, like Albany, into madness. Initially, this disorder takes an active form—to use Jane Austen's distinction in *Love and Friendship*, Cecilia follows the most healthful means of distraction by running mad—but she is gradually reduced to an immobility that is a type of that which kills Albany's mistress. First restrained and deprived of human contact by those around her—"she found herself shut up in a place of confinement, without light, without knowledge where she was, and not a human being near her!" (X, 877)—this restraint finally reduces her to "utter insensibility" and a sort of automatic negation that grimly parodies the dead woman's refusal of both Albany's help and her own life. Asked by Delvile if she is "gone so soon," Cecilia "now suddenly, and with a rapid, yet continued motion, turned her head from side to side, her eyes wildly glaring, yet apparently regarding nothing" (X, 886). Even this negative gesture soon fails her, however, and she lapses into total stillness, an icon of reproach against Delvile and his father: "She was wholly insensible, but perfectly quiet; she seemed to distinguish nothing, and neither spoke nor moved" (X, 890). While Cecilia recovers, her near-death from this illness—a refusal of a life that has become too cruel to bear—suggests parallels with the grimmer story of Albany's mistress. And, significantly, while the result of Albany's promise to work with Cecilia "till not a woe shall remain upon your mind" (VIII, 695) is a tenuous calm for the heroine, soon disrupted by the masculine sexual suspicions that drive her into madness, the fulfillment of the promise is a kind of rebirth for Albany: "These magnificent donations and designs, being communicated to Albany, seemed a renovation to him of youth, spirit, and joy!" (IX, 755). Work may be an answer to ruined hopes for men in the ideology of romantic love, but it offers limited alternatives to women, who are likely to be disempowered by both love and work.

A course of good works in life offers Cecilia, at best, a rather tenuous consolation for lost or frustrated hopes of romantic love, and it does not offer her any sense of renewal, as it does Albany; instead of leading to possible or even illusory gains, Cecilia's schemes for happiness through philanthropy are, at very best, a means of mere containment, of not losing what personal control she has. Employments, however virtuous, contribute to the static or regressive view of female life that I have discussed earlier, in chapter 2, and only romantic love—which, ironically, militates against the heroine's empowerment in the course-of-life plot— holds out the ideological possibility of hope, of transcending the cultural limitations placed on female life-development. Burney defines Cecilia's progress in finding a course of life as a series of steps forward and back, consistently leaving the heroine in pretty much the same place of virtuous, hopeless "forbearance." Cecilia's progress in romantic love is a different kind of forward-and-back game, one more informed by a repeating pattern of hope and disappointment than by static forbearance. Romantic love—its growth, deferrence, loss, and recovery—is an extremely dangerous venture, a gamble in which the stakes are either a transcendence of female life's socially determined limitations or a complete lapse into immobility and a killing stillness. If employments offer Cecilia a safe but hopeless stasis, love both offers her an escape from a life of forbearance and threatens the risk of a stasis even more complete and deadening.

Like the old women's race in *Evelina*, the treatment of female old age in *Cecilia* exposes the cultural attitudes that devalue female maturity and threaten even young women with ultimate powerlessness. The mindlessly cruel Sir Robert Floyer, for instance, would "go a hundred miles a day for a month never to see" again such a sight as "a old woman with never a tooth in her head sitting at the top of the table" (I, 77). Female old age is disgusting and improper, in Sir Robert's view, especially when in a position of some authority, as in the case of Lady Margaret, to whom he refers. Just as Lord Merton's treatment of old women exposes the sexual and economic exploitation at the core of his gallantry toward the young and beautiful, Sir Robert's abuse of Lady Margaret underscores his predatory behavior toward Cecilia. Burney explicitly attributes this type of misogyny, not just to the rakish Sir Robert, but to a whole social convention of thoughtless abusiveness to women. At the Harrels' masquerade, one of the maskers "greatly enjoyed and applauded by the company" is "an apparent old woman, who was a young man in disguise, and whose hobbling gait, grunting voice, and most grievous asthmatic complaints" (II, 110) are particular sources of amusement. As Mary Russo suggests in her study of the carnivalesque image of the "female grotesque," the man's masquerade in the culturally disturbing guise of female old age implies the power to take it off and resume male authority, while simultaneously encoding the feminine powerlessness associated with his disguise.[8] The young man gestures toward his own strength by assuming the parodic form of female weakness. In this case, to put on the weakness of old age in a specifically feminine form distances the masculine from the threat of such weakness by categorizing it as feminine, not really having to do with the future of the young man himself. Young Delvile disrupts this gesture of male power by exposing the falsity of its gender-linked representation of age and weakness. His general attitude of repugnance for such jokes recommends him to Cecilia on their first meeting; he generalizes the ridicule of age from that of *women* specifically to that of *humanity*. By extending the joke's object of abuse from women to human beings, Delvile reveals the sleight-of-hand shabbiness of associating a weakness common to humanity with the feminine: "its sole view is to expose to contempt and derision the general and natural infirmities of age! And the design is not

more disgusting than impolitic; for why, while we so carefully
guard from all approaches of death, should we close the only
avenues to happiness in long life, respect and tenderness?" (II,
110-11). Delvile's generalization deflates a joke that is harder to
see as funny if women are conceived of as human as well as
female. Cecilia is "delighted both by the understanding and
humanity of her new acquaintance" (II, 111). And, as Lord
Orville's love offers to Evelina the possibility of escaping such
cruelty and ridicule as old age brings to women, Delvile's esteem
for Cecilia seems to carry the promise of a life that transcends the
static or regressive pattern of female aging: " 'Not only her
minority, but her majority,' cried young Delvile, warmly; 'and
not only her maturity, but her decline of life will pass, I hope, nor
merely without reproach, but with fame and applause!' " (II,
151).

While Evelina's growing hopes for her future are not consciously linked to her feelings for the man who gives rise to them,
Cecilia's are. Her first suspicion that Delvile might return her
affection "opened to her views and her hopes a scene entirely
new," and she (rather prematurely, as it turns out) "looked forward with grateful joy to the prospect of ending her days with the
man she thought most worthy to be entrusted with the disposal
of her fortune" (III, 245). As Cecilia discovers, the dangerous
other side of hope is disappointment. Delvile does indeed return
her love, but his family's pride prevents him for a long time from
even thinking of marrying Cecilia. When his recognition of
Cecilia's love enables him to rebel (with filial moderation) against
his family's standards of class and family in his choice of a wife,
he is again stopped cold by the name clause in her uncle's will,
which requires her husband to take the family name of "Beverley"—a debasement that the Delviles never bring themselves to
accept; it rather must be worked around by yet more tortured
turns in the love plot. When Cecilia and Delvile finally do make
their marriage public, the Delviles choose to give up her uncle's
fortune rather their son's name. Repeated disappointment in

Delvile's love calls forth Cecilia's repeated, philosophic resignation, but resignation, in this novel, is not equal to the force of
romantic love: the love plot of *Cecilia* suggests that such resignation does not, finally, solve the dilemma of the heroine in love.
Separated from Delvile by her acquiescence to his family's wishes
and Delvile's own reluctance to displease his family, Cecilia hears
an account from the physician Dr. Lyster of Delvile's resignation:
"Cecilia's eyes glistened at this speech; 'Yes,' said she; 'he long
since said 'tis suspense, 'tis hope, that make the misery of life,—
for there the passions have all power, and reason has none. But
when evils are irremediable, and we have neither resources to
plan, nor castle-building to delude us, we find time for the
cultivation of philosophy, and flatter ourselves, perhaps, that we
have found inclination!' " (VIII, 680). Dr. Lyster seems to intuit
the danger for Cecilia implicit in this Johnsonian stance of resignation, and rather patronizingly responds that "I must not have
you give way to these serious reflections. Thought, after all, has a
cruel spite against happiness; I would have you, therefore, keep,
as much as you conveniently can, out of its company. Run about
and divert yourself, 'tis all you have for it" (VIII, 680). The doctor
prescribes motion, even relatively meaningless motion, as an
alternative better than giving in to the melancholy acceptance of
circumstances. His recommendation, "Let those who have leisure, find employment, and those who have business find leisure" (VIII, 681), suggests a gender-blind redistribution of work
and play that is improbable in Cecilia's—and Burney's—society.
It does not account for the particular socially defined contingencies of femininity in eighteenth-century culture: the pro-
found and debilitating nature of the stasis that infects women's
lives and the powerlessness of employments to change the essentially deadening nature of that stasis. Stillness proves, indeed, to
be a potentially killing danger to Cecilia; ironically, while romantic love impels the heroine to run from the danger of emotional
stagnation, it also causes Cecilia to immobilize herself, however
unintentionally. Cecilia lapses into a sort of catatonia as a result of

the hysterical exertions that her love for Delvile drives her to, and she must, like Sleeping Beauty, be brought back to life, sense, and the redeeming power of romantic love by the somewhat belated concern of her "prince," Delvile, who finally assumes the role of supportive protector at the end of the novel. The romance plot treacherously enables female action only to stop it; the course-of-life plot that involves Cecilia in nonromantic plans for how to use her time maintains the stasis that seems the most pleasant possibility for a woman, whose options are necessarily impinged upon by the ideology of love and marriage, whatever personal choices she seeks to make. Cecilia's course-of-life plot is necessarily truncated by the ideological imperatives of romantic love in feminine life.

In *Cecilia,* Burney begins to explore some of the issues of female life outside the ideology of romantic love—issues that probably receive the fullest treatment in her last novel—*The Wanderer; or, Female Difficulties*—which dramatizes the economic, social, and psychological difficulties of a woman trying to make a living outside of the ostensibly protective structure of domestic, family life in late eighteenth-century England. *Cecilia's* double plot evinces a probable ambivalence in Burney's attitudes toward her own situation as a young woman then taking her first steps into the public space of literary professionalism. The feminine identity invested in the heroine remains safely defined by the domestic, familial terms successfully established by the plot of romantic love, but the novel explores, through displacement and doubling, the problems and possibilities of a course of life outside the ideological limits of that plot. The story of Belfield's search for a satisfactory course of life parallels and, I would argue, amplifies the ideological exploration implicitly but incompletely articulated in Cecilia's search for a way to make her time mean-ingful when she is not happily in love. The character of Belfield presents an illustration of what happens to a man who is unsuited to find happiness through either his occupations or romantic love; through his story, Burney dramatizes the contradictory and sometimes destructive effects of investing, through education, cultural values and aspirations in any class that does not have the material means to act on those values and aspirations—be that class defined by gender or economic factors. Like Delvile's generalizations about human weaknesses from evidence having to do specifically with the female social problem of old age, Burney's doubling of Cecilia's course-of-life plot in Belfield's search for employment may serve a dual function: while it draws attention away from the gender-linked specifics of social problems—perhaps strategically—it also allows her to treat seriously a difficulty that might otherwise be dismissed as merely female, a dismissal perhaps all too likely in a society that rationalized a plethora of social abuses as women's religion- and tradition-determined lot to bear. The contradiction in Belfield's character—he is educated for a way of life that his economic circumstances do not support—serves as an indirect comment on contradictions implicit in eighteenth-century feminine social identity: Belfield experiences desires for a quality of life and social status beyond the range of his economic and class-determined abilities.

One reason for employing a male character in the exploration of this particular topic might have been that Burney, who habitually created heroines capable of error but consistently morally upright, may have felt more comfortable in portraying a male character ambivalently—as likeable but morally flawed—an ambivalence that allowed her more play in her exploration of the course-of-life subject. Belfield is a morally complex character who is difficult to reduce to a simple "good" or "bad," and Burney seems to make little attempt to reconcile the ambivalence she invests in his character. The only son of a well-to-do London merchant, Belfield receives the best education that his father can buy, the old man expecting him, somewhat unrealistically, to become the "best scholar in any shop in London." The habit of intellectual pursuits he gains at Eton makes him discontented, however, with returning to his father's shop, and the old man sends him on to university, in hopes that making him a "*finished student*" will teach him "a little more sense" about the worth of his business (III, 208). The result of this plan is the total unsuitability of Belfield for his business and the eventual financial ruin of the young man, his mother and unmarried sister. Like Robinson Crusoe, Belfield aspires to a station in life above the one in which he was born; like Fanny Burney, his education pushes him beyond the ideologically determined limits of that "station." He becomes—not an outcast—but a social and familial liability, a care and frustration to his friends and a source of real pain and deprivation to his sisters, as Henrietta testifies, "for I, and all my sisters, have been the sufferers the whole time: and while we were kept backward that he might be brought forward, while we were denied comforts, that he might have luxuries, how could we help seeing the evil of so much vanity, and wishing we had all been brought up according to our proper station, instead of living in continual inconvenience, and having one part of a family struggling with distress, only to let another part of it appear in a way he had no right to?" (III, 240). The novel sustains a pronounced ambivalence towards Belfield's rejection of his station, however; Henrietta seems to see the "vanity" as more her parents' than her brother's, and she is firm in her conviction that her brother not only has her affection but deserves it. Henrietta targets the lopsided distribution of cultural and economic advantages that privilege the male—not Belfield himself, who is the unwitting tool of this injustice. While Belfield is not without blame for his sisters' sufferings, he escapes the ultimate responsibility for them and is even given a certain value by his refusal of his station: the narrator speaks of his spirit "soaring above the occupations for which he was designed" (I, 7), a bit of praise that parallels her panegyric on Cecilia's father, "in whom a spirit of elegance had supplanted the rapacity of wealth" (I, 1). Belfield's aspirations to gentility seriously injure him and those he loves, but the novel, which characterizes the self-satisfied businessman and merchants as low or at best severely limited—the repulsive, miserly Briggs, the crass and complacent Hobson, for instances—seems both to blame and to congratulate Belfield for rebelling against his destined employments. This ambivalence echoes some of Burney's fears about how her writing for the public might result in harm or discredit to her family, especially to her father—fears voiced in *Evelina's* dedication to the "author of my being": "Obscure be still the unsuccessful Muse, / Who cannot raise, but would not sink, your fame" (1). The ambiguous moral value that Burney places on Belfield's desire to go beyond his class limits reflects, perhaps, her ambivalence about her own transgressions against gender limits. It also articulates, in general terms, the doubleness of Burney's attitudes toward human action that exceeds socially determined boundaries—the glory and the risk of breaking through limits.

The moral ambivalence of Belfield's character repeats a writerly strategy that Burney had employed since the character of Evelina, who, although thoroughly virtuous, is, as Burney's preface tells us, "no faultless monster that the world ne'er saw," a fallibility extremely useful to illustrating the social difficulties of a young lady new to society: perfect characters do not make the mistakes that reveal contradictions built into their position. Belfield's particular fallibility pertains to work, not love or etiquette, and his story illustrates the employment difficulties of a young man new to the need to make a living. These difficulties take a form that transposes into male terms Cecilia's search for meaningful employment: like the stream of life in Pope's "Cobham," Belfield's course of life is a discontinuous progress of bewildering rapidity, a course of motion from one equally unsatisfying employment to the next, very different from the static quality of Cecilia's long, slow filling-in of time during hiatuses in her engagement with romantic love, and one that is consonant with masculine rather than feminine patterns of development in mid-eighteenth-century ideology. But however frenetic Belfield's motion, it does not amount to much more economic, social or psychological progress than Cecilia's standing still. Like Cecilia, Belfield finds himself, contrary to his expectations, consistently disempowered by what he does.

Unanswered by Belfield's attempts at law and the military, the question of his employment is thrown to his friends, particularly Delvile. He is settled into the house of a nobleman as a tutor to his son, but his quickness to take offense at what seem to him his patron's liberties with a social inferior drives him back on his own resources. Belfield's sensitivity to insult derives from his social and economic powerlessness and parallels in a displaced form Cecilia's gender-linked vulnerability to public exposure in her charitable career with Albany. Like Cecilia, Belfield continually tries to find an employment that will allay instead of aggravating his social vulnerability. Within an extremely short time, he embarks with equal enthusiasm, first, on a career as a day laborer, and second, as a hack writer. The attraction of his first career is "labor with independence" (VIII, 645): like Cecilia, Belfield continually seeks employment that will empower him, despite his state of economic dependence, and continually fails to find it. Physical weakness and psychological unsuitability disable Belfield from continuing in this course, for, as he explains, "it will not do to war with the general tenor of education" (VIII, 718). His education makes it constitutionally impossible for Belfield to engage in the nonintellectual, purely physical labor suitable for the lower classes of his gender. His inability is a mirror-image inversion of Cecilia's revulsion against losing herself, like Mrs. Harrel, to the mindless social play traditionally suited to *her* gender. Both young people have been educated beyond their class- and gender-defined roles, so that the occupational possibilities open to them seem to degrade *what they have become.* Cecilia's dismay at her sense of social isolation, her intellectual barrenness is echoed in Belfield's comments on his experience as a day laborer: "The life I led at the cottage was the life of a savage; no intercourse with society, no consolation from books; my mind locked up, every source dried of intellectual delight, and no enjoyment in my power but from sleep and from food. Weary of an existence which thus leveled me with a brute, I grew ashamed of the approximation, and listening to the remonstrance of my understanding, I gave up the precipitate plan, to pursue one more consonant with reason" (VIII, 722). Belfield encounters a class-defined occupation that alienates the worker from his own society and mind, doubling Cecilia's encounter with mindless, alienating pastimes in London society—an "occupation" associated, as we have seen in chapter 4, with her gender. Burney uses a class-linked system of work roles that result in alienation from self and society in order to amplify her critique of a gender-linked system of occupational roles.[9]

Given Belfield's significance as a sort of mirror for the ideological position specific to femininity in eighteenth-century culture, his attempt at a career in authorship carries a particular relevance to Fanny Burney's position as a woman trying out a career in writing in 1782. When Belfield turns from hard labor to writing, his enthusiasm is, as before, focused on his hope of turning weakness into strength:

"From my earliest youth to the present hour," continued Belfield, "literature has been the favourite object of my pursuit, my recreation in leisure, and my hope in employment. My propensity to it, indeed, had been so ungovernable, that I may properly call it the source of my several miscarriages throughout life. It was the bar to my preferment, for it gave me a distaste to other studies; it was the cause of my unsteadiness in all my undertakings, because to all I preferred it. It has sunk me to distress, it has involved me in difficulties; it has brought me to the brink of ruin by making me neglect the means of living, yet never, till now, did I discern it might itself be my support." [VIII, 721]

This enthusiastic beginning ends, like the one before, in the realization that this employment leaves him just as without autonomy as the previous ones: "to write by rule, to compose by necessity, to make the understanding, nature's first gift, subservient to interest, that meanest offspring of art!" (X, 862).

It is hard to miss the commentary on Burney's own situation as she wrote *Cecilia*: writing by her father's "rule," composing by the "necessity" of her friends' urging, and "subservient" to the dictum of her mentor, Samuel Crisp, to follow up her financial "interest" after the success of *Evelina*, Burney must have written Belfield's complaint with real feeling. Despite—or perhaps because of—the novel's assertion of the differences between masculine and feminine employments, the addition of the story of Belfield comments on and reflects the experience of both Cecilia and Fanny Burney. Belfield's story serves to amplify the problems Burney explores through her heroine's search for employments—but it also throws into relief the significant differences in the answers that men and women find to the question of course in life. Belfield's story of nonprogressive progress differs from Cecilia's thwarted search for employments in two important particulars: first, Belfield's personal nature, however attractive, is given, at the novel's end, as much responsibility for his nonprogress as the social and familial circumstances of his repeated failures—"The injudicious, the volatile, yet noble-minded Belfield, to whose mutable and enterprising disposition life seemed always rather beginning than progressive…" (X, 918)—whereas the novel stresses that merely personal flaws are *not* responsible for Cecilia's difficulties. The end of the novel winks at Belfield's "injudicious . . . yet noble-minded" character while emphasizing the "upright mind of Cecilia, her purity, her virtue, and the moderation of her wishes" (X, 919). Belfield, then, represents the deviation from a masculine ideal, someone fallen out of the moral and social system that rewards masculine progress. Cecilia's failure to progress in the realm of employments is not attributable to personal flaws, but rather, to all appearances, built into the ideology that consigns female success to attaining a happy marriage. Second, the resolution of their respective careers emphasizes gender-linked assumptions about male versus female happiness. Belfield falls back into the course defined by masculine ambition and a sense of progress: "By the constant friendship of Delvile, he consented to accept his good offices in again entering the army; and, being fortunately ordered out upon foreign service, his hopes were revived by ambition, and his prospects were brightened by a view of future honour" (X, 918). Cecilia's ending, on the other hand, rewards her personally deserving nature with personal affection: "The upright mind of Cecilia, her purity, her virtue, and the moderation of her wishes, gave to her in the warm affection of Lady Delvile, and the unremitting fondness of Mortimer, all the happiness human life seems capable of receiving (X, 919). Resolution to Belfield's and Cecilia's plots is reached only by relegating love and work to the genders respectively assumed to take the most interest in one or the other. Burney resolves the conflict between the two—a conflict that has torn apart Cecilia's life—by polarizing the novel's two major themes—love and work—along the opposing lines of gender.

This resolution is, I would argue, rather a slicing of the gordian knot of love and work than a solution to the problems that the novel poses about the relationship between the two in women's lives. While gender-linked ideology restores a conventional order to the novel's ending, Burney fosters this thematic contradiction by leaving unresolved the issues of personal versus social power raised by Cecilia's dual search for love and work. Again, Belfield's search for employment serves to make explicit the conflict implied in Cecilia's—and Fanny Burney's—experience. The contradiction between individual autonomy and social control—the issue of the individual's power to act against social convention—is addressed directly in a debate that takes place between Belfield and Monckton at two points in the novel. Early in the story, before Cecilia makes her entrance into London, Belfield argues for acting out of the "light of your own understanding," regardless of social convention. Monckton opposes him with the "necessity of accommodating himself to such customs as are already received": "the opposition of an individual to a community is always dangerous in the operation, and seldom successful in the event" (I, 10). The discussion reaches no conclusion because the empty-headed Captain Aresby is bored and asks the accommodating Mr. Morrice to "start some new game." Morrice responds with the unmeaning "A hare! a hare!"—a distraction that calls attention to nothing—there is no hare—and merely serves to return the conversation to mean-

ingless social chitchat. The reader who has not been diverted by
Morrice's hare will notice by observation of his character, however, that "accommodation" is not always a rational or even
respectable form of behavior: adherence to social customs can be
as silly and unmeaning as the flightiest individual's whim. Indeed, the indulgence of whims often seems to constitute a kind of
custom. But Belfield's disastrous career provides sobering evidence of the harm that individual deviation from custom and an
exclusive dependence on one's own understanding can do: besides the hurt he does himself, Belfield most seriously victimizes
the women who depend upon him. The text disturbs any easy or
complacent answers to the questions that the debate raises, but it
makes clear that women are, in one way or another, the ones
inevitably most harmed in the struggle to adjust personal autonomy to the imperatives of social form.

    Later, this debate touches directly on the issue of writing.
Belfield is again arguing the virtues of acting independently, this
time specifically as a writer. Responding to Monckton's sarcastic
remarks about writing for hire, Belfield asserts that "my subjects
shall be my own, and my satire shall be general." He will not
serve petty, personal interests, but will instead adhere to his own
ideal of literature, an intention that Monckton dismisses as
"knight-errantry." During this discussion, Belfield gives a spirited defense of writing as a quixotically noble pursuit: " 'Tis a
knight-errantry," answered Belfield, laughing, "which, however
ludicrous it may seem to you, requires more soul and more brains
than any other. Our giants may, indeed, be only wind-mills, but
they must be attacked with as much spirit, and conquered with as
much bravery, as any fort or any town, in time of war should be
demolished; and though the siege, I must confess, may be of less
national utility, the assailants of the quill have their honour as
much at heart as the assailants of the sword" (VIII, 721).
Belfield's defense of the writer's "honour" gains poignancy in the
context of Burney's personal conflict between writing what she
chose and writing out of duty to others. The quixotic Belfield
temporarily vanquishes the cynical Monckton on this point in

a victory parallelled by Belfield's earlier short-lived conquest, in the guise of the knight of the woeful countenance, over Monckton, dressed as a devil, at the Harrels' masquerade. But the impotence implied in the quixotic stance, the defensiveness suggested in "only windmills," and the brief duration of Belfield's triumph over Monckton—he soon admits to the hateful necessity of writing by rule—place his victory in an ambiguous light. As he admits about another of his ill-conceived plans for making a living, "We may blame, despise, regret as we please, but customs long established, and habits long indulged, assume an empire despotic, though their power is but prescriptive" (VIII, 718).

The debate between Belfield and Monckton focuses on, without resolving, the problem of the writer's personal autonomy versus her responsibility to submit to the rule of custom. This problem was one of great personal importance to Burney in the year 1782, but it also has resonances beyond her particular situation, resonances of the general problem of the woman writer who was already, in a sense, breaking with a custom that limited the acceptable, middle-class social articulation of her gender to domestic, personal terms—terms that did not include becoming a popular writer of fiction. *Cecilia* is not, however, a novel expressing the defeat of the woman writer at the hands of received ideology. Rather, it maps out the newly emergent social and psychological terrain of women's literary production that Burney had entered when she went public as a middle-class, respectable woman novelist. *Cecilia* charts the contradictions between romantic love and a course of life, between affection and work, personal autonomy and social duty, as part of the identity she defines for herself through her fiction. Burney's novels reflect how she saw herself, as that contradictory being—a woman writer. But her novels are not simply so many biographical mirrors; rather, they represent a process of self-knowledge as a social product, an imaginary working through of Burney's sense of herself in a social context that often seemed an "empire despotic," however "necessary."

SIX

The Receptive Reader and Other Necessary Fictions

When Fanny Burney wrote *Evelina; or, the History of a Young Lady's Entrance into the World* in the mid-1770s, she was by no means entering into literary territory that was untouched by the female pen; scores of women had written and published novels prior to *Evelina*, giving Burney a clear, if not entirely unsullied precedent for going into print. (Some, indeed many, women novelists of the first half of the eighteenth century would not have been considered "nice to know" by the middle-class, respectable Burney.) This precedent enabled the act of writing without, however, making clear the authority by which that act was performed. Was the successful woman novelist notorious or simply famous? A prodigy or a freak? By what right could a woman claim a public audience and, hence, a public voice? The development of Burney's self-concept as a writer, revealed in her diaries, journals—and perhaps most candidly in her fiction—yields some specific answers to these questions.

Evelina was published anonymously, practically without the knowledge of Burney's friends or family, and its best-seller-like success transformed the unknown younger daughter of Charles Burney into a literary figure, a woman with a public identity. A close reading of *Evelina* in conjunction with Burney's early diaries and journals reveals that the young novelist had thought deeply and carefully about the extent and limits of female creative control—as *power*, the ability to manipulate how others see and, hence, define the writer's identity. Being read, we can see from

Burney's early journals and from *Evelina*, is a means to self-definition: by becoming known to a private audience, Burney creates herself. This power to control one's self-image is, however, problematic once it extends beyond the private, personal influence that contemporary ideology defined for Burney as the proper exercise of female power; moved into the public realm, it signals its own limitations and the dangers of failure that surround the woman who attempts to wield it. Hence, the ability to write herself into a secure psychological position as a woman novelist is, for the Burney who wrote *Evelina*, a complex rhetorical process that calls attention to its own strategies and limits.

When *Evelina's* success forced Burney into the public life of literary London, the claims to a public voice implicit in her writing came into conflict with that part of her femininity which did not authorize power outside the realm of the personal. Writing was still a means to self-definition, but it also implied a kind of authority—a public, not a personal sense of control—that disconnected power from the private self in which Burney's journals, written after the success of *Evelina*, show her seeking to invest writerly authority.

Cecilia, published four years after *Evelina*, reveals the self-alienation, even madness that was implicit for Burney in public acts of power, the fear that writing for a public audience alienated her from her private sense of self as a woman; in this act of revelation, however, *Cecilia* balances fear against control, loss of identity against self-expression, in a fictional embodiment of the ideological contradiction between the public writer and the private self. *Cecilia, Camilla* (1796), and *The Wanderer* (1814) all portray the heroine's key act of power—the turning point in the plot by which she gains social definition in the novel—as both an act of self-alienation, a splitting-off of the act of control from the personal, desiring self that authorizes it, and as a successful strategy of social manipulation. The self-defining and self-referential limits of Evelina's power reflect Burney's contradictory desire to create a public identity as author and then to deny that identity by burying it in anonymity; Burney's later heroines express the social and personal terms of female authorial control as contradiction, as the unresolved and disjunctive result of her ideological circumstances as woman and as writer.

The journals that Fanny Burney wrote over the course of a long lifetime seem, for her, to have been more important as a process of maintaining a sense of emotional relationship with her readers than as an artistic product. From *The Early Diary* to the latest volumes of the *Journals and Letters*, Burney's personal writings—consisting of diaries, letters, and journals—are filled with references to her need for the personal approval and understanding of a relatively few individuals. Her letters to the royal family, for example, are starched with respectful formality, yet her claims to the attention of Queen Charlotte and her daughters are as personal in kind, though not in degree, as her claims to the understanding and interest of her beloved father or the elderly friend of her youth, Samuel Crisp. Writing her journals for a small, familiar audience—her closest family and friends—allowed her to bury any consciousness of writerly control over her readers in claims to her audience's affection for her, the emotional control that intimacy gives the writer over a familiar audience. The joy of writing was, for Burney, the loving response she hoped to gain from her readers. If a real, emotionally supportive audience gave Burney energy as a writer of journals, as a novelist she faced a less immediate, more complex writing situation. Burney apparently published *Evelina* with little expectation of the notoriety the novel would bring her, and perhaps without a clear sense of who her audience actually was or how they would respond.

Evelina is a Cinderella-like story of a virtuous young woman rewarded, against all worldly odds, with the financial and emotional security of marriage to a contemporary Prince Charming.[1] It also includes, in its fairy-tale plot, a writerly form of wish-fulfillment: the heroine's power to gain the love of those who can provide security is a fictionalized version of the emotional control over audience that Burney saw as her best or, at least, most appropriate claim to power as a writer of journals. In the novel, Burney draws an idealized scenario in which Evelina creates, through her emotional power over a few others, a kind of buffer against a society that treats women rudely, even cruelly.[2] The fiction, then, reveals even more graphically than the journals the practical necessity for the young woman's—and the young woman writer's—dependence on personal support to sustain her efforts at self-expression in a society that often does not take young women either seriously or kindly. Burney's first novel expresses her desire to control, through writing, her own emotional value in the eyes of others, but it also suggests Burney's highly self-conscious, self-analytical sense of her desire to create through writing a better personal identity—for herself and for women in general—than her culture afforded her. Burney hoped to generate for herself and her readers a sense of female worth grounded in the affective value of the heroine, but her fiction shows us that her hope was self-consciously sustained through and limited by her estimation of her own abilities; it was never a sentimental reliance on her culture's ability to recognize and reward female worth.

At first blush, *Evelina* seems predicated on a feminist's nightmare version of social identity. Throughout the novel, Evelina is misinterpreted according to reductive social formulae for categorizing young women—sexual prey, country bumpkin, selfconscious temptress—that fail to take into account her personal moral and intellectual worth. The real Evelina does not socially exist (except for her readers, outside the fiction) unless recognized by a few men powerful enough to gain her the respect that she deserves. Lord Orville (the Prince Charming–like hero) translates Evelina's personal value into terms that her society understands, by giving her the name of his betrothed, and her father, Sir John Belmont, provides the additional social signifiers of money and an aristocratic family position. Mr. Villars, her guardian and chief correspondent, provides Evelina with a sense of her personal value that, although it does not translate into the social identity that the wealthier and younger men can bestow, seems Evelina's main source of moral self-respect. Women can and do approve of Evelina in the novel—Lady Howard, Mrs. and Miss Mirvan all see the heroine's value—but their support is always bounded by male control and cannot carry the moral, monetary, and social clout of Evelina's select male audience. This male-directedness is, on one hand, surprising in light of the important role that women—Burney's sisters (especially Susan Phillips), Hester Thrale, Frederica Locke—played in the writer's personal life, and, on the other, not surprising at all given Burney's correct recognition that men, in her society, had more power than women (particularly in the sphere of public recognition where Burney was so gingerly treading). In any case, Evelina achieves social identity through being read correctly by a small group of supporters, primarily male. But much of the novel focuses on the sheer difficulty of this "reading" process. Women in the novel either do or do not recognize Evelina's worth—they are immediately either capable or incapable of loving her. But the means by which men come to know, love, and give being to Evelina are central to the novel because they cannot be assumed but are problematic, a source of anxiety, the unconsciously assumed focus of Evelina's energy and the self-consciously assumed focus of Fanny Burney's.

Burney expresses Evelina's power to control how she is read by embedding metaphors of reading and writing in her narrative of the heroine's growing personal importance to powerful male protectors. Richardson's Pamela and Clarissa had, of course, left Evelina their precedent by making writing the perfect passive-aggressive technique for manipulating how ostensibly more powerful males see and define female identity, and the metaphor came readily to Burney's hands. She herself knew the effectiveness of providing her personal audience with a literal text through which they could know her, the journals and letters that she produced in such huge quantities throughout her life for her father, sister, friend and mentor "Daddy" Crisp, husband, and, finally, son. Hence, the process by which Evelina is read is a paradigm of how Burney herself sought to form her own image in the eyes of others.

Evelina is not a blank page upon which men write their perceptions. Indeed, literally taking pen in hand to correct Orville's possible misreading of her behavior in the Branghton carriage-borrowing episode, Evelina writes an apology in which she explains herself, telling him how to interpret the appearances that informed against her. The letter, of course, miscarries and produces a forged note in response from Sir Clement—one of Evelina's most dangerous misinterpreters—which Evelina takes as Orville's insulting misreading of her attempt to explain herself. This apparent misreading by Lord Orville shakes Evelina's perception of herself, as she writes to Miss Mirvan—"I believe you would hardly have known me;—indeed, I hardly know myself" (172)—and Evelina's failure to recognize herself is specifically connected to a sudden failure of language: "no words, no language can explain the heaviness of heart with which I made the journey" home following the receipt of "Orville's" letter (254). She finds that she "cannot journalise; cannot arrange my ideas into order" (255). This apparent misreading by a powerful and attractive male affects, temporarily, Evelina's sense of control over language and hence her ability to know or make herself known. The best she can do is express her disintegration to a female audience who, Evelina seems to feel, will automatically accept and understand the emotional subtext of her linguistic fragmentation.

The metaphors of reading and writing which make clear the power of language to effect self-definition through control over others emerge when Evelina, "not herself" after Orville's apparent misreading of her, rediscovers that self through the recognition of Mr. Villars. Caught in a self-forgetful reverie, Evelina tries to recover her composure by asking Mr. Villars "if he had been reading?":

He paused a moment, and then said, "Yes, my child;—a book that both afflicts and perplexes me!"

He means *me*, thought I; and therefore I made no answer.

"What if we read it together?" continued he, "will you assist me to clear its obscurity?"

Evelina's difficulty in finding "what to say" leads her to offer Villars alternative reading matter——"Shall I fetch you another book?—or will you have this again?"—a ploy that Villars rejects, demanding to come back to the original text of Evelina herself (263–64). Finally, Evelina speaks, not directly, but through the text of her London journal, to which Villars refers in order to discover the state of her present thoughts. By comparing this text with the text of the forged note, Villars comes to an understanding of Evelina that helps her see herself afresh (and favorably) in relation to her two male "readers": "But why should I allow myself to be humbled by a man [Orville] who can suffer his reason to be thus abjectly debased, when I am exalted by one [Villars] who knows no vice, and scarcely a failing,—but by hearsay?" (266–67). Burney associates the act of knowing her heroine with textuality: the recognition of female worth is attained through a process that can only be described as "reading," since to know Evelina is to have read her texts. Because female social value is predicated on masculine recognition of a woman's personal "text," this process of self-identification is infused with both the risk of misreading and the potential for female, authorial control.

Villars is Evelina's best reader, the audience to whom she writes the most and by whose responses she knows herself. Orville, and to a considerably lesser extent, Sir John, also learn the art of Evelina-reading as they assume from Villars the role of responsive audience. *Evelina* playfully intertwines mentions of books and reading with the process by which Orville and Sir John assume their proper roles as audience to the heroine, carrying out the motif begun in the reading scene at Berry Hill.

Appropriately, Evelina reveals her love to Orville when she is ostensibly looking for some books for Mrs. Selwyn:

And here, while I was looking for them, I was followed by Lord Orville. He shut the door after he came in, and approaching me with a look of great anxiety, said, "Is this true, Miss Anville, are you going?"

"I believe so, my Lord," said I, still looking for the books.

"So suddenly, so unexpectedly must I lose you?"

"No great loss, my Lord," cried I, endeavouring to speak cheerfully.

"Is it possible," said he, gravely, "Miss Anville can doubt my sincerity?"

"I can't imagine," cried I, "what Mrs. Selwyn has done with those books."

The comedy continues with Mrs. Selwyn presenting one of the three "lost" books to each of the lovers and taking one herself to "give employment to us all" (351-52). The comic business of the books lightly underscores the nature of their relationship and Orville's role as appreciative reader, interpreting Evelina's text to the world and affirming its value with responsive approval. Evelina seeks a similar reader in Sir John when she wishes that he "could but read my heart!" (384), but the text of her mother's letter interposes between her father and the text of Evelina's heart. Sir John is yet her dead mother's audience—her reformed and repentant betrayer—and at first sight all he can read in Evelina's face is an "image of my long-lost Caroline!" (372). But the mother's literal text, in this case, speaks for the daughter's metaphoric one: Caroline Evelyn's posthumous letter asserts, like Evelina's speech, the power of a woman's words to make men see her as she would be seen, to interpret her as she would be interpreted. The texts of the mother's letter and the daughter's heart combine to bring Sir John a vivid realization of unjustly misinterpreted female value.

Orville is, of course, Evelina's most important reader at the end of the novel, and he offers a paradigm for the readerly reassurance that Burney looked for in an audience. Orville offers

Evelina a response that will affirm her self-worth no matter what story she tells him. When she tries, before revealing the melodramatic history of the Evelyn family's misfortunes, to release him from his vows of allegiance to an apparently penniless and nameless girl, Orville professes the constancy of his feelings: " 'Never!' cried he, warmly; 'my heart is yours, and I swear to you an attachment eternal!—You prepare me, indeed, for a tale of horror, and I am almost breathless with expectation,—but so firm is my conviction, that, whatever are your misfortunes, to have merited them is not of the number, that I feel myself more strongly, more invincibly attached to you than ever!" (368). Orville is the perfect audience, "breathless" with anticipation and willing to affirm the worth of the teller whatever she tells him—a writer's dream, certainly, but also the projection into fiction of Burney's answer to the limited rhetorical powers of women in her society. Orville represents the steady, intelligent affirmation of female value through sympathetic listening, a male interlocutor who implicitly approves the female teller, no matter what the tale. The heroine's fictional power becomes a type of female authorial control in Burney's novels.

The will to control such an audience is, not surprisingly, more fraught with anxiety in life than in sentimental fiction, and the tension between a desire to manipulate audience and the fear of failing to do so informs the earliest of Burney's extant journals, which show her taking no chances with a real audience that might be too unruly for her to control. In the diary addressed to "Nobody," written between 1768 and 1774, Burney humorously endows her audience with a permanent capacity for unlimited approval: "Disagreement cannot stop our affection, Time itself has no power to end our friendship" (*ED* 1:5-6). This parodic fictionalization of an audience fools no one, least of all Burney, but it suggests that she found unshakeable sympathy and understanding requisite in her imaginative construction of an ideal audience. Not surprisingly, Burney's first venture with a real reader was a journal for her sister Susan, to whom Burney frequently refers as the other half of what she called "one soul" (*DL* 2:362)—like "Nobody," a sort of alter ego. Burney came out slowly and reluctantly as a writer of journals, trusting first those whom she absolutely knew best and expanding this circle very little in her lifetime: Samuel Crisp, an old family friend and her adopted "Daddy," her father Charles Burney, her friend Frederica Locke, her sister "Hetty," husband Alexandre d'Arblay, and finally, her son Alex. This tiny audience embodied, for Burney, a model of what she came to see as the psychological conditions necessary to writing, particularly writing that involved self-disclosure. When her sister Susan died, her anguished commentary, written to her sister Hestor, reveals the extent to which pleasure in writing depended on the steadying presence of a well-known and beloved audience: "The constant Journal—the never omitted memorandums of all that concerned me, which you know to have been kept up ever since I held a pen in my hand, during every absence from my earliest—darling confident—now suddenly broken off, and dissolved, has made the very action of writing labourious—painful—almost anguish to me" (*JL* 4:408). Emotional connection between the writer and reader was both the goal and justification of the journals (hence, Burney's violent objections to Crisp's attempts to show her journals to his acquaintance).[3]

As a novelist, Burney expresses considerable anxiety about her ability to gain and hold her audience's approving acceptance. The public prominence brought by the overnight success of her first novel seems as much an opening to more personal vulnerability as a reward, and, as I have noted in chapter 5, her reflections on the personal danger that fame brought to bluestocking Elizabeth Montague carry implications for her own situation: "Many as are the causes by which respect can be lessened, there are very few by which it can be afterwards restored to its first dignity. But where there is real affection, the case is exactly reversed; few things can weaken, and every trifle can revive it" (*DL*, 1:462). The fusion of writerly and emotional control that Burney seems to have desired for herself as less dangerous than a depersonalized aesthetic is translated into the sentimental triumph of her heroine, Evelina. In her first novel, Burney envisions the security and success that she hopes to gain through the affective power of writerly control, but her management of the eighteenth-century sentimental novel's discourse also reveals the difficult and self-consciously performed labor of sustaining that power against the vulnerability and failure built into acts of female authorial control.

Burney deploys fictional conventions that reward female virtue with the love of a male protector, while simultaneously calling attention to their deployment. Evelina's creativity, like Burney's, is the offspring of a specific need: both the real and the imaginary woman seek redemption from the assumptions and attitudes that devalue female life into a poor and depressing business. And both locate redemption in the security of loving personal relationships. But Evelina's fairy-tale romance with Lord Orville, who saves her from a society full of dangers to young women, suggests that such beleaguered young women— be they heroines or novelists—are sometimes forced to look beyond the realities of their society to find the emotional support that means personal safety. Evelina's sallies into the brighter air of imagination are not without consciousness that she is, in a sense, dreaming, nor, I suspect, were Burney's. From the reality of Holborn, Evelina begins to see her acquaintance with Lord Orville and the self-elevation she experienced through it as a "dream," "some visionary fancy," "a romantic illusion": "I now re-trace the remembrance of [Orville's politeness], rather as belonging to an object of ideal perfection, formed by my own imagination, than to a being of the same race and nature as those with whom I at present converse" (172). In fact, Evelina's actual encounter with Orville was not without pain and embarrassment, but in her need to transcend the shabby realities around her—the grossness of her egregious grandmother, Madame Duval, the mercenary impertinence of her cousins Branghton—she transforms it into a dream-vision with Orville as "an object of ideal perfection." Evelina creates Lord Orville, just as her author does. Burney seems to be suggesting a tenuous but crucial connection between female creativity and the redemption of female life, which reflects her personal coupling of writing with the need to be loved and known as valuable. What Evelina creates is, of course, a conventional Prince Charming, the patriarchy's reward to good girls, but Burney seems to invest in Evelina's language a consciousness of her own imagination's powers to evoke such gratifying visions.

Evelina, rescued princess that she is, is not sprung from her trap without the sense that her fairy tale depends upon the power of female creativity to sustain it, and that the social circumstances of a "young lady" render perilous the use of this power. It is dangerous for a woman to assume creative power in a context that allows her little control over her social circumstances, and Evelina's conjuring of Orville places her in danger of a sickening fall from illusion, as Villars points out to her:

> Young, animated, entirely off your guard, and thoughtless of con-sequences, *imagination* took the reins, and *reason*, slow-paced, though sure-footed, was unequal to a race with so eccentric and flighty a companion. How rapid was then my Evelina's progress through those regions of fancy and passion whither her new guide conducted her!— She saw Lord Orville at a ball,—and he was *the most amiable of men!*—She met him again at another,—and *he had every virtue under Heaven!*
>
> I mean not to depreciate the merit of Lord Orville, who, one mysterious instance alone excepted, seems to have deserved the idea you formed of his character; but it was not time, it was not the knowledge of his worth, obtained your regard; your new comrade had not patience to wait any trial; her glowing pencil, dipt in the vivid colours of her creative ideas, painted to you, at the moment of your first acquaintance, all the excellencies, all the good and rare qualities, which a great length of time, and intimacy, could alone have really discovered. [308-09]

Villars' warning against the danger of imagination is no new thought in 1778, of course, but it accurately suggests the vul-

nerability of a woman—real or fictional, Burney or Evelina—
who has created her own audience without bothering to check it
against social reality. Orville is to Evelina what "Nobody" was to
Fanny Burney—though far riskier—an audience who will not
fail to affirm her self-worth, and who exists within her power as
surely as he is her own creation. Unfortunately, as Villars points
out, Evelina has come to believe in the social, as well as personal
and imaginative virtue of her hero, and her "Nobody" becomes a
"Somebody" whose autonomous reality may betray her reliance.
Villars warns her of this danger and confirms what she had
previously suspected: Orville is, indeed, a "visionary fancy" that
she has conjured to mitigate the isolation and oppression of her
social life at London and at Bristol Wells.

Evelina's fictional situation reflects Burney's own dilemma as
a woman who sought solutions to female difficulties among
conventional, patriarchal answers. Writing gave her aesthetic and
imaginative choices among the options for women in patriarchal
society that were not matched by her social and personal
powers.[4] Burney could, in other words, easily endow her fictional heroine with the secure, emotionally based power over
males that she, herself, could only gain with considerable difficulty, if at all, in life. Fiction is, then, as dangerous, in setting up
false expectations, to Fanny Burney as Lord Orville is to Evelina;
as Villars says, the age did not encourage women to trust to
appearances, particularly when perception is brightened by
hopeful illusions about the disinterested generosity of male
power. Such illusions are the stuff of novels that end happily for
their heroines. Burney seems aware of this danger to personal
sanity and safety, and she projects it into her heroine's Cinderella
story. The dangers that track Evelina's entrance into the world are
ones that Burney knew: disappointment, powerlessness, and
regret for lost hopes. Balanced against these dangers is her ability
to sustain the fantasy of patriarchal benevolence, the rewards that
await female virtue, and, given the grimness of her alternatives, it
is not strange that she chose the fantasy.

In a telling passage dated 1768 in *The Early Diary*, Burney records her conversation with a "Mr. S." who claims that Richardson's Sir Charles Grandison is "too perfect for human nature." Burney responds that "it quite hurts me to hear anybody declare a really and thoroughly good man never lived. It is so *much* to the disgrace of mankind." When Mr. S. patronizingly admires her "innocence and credulity of heart," however, she worries that such innocence may expose one to danger. Mr. S. answers that since danger cannot be avoided in any case, Burney is better off believing in the possibility of a "really and thoroughly good man" (*ED* 1:36–37). Three years later, she seems to confirm Mr. S.'s fatalistic endorsement of innocence as the least culpable approach to a no-win situation: "What can one think of the natural disposition of a young person who, with an eye of suspicion, looks around for secret designs in the appearance of kindness, and evil intentions in the profession of friendship? *I* could not think well of such apprehensions and expectations in youth. A bad opinion of the world should be dearly bought to be excusable" (*ED* 1:110–11). In this passage, Burney presents innocence as a self-consciously formulated strategy for coping with a lack of real options. Accordingly, the "innocence" that allows Evelina and Fanny Burney to believe in Lord Orville as a Grandisonian protector is a considered choice, made with full knowledge of its danger, among the few solutions offered by patriarchal culture, and Burney's presentation of Lord Orville calls attention to the dangers as well as the desirability of believing in such creations.

Hence, *Evelina*'s happy ending is literary schizophrenia of a particularly calculated nature; it is withdrawal from reality as a coping mechanism or strategy. Yet the text is not, in this sense, totally "insane," but rather a split or doubled embodiment of Burney's self-consciousness, expressive of the dangers and the limits of the very solutions it advocates. This reflexivity—in the form of a sentimental artifice that calls attention to its artificiality—is less a case of literary cleverness than a manifestation

of the contradiction inherent in Burney's position as woman
writer. In that role, she implicitly claims a public voice that felt
awkward and unwieldy to what Mary Poovey has aptly named
the Proper Lady in her character, the woman who saw herself in
essentially private—not public—terms.[5] The contradictory
nature of this ideological position both gave authority and took it
away, leaving Burney licensed to use the affective power of
eighteenth-century sentimental literary conventions and, at the
same time, leaving her inclined to see that power as unauthorized
and unreliable unless grounded in the personal affection that
justified more fully established uses of feminine power in the
domestic sphere. Hence, *Evelina* asserts the heroine's power to
define herself through others' controlled estimations of her, while
suggesting how tenuous this power is, how much it depends on
human emotion's proper—and lucky—deployment. The public
success of *Evelina* disturbed this tenuous, compromised resolution of Burney's contradictory feelings toward authorial power.
Instead of feeling that her right to a public voice had been
validated, Burney seems to have transposed public acclaim to a
personal level: her success either made her all the more personally
valued or—devastatingly—exposed her to personal degradation.

Burney's feelings about gaining a public voice remain curiously ill-defined, as if she were masking feelings of invasion with
indifference—"I have an exceeding odd sensation, when I consider that it is now in the power of *any* and *every* body to read what I
so carefully hoarded even from my best friends, till this last
month or two,—and that a work so lately lodged, in all privacy
of my bureau, may now be seen by every butcher and baker,
cobler and tinker, throughout the three kingdoms, for the small
tribute of three pence" (*ED* 2:214). But whether Burney is, as I
suspect, shielding herself from a role that felt untenable to her or
whether she actually gave the public nature of her work as little
attention as appears from her journals, she shows only slight
concern for the reading public at large, and the audience that
seems to matter to her was known to her in person or by name:

her family (in particular her father), friends, and the literary circle to which her father had access through his relationship with the Thrales.[6] Public success, for Burney, did not mean the anonymity of writing in the privacy of a closet for unknown readers. It meant, rather, being exposed to real, specific individuals who would feel personally let down if she did not live up the success of her novel. She writes, after reading Susan Burney's account of her praises in the mouths of Hester Thrale and Samuel Johnson, "I tremble for what all this will end in. I verily think I had best stop where I am, and never again attempt writing: for after so much honour, so much success—how shall I bear a downfall?" (DL 1:126-27). It is hard to say, however, whether the responses of the famous unknown thrilled and terrified her more than those of her father; both seem to have had equally personal, specific significance to Burney, and both created enormous anxiety— about continuing to please, about whether or not the people who praised the novel would be disappointed by Burney, the woman.[7]

Burney's anxiety was partially and temporarily relieved after she became intimate with Johnson and the Thrales, during the time just previous to writing *Cecilia*.[8] Her journals express a sense of feeling personally known and valued; she says of Thrale that "had I been the child of this delightful woman, she could not have taken more pains to reconcile me to my situation" (DL 1:98), and somewhat later Burney adds that "I flatter myself that if he [Johnson] were now accused of loving me, he would not deny it, nor as before, insist on waiting longer ere he went so far" (DL 1:181). But her growing personal security with her new literary friends does not seem to have affected her continuing insecurity as a writer. As she worked on a play, "The Witlings," her journals reveal her trepidation at another public display of her art struggling against her brief, tenuous sense of personal security with her new audience. This precariously established balance between contradictory feelings—that her new-found public role both augmented and debased her personal value—was upset by a mild lampoon on "dear little Burney" published in *Warley: a satire.*[9] She had previously expressed her fears that writing might expose her to "the horror irrecoverable of personal abuse" (*DL* 1:127); given her need for personal approbation, this extreme, almost phobic response seems inevitable rather than prissy. "Personal abuse" denied the efficacy of her writerly control over how she was seen, and when "the worst" happened, and Burney's name was dropped in a lampoon, she was "for more than a week unable to eat, drink, or sleep for vehemence of vexation" (*DL* 1:161). The soothing effects of Johnson's concern over her distress and the flattering encouragement of her family and Hester Thrale probably helped her to continue writing the play (*DL* 1:158-60, 182-83), although her conviction that "no success could counter-balance the publishing of my name" (*DL* 1:166) remained firm after the *Warley* incident. Under continuing encouragement, she went on with "The Witlings," deciding, however, to "keep my own counsel; not to whisper even the name of it; to raise no expectations, which were always prejudicial, and finally, to have it performed while the town knew nothing of whose it was" (*DL* 1:208). Unfortunately, the protective mask of anonymity proved unnecessary; Dr. Burney and Crisp, apparently concerned that "The Witlings" was a too-obvious satire of the bas bleu, advised her to suppress the play.[10]

Burney seems to have seen their advice as "disapprobation" of a personal nature, not as a political strategy for the good of her career. She responded to her father and "Daddy" Crisp like a chastened, slightly resentful child determined not to be caught in the wrong: "I will never proceed so far again without your counsel, and then I shall not only save myself so much useless trouble, but you, who so reluctantly blame, the kind pain which I am sure must attend your disapprobation. . . . I have long thought I have had more than my share of success already" (*DL* 1:258-59). Burney's next project shows how seriously she meant never to "proceed so far again without your counsel"; with the writing of *Cecilia*, Burney turned to her paternal mentors for actual creative direction as well as emotional energy, beginning "hard fagging" at the novel that Crisp and Dr. Burney urged her to write. Resolving to exert herself so as not to appear "sulky" over her mentors' suppression of the play (*DL* 1:258), she wrote in order to rewin a secure sense of approval from the men who personally mattered most to her.

Burney's attitude toward her work in her later career as a writer shows a chronic need to reaffirm the early relationship with paternal mentors who made her feel safe as a writer. After her return to the Burney household from court, she sees the pleasure, almost the point of her work on a long poem as the gaining of Charles Burney's approval: "This is a delight to my dear Father inexpressibly great: and though I have gone no further than to let him know, from time to time, the species of Matter that occupies me, he is perfectly contented, and patiently waits till something is quite finished, before he insists upon reading a Word. This suits my humour well, as my own industry is all gone, when once its intent is produced" (*JL* 1:73). With *Camilla* as well, Burney placed her father's praise high in her gratifications as a writer: "with the utmost truth I can aver, never, in all their amazing circle of success have procured me any satisfaction I can put on a par with your approbation of them." Charles Burney's approval—"that approbation I *most* prize of all approbations in this lower sphere" (*JL* 3:255-56)—seems to have had more value to Burney than public opinion; the mixed reviews on *Camilla* do not seem to have disturbed her greatly, being only what Burney rather expected now that Johnson, Burke, and Reynolds no longer protected her with their praise: "But those immense Men whose single praise was Fame and Security, who established by a Word, the two elder sisters, are now silent" (*JL* 3:205). Burney persists in seeing audience response in specific, personal terms; I suspect that doing so gave her the semblance, at least, of a comforting fusion between the authorial control that her culture gave her reason to mistrust and the more known, more fully reassuring authority of the beloved over the lover.

The journals and letters written in 1813 during Burney's preparation to return to England from France with the manuscript of her last novel, *The Wanderer*, reveal how Charles Burney had assumed the psychic function of fusing Burney's public role as writer with her private identity of daughter, wife, mother: "Could I but have had my work for my dearest Father, the certainty of giving him so much pleasure, and of reaping hence ourselves so abundant an harvest, would have made affection, filial affection, and conjugal and maternal interest unite to give me fortitude for bearing my personal regret [at the absence from her husband]" (*JL* 6:675). Burney writes of her "true, heart-dear Joy in making such a presentation to my beloved Father; Joy, there at our meeting, in giving HIM so great a satisfaction, will indubitably take the lead. It will necessarily be one of the most blessed moments of my life, for it is what, I know, beyond all things in the world, he most wishes" (*JL* 6:690). After a ten-year separation from her elderly, failing father and with little notion of what Charles Burney's real interests and condition were at the time, Burney constructs a climactic reunion scene between father and daughter that not only recapitulates *Evelina*'s dedicatory poem addressed to the "author of my being," but also is a sort of reverse echo of the fictional Mr. Villars' wish to embrace Evelina before his death. The imagined emotional encounters between father and daughter are, in the case of both journal and novel, fictions, projected affirmations of female affective power in the hands of the heroine/writer. This is not to say that Burney could not tell the difference between life and art or the personal and the public. Rather, writing—both of journals and of fiction—gave her a way of imaging the results of affective rhetoric as well as a means of exerting it. And her image of affective control over audience, in both her fiction and her journals, consistently binds together authorship and traditionally feminine modes of cultural empowerment. Burney collapses the distance between writing as a public act and writing as a personal mode of relating—not out of confusion, but in order to extend and consolidate her sense of control.

But while Burney's personal concept of audience probably gave her a useful justification for continuing to write, it does not mask, in her fiction, the ideologically contradictory and divisive nature of female authorial control. The contradictions between public and private, active and passive roles for women reach a tenuous resolution in the reflexivity of *Evelina*. In the novels that followed, Burney discloses more fully than in *Evelina* the psychic cost of the contradictions inherent in her profession; whereas *Evelina* merely calls attention to the artificiality of the power granted to women in the sentimental novel, *Cecilia* is far more explicit about what is at risk in the woman writer's work: self-alienation, madness, and mental disintegration haunt the process by which the heroine gains control over her audience and, hence, her own identity.

Cecilia marks a shift in Burney's fiction from a romance plot that points to its source in female creative desire—signalling its own generic limits—to a plot that emphasizes far more painfully the tenuousness of female creative control over audience. Cecilia, like Evelina, finds her best, happiest self in marriage with the man of her choice, and, as in *Evelina*, the heroine reaches that goal through the hero's learning to read her character accurately—a painful process, fraught with mishaps and difficulties, by which he comes to appreciate her real worth. While Evelina suffers under Orville's possible and real misreadings of her—as simpleton, bumpkin, or object of sexual jealousy—Cecilia is nearly destroyed by Delvile's inability to see her accurately, an inability that persists even after the lovers are avowed and wed. Each heroine finally brings the hero to a correct reading of her, and they do so in ways that suggest a parallel between their power to control and the author's power to create the hero capable of such a reading—an implied analogy that, by calling attention to the tenuousness of a female control grounded in fictional rather than social convention, points to the enormous risks implicit in female creative power. Whereas this self-referential process in *Evelina* is arduous, suggestive of the difficulties inherent in commanding sentimental or authorial control, in *Cecilia* it is torturous, sug-

gesting the near-self-destruction risked by the authorial manipulation of audience.

Evelina unconsciously creates Lord Orville—happily, as it
turns out. But Cecilia's conscious attempts to see a lover in
Delvile reflect a dark side of Burney's self-conscious manipulation of literary romantic love: by creating a false happy ending
and by suffering a more intense form of the disillusionment that
Evelina momentarily feels and then evades, Cecilia reflects her
author's awareness of her own psychic risk in creating sentimental fantasies of female happiness. Like her author, who knows a
sentimental hero when she sees one, Cecilia quickly recognizes
Delvile's potential as her avowed lover and eventual husband.
Furthermore, she believes, like the author of *Evelina*, that love
will override practicalities, will "make every obstacle to the
alliance seem trifling, when put in competition with mutual
esteem and affection" (IV, 287). Delvile, however, sets a precedent
for subsequent Burney heroes in being far denser than Orville in
reading the heroine. Whereas Orville bears out Evelina's unworldly assumption about the power of love over finance and
family pride, Delvile is bound into a contradictory line of behavior by the familial and social expectations that Cecilia, in her
first sanguine perception of his love, dismisses so lightly. And,
even when hero and heroine become first avowed lovers and then
husband and wife, Delvile continues to misread Cecilia, interpreting her behavior in the light of circumstances and appearances that link her sexually with other men. His misguided
jealousy leads him, at the crisis point in their relationship, to run
from Cecilia, apparently intent on violent revenge, an act that
finally, as the culmination of misreading upon misreading, drives
Cecilia into madness. The emotional control secured to Evelina
by the title of "wife" is, in *Cecilia*, as unreliable as the created
vision of patriarchal benevolence that both heroines weave
around their men. Marriage, the relationship that ensures Evelina's self and security, renders Cecilia voiceless and powerless; in a
dramatic mad scene, she cries out that "no one will save me now!

I am married, and no one will listen to me!" (X, 881). Cecilia's attempts to "make sense" of herself to the hero break down into a state of madness and meaninglessness that has disturbing implications for women's ability to use language as affective control: speech, in Burney's second novel, not only fails to gain the heroine a just interpretation; it turns against her, alienating her from the hero—and herself.

Cecilia's ability to name, to give linguistic form to her sense of herself in relation to Delvile, becomes a mad parody of female creativity. She speaks her husband's name as if it—the name itself, the verbal token of her claim to power over her husband—were a child, a being made as well as known, which has turned treacherously upon its maker: " 'Tis a name,...I well remember to have heard, and once I loved it, and three times I called upon it in the dead of night. And when I was cold and wretched, I cherished it; and when I was abandoned and left alone, I repeated it and sung to it" (X, 885). In *Cecilia*, creative control—betrayed by its object in a biblically resonant triple denial—disintegrates into a mad parody of maternal power over the masculine. Ironically, this act of madness works for Cecilia as her saner attempts to secure affective control over Delvile do not. Although her fantasy loses its grounding in reality, Cecilia unconsciously uses its affective power to regain her control: her madness is the dark, unconscious side of Evelina's fantasy, her power to command the male protection she needs in order to survive. Loss of control over her own mind allows her to shock Delvile into a just interpretation of her integrity, giving her, finally, the control over the hero's mind that she has forfeited over her own.

Burney turned to the literary convention of "running mad" to express female desire, the will to power, through emotional blackmail of the particularly risky sort that walks a fine line between the creation and the immolation of self. *Cecilia*, then, stresses the contradictions implicit in acts of female creative power—between the public and private, art and artlessness—that *Evelina* precariously resolves through a self-referential assertion of authority. The self-alienation of *Cecilia* is a more extreme form of the contradiction implicit in *Evelina*, an exaggerated version of Evelina's sexual unselfconsciousness—her "delicate" dissociation from her own sexual impulses. Cecilia's madness suggests Burney's awareness, on some level, of the danger implicit in her heroine's affective power over hero and reader. And Burney's self-consciousness sets her apart from—without denying her implication in—the self-destructive potential of Cecilia's attempts to manipulate audience. Cecilia wins over husband and father-in-law by running mad; Fanny Burney gains patriarchal recognition by writing in a form in which the threat of her own self-alienation is implicit.

Evelina does, however, suggest, in half-submerged form, the dangers that patriarchal discourse can entail for the woman writer—dangers that *Cecilia* makes clear. Burney's first novel also culminates in the heroine's envelopment in male authority, a milder, benign version of the self-alienation to which Cecilia is reduced to gain affective control over her male audience. Looked at carefully, Evelina's fairy-tale union with Lord Orville is a sort of love-death in which the record of female consciousness is buried in the text of conventionally defined female "happiness." Evelina's closing account of her marriage brings to a climax Mr. Villars' longings for the almost sexual consummation of reunion with her by blurring, I think deliberately, the line between her sexual union with her husband and her anticipated reunion with her guardian. Evelina's affirmative answer to Villars' desire to die in her arms seems as much her "end" as it is his:

All is over, my dearest Sir, and the fate of your Evelina is decided! This morning, with fearful joy, and trembling gratitude, she united herself for ever with the object of her dearest, her eternal affection!

I have time for no more; the chaise now waits which is to conduct me to dear Berry Hill, and to the arms of the best of men. [406]

The arms that enfold Evelina in death are almost indistinguishable from those which embrace her in marriage, and, in a sense, it matters little whose arms hold her with what intent: both afford release from the ambiguities of power used within an ideological context—the public sphere—that assumes her powerlessness. Evelina runs happily (though with with "fearful joy" and "trembling gratitude") to her "end," of course, a willing Isolde to the Villars/Orville Tristan, but Cecilia's dash into arms that temporarily betray her has more of auto-da-fé than *liebestod* about it. In *Cecilia*, the heroine is not so much enveloped as she is cannibalized by the ostensible protection of masculine authority.

Cecilia's hysteria allows her language to express a gothic side to the novel's fairy tale of romantic love. Her ravings about Delvile, her husband and "prince," reflect the psychic reality of her brutally frustrated attempts to be known and hence protected by him. The prince becomes an agent of blood, the source and center of a terrifyingly vague violence whose lack of a clear object makes it all the more threatening: "Oh, if he is yet to be saved, if already he is not murdered...he is only in the next street, I left him there myself, his sword drawn, and covered with human blood!" Delvile's death is the imagined result of his violence, but the visionary "poniard" in "his wounded bosom" reflects Cecilia's "bloodied" vision of her marriage as well: "Oh, it was a work of darkness, unacceptable and offensive! it has been sealed, therefore, with blood, and tomorrow is will be signed with murder!" (X, 880-81). Cecilia refers to her own guilt, of course, in consenting to a clandestine marriage to Delvile after his father had refused consent, but hysteria allows her language to express more than a sense of her own wrong-doing: it also suggests her fears at being trapped in a situation in which male violence aggravates her mistaken action into an ultimate act of destruction. Cecilia is afraid *for* Delvile, but she is also afraid *of* him, a condition that Burney can express by disjointing and decentering her heroine's sense of relationship between self and the other, the patriarchal reality. Failing to recognize Delvile, Cecilia makes explicit the threat that she feels:

Cecilia now, half rising, and regarding him with mingled terror and anger, eagerly exclaimed, "if you do not mean to mangle and destroy me, begone this instant."

"To mangle you!" repeated Delvile, shuddering, "how horrible!—but I deserve it all!" [X, 884–85]

The plot contingencies of Cecilia's madness allow her to make this accusation—she thinks Delvile is the villain, Monckton; they also allow her to become again the loving, gentle heroine after the delirium has passed, so that Burney can incorporate in her novel both the expression of female anxiety and the reconciliation that is important to her heroine's happy ending. But insane, Cecilia can state a truth that does not become the lips of a conventional heroine: the psychic and social pressures created by her love for Delvile have indeed "mangled" her, and by his own admission, at that. Madness, then, is both rhetoric—a communicative act that is specifically pointed at gaining the desired effect on men who have power over women's lives—and a way of naming the threat of self-victimization implicit in acts of female power in the context of a male-controlled society—and literature.

In each of Burney's novels written after *Evelina*, a moment comes in the course of the heroine's troubled romance when the familial, sexual, and social pressures of her attempts to gain a just "reading" culminate in a crisis of self-alienation. Also at that moment, the hero comes to his own crisis in the course of his feelings for the heroine by observing her pain and debilitation. Delvile discovers Cecilia in her madness; Edgar finds his estranged fiancée, Camilla, teetering at the brink of a self-willed death. Harleigh, of *The Wanderer; or, Female Difficulties*, witnesses Juliet's sane but even more chilling abdication of self as she turns herself over to the husband whom political circumstances in France have forced her to marry—this time, a specifically sexual form of alienation from self. At this crisis point in all three of Burney's novels after *Evelina*, the heroine's temporary loss of self-control ultimately leads to a right understanding with the man of her desires—and the rhetorical purpose of female self-abdication is fulfilled. But in each case, the actual moment of encounter between the estranged lovers focuses on the emotional distance that the hero must overcome to understand his beloved, and on his weakness and inability to do so, suggesting that the female crisis of self-alienation needs to be read as more than a cry for patriarchal help: it is also Burney's clearest expression of the damages that the articulation of women's feelings—an affective act of power—inflicts on the female ego in a male-dominated world and art.

In *Cecilia*, Delvile persists, for a while, in misreading Cecilia's insanity as reproach and rejection; when he finally realizes that she is out of her senses, her madness "turns him to stone," leaving him weak and unable to help her either emotionally or physically: "Delvile now attempted to carry her in his arms; but trembling and unsteady, he had not strength to sustain her; yet not enduring to behold the helplessness he could not assist, he conjured them to be careful and gentle, and, committing her to their trust, ran out himself for a physician" (X, 886). The hero can only help the heroine by running away, a pattern that is repeated in *Camilla*, when the sight of the heroine's hand stretched out to him from behind the curtains of a sickbed causes the hero to flee the tormenting presence of his beloved. In both discovery scenes, the man blunders helplessly out of the room, leaving the woman isolated in a psychological darkness which is a type of death, or at least its prelude: "Declining all aid, Camilla continued in the same position, wrapt up, coveting the dark, and stifling sighs that were rising into sobs."[11] "Cecilia resisted them with her utmost power, imploring them not to bury her alive, and averring she had received intelligence they meant to entomb her with Mr. Monckton" (X, 886). Although more rational than Cecilia's ravings, Camilla's stillness is more chilling, since she seems to be "coveting" the living death that Cecilia, however irrationally, thinks she is fighting off. In both novels, the heroine's moment of most extreme alienation from herself and her life is, ironically, the crisis that gains her the patriarchal reward she desires. But Burney also seems to be embedding in this rhetoric of female madness the cost of alienation from one's self and from the patriarchal other that results from attempts to communicate female being in a world that assumes the suspect or insubstantial nature of female acts of power.

In *The Wanderer*, the hero is cut off from the heroine in her moment of crisis by the institutions of a society that, in Burney's view, has gone wrong at the core of its moral order. Instead of symbolic curtains or the heroine's own disordered mental state, marriage (ironically) alienates the hero from the heroine: Juliet has been forced to wed a brutal French Republican through the hope of saving those she loves during the Reign of Terror. She flees to England, but when she is discovered by her husband, numbly submits to the obligation of obedience that the institution of marriage entails for women. The discovery scene dramatizes her own self-abdication; it also focuses on the psychological alienation of her lover, Harleigh, who witnesses it: "A sudden sensation, kindred even to hatred, took possession of his feelings. Altered she appeared to him, and delusive. She had always, indeed, discouraged his hope, always forbidding his expectations; yet she must have seen that they subsisted, and were cherished; and could not but have been conscious, that a single word, bitter, but essentially just, might have demolished, have annihilated them in a moment."[12] Harleigh shifts quickly into pity for Juliet's plight and elation at the evidence that, although married to someone else, she still loves him. But Burney seems to have included this moment of near-hatred with a kind of instinct for the gap that separates male from female in the misreadings, revisions, and re-revisions that constitute "communication" between the sexes. In *The Wanderer*, a whole social order, rather than personal and familial pressure, is responsible for female alienation from self, her male lover, even sexuality itself—the Revolution serves as a sort of gothic objective correlative for the madness that Burney seems to think is implicit in female attempts to control male response, the madness of trying to merge the female will with an enabling male other.

The connection between the act of control implicit in writing and the heroine's sentimental ability to move the hero becomes, perhaps, clearest in *Camilla*, a novel that Burney wrote with the renewed sense of financial urgency that the birth of her son brought in 1794. Burney wrote this novel with a clear practical purpose in mind—the security of her family—and perhaps because of this acceptably feminine motivation seems to have taken a pleasure in writing it that was missing from the composition of *Cecilia*. Yet *Camilla* is still more explicit than *Cecilia* in its symbolic connection of writing with a power that turns back on the woman who wields it. Like Cecilia, Camilla is offered the promise of marriage early in the novel, and, like Cecilia, is put through a purgatory of doubt and loss after a promising beginning. Edgar, like Delvile, misreads Camilla through a too-scrupulous deference to a (patriarchal) moral authority figure. Edgar's caution produces the same results as Delvile's jealousy, and Camilla, ill and desperate, has a nightmare just before her rediscovery by Edgar that parallels Cecilia's waking delirium. This dream sequence, as Julia Epstein wisely points out, is the culmination of a linguistic struggle that occupies Camilla throughout the novel. Whereas Evelina artlessly controls her audience and determines her own "reading," *Camilla* dramatizes the debilitating struggle underlying the ostensibly unselfconscious expression of female identity and links that struggle to writing—the heroine's abortive attempts to make herself known on paper. The nightmare sequence in *Camilla* writes large the implications of this process, Epstein explains.[13] Camilla falls asleep, wishing herself dead and out of the troubles that her naiveté and Edgar's implacability have led her into; Death comes to her and demands that she write "thy claims, thy merits to mercy." Her hand "involuntarily" grasps "a pen of Iron, and with a velocity uncontrollable" writes out the "guilty characters," which become "illuminated with burning sulpher." Death tells her, "These are thy deserts; write now thy claims," but when she grasps the pen a second time it makes no mark on the page (875). This scene expresses the pain and difficulty of a woman struggling to redeem herself through a medium that she is not fully authorized to control. Burney, probably like other women, found herself writing out of patriarchal assumptions about writing as an act of power in which her oppression and even destruction were implicit. Hence, self-expression is closely allied with self-condemnation: the "iron pen" will write Camilla's guilt, but not her "claims."

Camilla's nightmare also expresses the disintegration of female personality implicit in Cecilia's earlier madness. The act of writing is accompanied, in the heroine's dream, by a cacophany of voices that seem to emanate from within her, most angry and accusatory, others querying or defeated:

> When again she made a feeble effort to rid her oppressed lungs of the dire weight that had fallen upon them, a voice hollow, deep, and distant, dreadfully pierced her ear, calling out: "Thou hast but thy own wish! Rejoice, thou murmurer, for thou diest!" Clearer, shriller, another voice quick vibrated in the air: "Whither goest thou," it cried, "and whence comest thou?"
>
> A voice from within, over which she thought she had no controul, though it seemed issuing from her vitals, low, hoarse, and tremulous, answered, "Whither I go, let me rest!"…Quick then another voice assailed her so near, so loud, so terrible…she shrieked at its horrible sound. [874-75]

The voices multiply until she is assailed "by hundreds, by thousands, by millions, from side to side, above, below, around" (876). Camilla is beset with a nightmare chorus of her own feelings, the seemingly alien voices of her overwrought mind; the attempt to write her own self-defense is not only painful, but is accompanied by a splintering of self into dissociated fragments. Camilla's nightmare passes, of course, like Cecilia's madness and Evelina's greensickness: even Juliet's brutal husband conveniently dies so that she can marry Harleigh. Burney repeatedly asserts the power of successful romantic love to banish the female nightmare, at least in novels, but she also asserts, more and more forcefully after *Evelina*, that happy endings are created at great risk to the woman who holds a pen in a world that defines public, writerly power as male. For Burney, writing meant a self-division that could either be carried off in reflexivity or painfully expressed in images of self-estrangement; the split between public and private along the lines of gender created internal contradictions in the most "respectable" and successful of eighteenth-century women novelists that her fiction does not fully resolve. I would argue, however, that the dissonances of Burney's fiction reveal not aesthetic failure but an impressive ability to resist false unities and resolutions designed to mask the real difficulty of her historical and personal circumstances. Burney's novels body forth contradiction, allowing her power over her identity as a woman writer and giving her the ability to confront her audience with the often-painful evidence of the difficulty in sustaining that identity. There is nothing easy and a great deal that is courageous in Burney's assimilation and management of the ideological dissonances that assailed her, like Camilla's nightmare voices, when she picked up her pen.

SEVEN

CAMILLA and THE WANDERER
Male Authority and Impotence

Fanny Burney's experience with authorship brought her, I have argued, to a heightened awareness of the contradictions implicit in her ideological position as woman and as writer in the late eighteenth century. In plotting the course of Burney's progress toward this awareness, I have focused almost exclusively on her first two novels as documents that mark the threshold of Burney's writerly entrance into the world of literature and public authority. In doing so, I have adhered to my study of the emergent development of a woman's writerly self-consciousness, but I have also left room for some misunderstandings of my own intentions in limiting my study of Burney's fiction to her two earliest works. I hope that my use of the metaphor of "entrance" in studying Burney's first two novels does not suggest that I see the last two novels as anticlimactic; in fact, I see them, in the light of my own feminist, politicized aesthetic, as the realization of possibilities for female writing that I see her discovering in the first two novels. *Camilla* (1796) and *The Wanderer; or, Female Difficulties* (1814) are not, in my view, mere repetitions of the patterns I have set forth here, but complex, and in some ways, richer developments from them.

To do justice to these developments would be to write another book—or other books—an undertaking presently in the hands of abler scholars than I.[1] But I offer here a sort of coda to my story of a writer's entrance into the world of authorship, which will, I hope, help lay to rest the fantasy that Burney somehow learned nothing other than fearful caution from her entrance into print. *Camilla* and *The Wanderer* both continue the work of Burney's earlier two novels in exposing, in increasingly bold, energetic, and explicit ways, the contradictions implicit in eighteenth-century female experience and in the experience of the woman writer. They also explore, more and more fully, the problematic relationship between the female artist as the manipulator of form and meaning and the ostensible authority of masculinity in male-dominated culture. Burney's last two novels expose contradictions in male authority over women—contradictions that, in turn, make the very social context for female creativity conducive to the woman artist's lack of control over her own social and economic condition.

The system of power relations in society, as Burney depicts it in her fiction, ostensibly gives women a kind of ideological power through the institutions of romantic love and marriage. This same system, however, also contributes to women's ideological devaluation as passive, morally weak and sexually suspect objects in relation to male power. Men, in Burney's fiction, are locked into the inverse of this contradiction. Whereas male characters in Burney's fiction are obviously and uniformly more socially powerful than the female characters, their power is often a sort of self-made travesty, a form of social control that is at absurd odds with their chronic ineptitude in romance and marriage. The system of power relations between the sexes locks both male and female into contradictory positions: male characters' weakness and incapacity as desiring subjects—as lovers and husbands—contradict socially sanctioned, economically reinforced masculine control, just as women's ideological position as the weaker other to male power contradicts their empowerment as desired object in the paradigm of romantic love. Burney's last two novels expose the absurdity and danger of a system of social relations that locks both male and female subjects in ideologically contradictory positions that disable and thwart human attempts at happiness—for both genders.

Both *Camilla* and *The Wanderer* are premised on the rigidity—

and illogic—of a system of economically motivated social customs that subordinate female action to male authority. The decision of Camilla's father, the Reverend Augustus Tyrold, sets the plot of *Camilla* into motion. He decides, at the novel's beginning, to indulge his feebleminded but wealthy brother, Sir Hugh, by allowing the child, Camilla, to live with Sir Hugh, whose ill health and poor education leave him with few resources for passing the time. Tyrold's decision is, the narrator tells us, motivated by "the love he bore his brother," but this male bond, as we learn in the next sentence, derives as much from economic motives as from brotherly love: "It seemed certain such a residence would secure [Camilla] an ample fortune" (13). Mrs. Tyrold, Camilla's mother, objects "against reposing a trust so precious where its value could so ill be appreciated," but complies out of obedience to her husband: "Had this lady been united to a man whom she despised, she would yet have obeyed him, and as scrupuously, though not as happily, as she obeyed her honoured partner. She considered the vow taken at the altar to her husband as a voluntary vestal would have held one taken to her Maker; and no dissent in opinion exculpated, in her mind, the least deviation from his will" (13-14). This beginning—in which a woman gives in to institutionalized male authority much against her better judgment—establishes a repeating pattern of plot developments in which women are placed at the mercy of incompetent and inconsistent male authority figures who, with varying degrees of malice or stupidity, mentally and physically torture the women within their control. This description of Mrs. Tyrold's obedience also gestures toward even darker possibilities implicit in women's subordination in marriage by naming what is *not* the case in this particular marriage: other women would not be able to obey even "as happily" as the reluctant Mrs. Tyrold.

The duty of female obedience in marriage also initiates the plot of *The Wanderer.* Juliet's adventures as a "female Robinson Crusoe, as unaided and unprotected, though in the midst of the world, as that imaginary hero in his uninhabited island" (5: 394)

are precipitated by her attempts to escape the social and sexual
obedience demanded of her by the forced marriage into which
she has been manipulated. Juliet's attempts to escape only lead
her inevitably back, however, to a compulsory submission that
repeats Mrs. Tyrold's grim sense of her marital duty; the subordination of women to men is, in both novels, the basis for plot
developments that dramatize the injustice of female suffering
within an economic and social system that empowers men who
often think and act with a contradictory weakness—a weakness
that imperils the women placed under their control. Camilla tries
futilely to be understood by Edgar, the hero whose capacity for
suspicions about the heroine's worth and integrity defies most of
the rules of logic and probability: courtship, supposedly the
means to woman's empowerment as the courted, desired object,
actually serves as the context for female debilitation at the hands
of incompetent or uncomprehending, powerful males. In *The
Wanderer*, the sexual vulnerability and economic powerlessness
imposed on the heroine by a forced marriage take on the nightmare quality of recurrent horror as Juliet runs from them only to
meet, again and again, the socially institutionalized fact of women's sexual and economic victimization. In both cases, the
romance plot that finally resolves the heroines' problems in the
happily-ever-after of married love also exposes the contradictory
nature of this resolution: in the working out of the very plot that
finally embeds female happiness in the ideology of romantic
love, women are economically debased, socially humiliated, and
psychologically maimed.

Camilla and *The Wanderer* both deploy the plot of blocked
romance to expose this implicit contradiction in the cultural
assumptions that place women's best chance at social empowerment in a system of courtship that debilitates at the same time
that it promises them hope for personal security and happiness.
In *Camilla*, multiple romances start, falter, and fail, in a series of
subplots that underline the frustration of the main loveplot between hero and heroine. In the main plotline, Edgar Mandlebert,

a rich, virtuous, but priggish young man falls in love with and asks to marry Camilla, the poor but attractive daughter of his guardian, Tyrold. He worries, however, that she is either unworthy of him or, alternatively, does not return his affection with sufficient ardor. The counsel of his tutor, Dr. Marchmont, whose misogynistic tendencies have been fueled by his own disappointments in marriage, aggravates these suspicions. Camilla, on her side, is constrained from clearing up the misunderstandings that Edgar so easily falls into by prescribed modes of proper female behavior in courtship, and the two lovers act out a veritable fool's game of miscommunication.[2]

Surrounding this plot of blocked romance, a number of other romantic possibilities flare and fizzle like so many damp firecrackers. First, the youthful Edgar has been drawn to flatter Camilla's beautiful cousin, Indiana, setting off expectations of romance in her and her uncle, Sir Hugh, as well as just about everyone else within the range of Sir Hugh's voice. In the meantime, a fortune hunter, Bellamy, courts Camilla's wealthy sister Eugenia, Sir Hugh's heir, and Eugenia falls in love with Melmond, a poor and romantic scholar, who, in turn, falls in love with the beautiful surface of the mindless Indiana (who is, in addition, the object of the fiery Macdersey's love). Bellamy is also romantically involved with Camilla's beautiful and foolish friend, Mrs. Berlington, while Sir Sedley Clarendel falls for and then denies his love for Camilla, who, in addition, inadvertently excites the romantic aspirations of young Hal Westwyn. These plots inevitably tangle and frustrate each other in a sort of absurdist's vision of romance; what emerges most clearly is the victimization of the women who become enmeshed in this tangle. The most sympathetic female characters are the most severely hurt: Mrs. Berlington is compromised and Eugenia brutalized and bullied by the romantic Bellamy. Camilla is nearly driven into a kind of suicide before Edgar finally comes to his senses and rescues her from her own self-destructive tendencies. The inevitable, institutionalized helplessness of women in a romance paradigm that ends in marriage—glossed over in the romantic resolution of Camilla's story—is given explicit expression in a minor subplot involving Miss Dennel, a silly young girl who falsely assumes that marriage might be a way out from under the patriarchal control of her father. Impatient with her father's authority over her as an unmarried girl, she hopes to gain more freedom through an early marriage. The inevitable happens: she finds herself more tyrannized by male authority in the form of a husband than she had been by her father when she was still Miss Dennel. Miss Dennel's case underscores the contradiction between women's supposed empowerment in marriage and their economic and ideological subordination to their husbands.

In *The Wanderer*, female powerlessness in romantic love is played out in a love triangle between Harleigh, the hero, Juliet, the object of his romantic aspirations, and Elinor, who, in turn, loves Harleigh. Instead of the absurd proliferation of romance in *Camilla, The Wanderer* shows us a triad of lovers rendered powerless by the conventions and institutions of romance, love, and marriage. There is considerable understanding and sympathy between Harleigh and Juliet, but the latter's secret marriage to a French Republican—a political marriage forced by Juliet's efforts to help her family—thwarts their romance. Juliet, who is actually the beloved object of the hero's desires, is prohibited from acting on her power, ironically, by her adherence to the forms of female marital duty, even though these forms are empty of all emotional conviction. Burney uses the character of Elinor, however, to make what is perhaps her most powerful statement of women's disempowered position in performing the customary gestures of romantic love that lead, in theory at least, to the institutionalized protection of women in marriage. Elinor deliberately breaks the rules of courtship that demand passivity and reticence from the woman; she resolves to throw off "unmeaning custom" and act "for myself" by arranging the disclosure of her love for Harleigh (1:342). Although Elinor's directness comes as something of a relief in contrast to the indirection of the heroine, who seeks to hide the marriage that renders her helpless, Elinor's own language discloses the suicidal nature of her attempt to break out of the bounds of accepted female behavior in courtship: "Let me wait the fated moment, and then—let the truth burst, blaze, and flame, till it devour me!" (1: 385). Finally, she is driven to attempt suicide (an act chillingly reminiscent of Mary Woll-stonecraft's historical reaction to unrequited love) when her attempts to break through the disempowering rules of courtship fail to win her the hero's love. Elinor is caught in a no-win situation in that neither breaking nor playing within the rules seems to change the essential nature of the game in which male power and female powerlessness are acknowledged in every move. Even Elinor's suicide attempt brings her into line within a system of masculine authority. When Harleigh counsels her to talk with a clergyman (another male authority figure) following her failed attempt, Elinor responds in another act of self-destructive rebellion: "She flung off her bandages, rent open her wound, and tore her hair; calling, screaming for death, with agonizing wrath" (1: 445).

Elinor's self-mutilation gestures toward a psychological tendency often apparent in women's attempts at rebellion. Adrienne Rich, in a perceptive reading of Charlotte Brontë's *Jane Eyre,* suggests that Jane's hysterical behavior as a child in the "red room" sequence of the novel reveals the tendency of female rebellion unmediated by social consciousness to turn in on the rebel, to convert its own energy into a weapon against the rebellious woman herself.[3] Elinor's hysteria at Harleigh's rejection of her confessed love for him takes a similar self-destructive form. Burney, however, is more explicit than Brontë about the social constraints on female behavior in romantic love that leave Elinor with no way out of the social system that forces her energy into self-destructive channels. At the end of the novel when Juliet is happily freed from her hateful marriage and united with Harleigh, Elinor must return to conventional female behavior—not because it is desirable, but because she has no choice: "must

Elinor, too—must even Elinor—like the element to which, with the common herd, she owes, chiefly, her support, find,—with that herd!—her own level?—find that she has strayed from the beaten road, only to discover that all others are pathless!" (5: 394). The "Wanderer" herself, Juliet, reinforces this theme of female choicelessness, the lack of paths off the beaten road of conventional female behavior. Forced by circumstances off the course of middle-class female life under the protection of the patriarchal family, Juliet finds that her own unwished-for deviation from convention—like Elinor's willed one—places her in socially and economically untenable positions. Making a living as a single, unprotected woman means being subjected to the grossest forms of unjust, reductive, and distorting interpretation: "How insufficient, she exclaimed, is a FEMALE to herself! How utterly dependant upon situation—connexions—circumstance! how nameless, how for ever fresh-springing are her DIFFICULTIES, when she would owe her existence to her own exertions! Her conduct is criticised, not scrutinized; her character is censured, not examined; her labours are unhonoured, and her qualifications are but lures to ill will! Calumny hovers over her head, and slander follows her footsteps!" (2: 197). Although Elinor is left odd woman out at the end of the novel, while Juliet is restored to the domestic safety of conjugal love, the parallel between the two women's experience beyond the boundaries of conventional middle-class female behavior casts some doubt on whose is the special case—the defeated Elinor's or the rewarded Juliet's. Leaving the beaten path of courtship, love, and marriage, the institutions that subordinate women to male control in the patriarchal family, is not a real option for either Juliet or Elinor. *The Wanderer* emphasizes the entrapment of women within the ideology of romantic love and marriage that *Camilla* exposes as itself claustrophobic, stifling to female self-expression.

Burney's last two novels portray the ideological double bind of women's place within the patriarchal family, how that power structure gives women the only socially available means to self-expression and personal control while simultaneously militating against them. *Camilla* and *The Wanderer* also address the complex and contradictory position of the woman who seeks to control the way she is seen, the woman as manipulator of appearances, as the maker of her own identity—in short, of the woman as artist. Female dress and the expressive—or disguising and transforming—nature of dress as a form of social signification are important, in Burney's last two novels, to the question of women's paradoxical entrapment by the very modes of institutionalized social behavior that are supposed to empower them. In *Camilla*, the rituals and institutions surrounding women's clothing become a locus of woman's contradictory position as both the sought-after treasure and the victim of romantic courtship. Conformity to bourgeois female dress codes becomes a type of conformity to more inclusive modes of socially institutionalized feminine behavior, the modes that hold women in their contradictory ideological position.

Recurring to a passage from Burney's *Diary and Letters* discussed earlier in this study may help clarify a specific kind of double bind that the imperatives of dress imposed upon the middle-class woman of Burney's day. Burney's 1780 response to Samuel Crisp's inquiry about the writing she was getting done while with the Thrales in London suggests, as I have argued, a contradictory attitude toward the particular rituals of dress that are a prominent aspect of the social duties of women much in public life. The passage is worth quoting again as an example of Burney's impatience with and her sense of lacking alternatives to conventions of middle-class femininity: " 'Fact! Fact!' I assure you—however paltry, ridiculous, or inconceivable it may sound. Caps, hats, and ribbons make, indeed, no venerable appearance upon paper;—no more do eating and drinking;—yet the one can no more be worn without being made, than the other can be swallowed without being cooked; and those who can neither pay milliners nor keep scullions, must either toil for themselves, or go capless and dinnerless" (*DL* 1:314). I have already suggested the contradictory attitude toward dress—as both a "paltry" duty and a necessary aspect of femininity—implied by this passage, but I wish to point out as well the specifically economic underpinnings to Burney's ambivalence in this passage. Crisp's concern for how much writing Burney was doing at this time was not, after all, an idle one; both he and Charles Burney were anxious, especially during the peak period of *Evelina*'s popularity, for Burney to secure herself, through writing, against an uncertain economic future. Burney was well aware of and in accord with this economic motive in allocating the use of her time to writing. She was therefore also aware that keeping up her social stock by keeping up sartorial appearances meant a corresponding drain on the potential economic resource that writing had become for her since *Evelina*'s success. Burney seems to accept this conflict between the need to play a conventionally middle-class, feminine social role and the economic anxiety that underlies that role as one of the inconveniences of her sex and class. Without the money that would make such preparations less time-consuming, Burney must toil at nonrenumerative work that, worse, cuts into time that she might have spent in more economically empowering ways. Conformity to social custom entraps the middle-class but impecunious young woman within her own impoverishment, perpetuating the means of her own economic oppression.

Camilla's experience with the imperatives of dress in public places shows a similar contradiction between social expectations imposed on middle-class young women and the economic necessity so often implicit in their position. Like the young Fanny Burney, Camilla has limited funds for financing the outfits that a public social life demands, and although even a small sample of public life teaches her that she would be economically safer and wiser to stay within the family circle where the demands of dress are less exacting, motives involving her relationship with Edgar lead her into dressing for a more public social scene. On several occasions throughout the novel, Camilla accepts an invitation to some place of public diversion on Edgar's account: either to see and reattach Edgar or to avoid him in the interests of getting over and concealing her attachment. The twists and turns in Camilla's courtship make her economically vulnerable in a manner that is specific to social expectations linked to her femininity. Although she is by no means extravagant, the decorum of the public feminine role demands expenses past her means. These expenses, in turn, combined with the money extorted from her by the rapacious Lionel—her thoughtless, scapegrace brother—result, through the means of a plot incredibly convoluted and complex, in the imprisonment for debt of Camilla's saintly father and her own nearly fatal, guilt-imposed illness. The plot ironically re-turns to the father whose decision had initially precipitated the novel's action; Tyrold's literal imprisonment for his daughter's debts gestures toward his own ideologically fixed position as patriarchal authority—and his contradictory helplessness within that position of power.

The contradictory strengths and weaknesses in the social posi-tions of both men and women are not privatized flukes, however, but structural contradictions in the social system itself. Camilla's foolishness in incurring debts is never the result of mere vanity, but rather a by-product of her thoughtless immersion in the social roles that her society encourages young women to play. The narrator praises Camilla for resisting the urgings of youthful vanity in dress, but matter-of-factly notes that a total resistance to spending money on clothes is incompatible with middle-class notions of femininity: "After a very short time, [Camilla's] little wardrobe exhibited a worse quality than that of not keeping pace with the last devices of the *ton*; it lost not merely its newness, but its delicacy. Alas, thought she, how long, in the careful and rare wear of Etherington and Cleves, all this would have served me; while here, in this daily use, a fortnight is scarce passed, yet all is spoilt and destroyed" (689). The "delicacy" intrinsic to social identity for women of Camilla's class (she is a poor, but respecta-ble clergyman's daughter and the niece of a baronet) must somehow be supported even if her social position does not carry with it the economic means of doing so. Sir Sedley Clarendel may, as the narrator points out, attend a public breakfast in dirty boots and a powdery coat, but ladies must be nicer—even if they can't afford it. Burney's juxtaposition of Camilla's socially determined role as a woman of delicacy against her lack of economic means to sustain that delicacy reveals a gap between the heroine's ideological position and her empty (although stylish) purse.

Burney's treatment of Camilla's clothes stresses this contradiction between economic power and ideological respectability in women's social roles. Specific items of dress become emblems of both her economic helplessness and of her hopes for re-empowerment as Edgar's beloved wife-to-be. Camilla finances, by borrowing money, a ball dress as a sort of ticket to a last-chance meeting with Edgar intended to win him back, and this dress comes to symbolize two contradictory aspects of the role of feminine love-object: it simultaneously calls attention to Camilla's economic vulnerability and to her hopes for gaining back her influence over her estranged fiance. Returning from her latest, failed attempt to convince Edgar that she is worthy to be his wife, Camilla is struck by the sight of "her bed completely covered with her new ball dress," a dress ordered in hopes of being seen and beloved by Edgar: "This sight was, at first, an aggravation of her agony, by appearing to her as superfluous as it was expensive: but wherever hope could find an aperture to creep in at, it was sure of a welcome from Camilla. Edgar was undoubtedly invited to the ball; why should he not be there?" (710). The dress suggests not only economic folly to Camilla, but the conventional feminine hope of a successful romantic conquest. Although Camilla is certainly above the manipulation of men through superficial attractions, a game played by her beautiful but empty-headed cousin Indiana, she buys into a system of courtship that offers her an elusive and tenuous power at the cost of aggravating her economic difficulties.

Camilla's apparently final loss of this power—the power of

romantic treasure—strips feminine sartorial splendor of its hopeful significance in the courtship game. Again, the novel gives us a
scene of female reflection in which Camilla looks at her clothes,
but this time she is without illusory visions of conciliatory
meetings with Edgar. Rather, she is confronted with the sheer
material costliness of her magnificent ball dress, a costliness that
makes its very beauty painful: "A more minute examination of
her attire was not calculated to improve her serenity. Her robe
was everywhere edged with the finest Valencienne lace; her lilac
shoes, sash, and gloves, were richly spangled with silver, and
finished with a silver fringe; her ear-rings and necklace were of
lilac and gold beads; her fan and shoe roses were brilliant with
lilac foil, and her bouquet of artificial lilac flowers, and her
plumes of lilac feathers, were here and there tipt with the most
tiny transparent white beads, to give them the effect of being
glittering with the dew" (721). The narrator's description of
Camilla's gorgeous finery in the context of her growing economic crisis and her desertion by the hero—a desertion that seems to
end hopes of economic as well as emotional security—serves to
rub in the contradiction between the role of feminine "treasure"
in the ideology of romance and women's real economic powerlessness to sustain the cost of such a role without a male backer.
The material evidence of a feminine economic disaster jostles the
reader's—and perhaps the author's—sensuous pleasure in this bit
of eighteenth-century fashion copy. The experience of reading
Burney's text reconstitutes, rather than resolves, the gap between
the promise of empowerment and the actuality of women's
economic helplessness in love and marriage.

The dress that Camilla invests in, to her own economic disad-
vantage, is required to meet the dress code of the social function
at which she hopes to reattach Edgar. Like Cinderella's ball dress
in many versions of the old fairy tale, it constitutes a sort of
conventionally agreed-upon packaging that is intrinsic to mar-
ketably marriageable feminine beauty. *Camilla* suggests what
might have happened had Cinderella, lacking a fairy godmother,

returned from the ball without the Prince, to face the bills run up in a futile attempt to rescue herself from poverty by romance. Uncritically and thoughtlessly buying clothes—or the ideological position of romantic treasure that they conventionally represent—can be economically disastrous for the young woman at the crucial age of courtship, a lesson that *Camilla* brings home. But Burney's third novel goes beyond establishing the double, empowering and defeating, nature of the feminine role in romantic love. *Camilla* begins to explore alternatives to a conventional acceptance of feminine ideology, again, through the metaphor of clothes and dressing up. In *Camilla* and *The Wanderer*, Burney deploys metaphorical possibilities for clothes that go beyond the bounds of signifying the passive ideological position of women in courtship—the position of Cinderella at the ball. Clothes in *Camilla* become the means of pushing at—and defining—ideological boundaries for gender- and class-based roles.

Camilla's disastrous acceptance of social convention in dress is counterbalanced by other characters' conscious eccentricities in dress, eccentricities that suggest the individual's attempts to subvert as well as conform to norms of social behavior. The heroine's often thoughtless—because innocent—acceptance of sartorial propriety in feminine attire is contrasted with the deliberate dressing habits of four characters who play out various possibilities for the power of dress as a deliberate manipulation of social convention. These characters are symmetrically opposed to each other in gender and in class: the aristocratic Sir Sedley Clarendel and Mrs. Arlbery seem, in their conscious flaunting of gender-specific dress conventions, to be paired against the lower class Mr. Dubster and Mrs. Mittin, whose clothes are integral parts of their attempts at manipulating class roles to their own advantage. Through the sartorial eccentricities and improprieties of these four characters, Burney both develops and delimits possibilities for individual expression through the deliberate use of dress as a means of creating a sometimes dangerous, sometimes liberating slippage in class- and gender-defined social roles.

Dressing up and dressing down enable these characters—not to *redefine* social roles—but to attempt, at least, to use culturally constructed roles to their own advantage. The extent to which they succeed or fail to empower themselves and the narrator's moral assessment of their attempts form a kind of commentary on the possibility for shaping social form to fit individual desire or need. In *Camilla*, the possibilities for ideological slippage in gender- and class-defined roles become a displaced comment, invested in other characters, on the heroine's entrapment in convention. *The Wanderer*, as we shall see, locates that slippage in the heroine herself. Juliet's multiple names and disguises dramatize the power and danger implicit in female manipulations of form and appearance.

Our first introduction to *Camilla's* Sir Sedley and Mrs. Arlbery emphasizes their respective nonconformity to standards of attire as a more or less successful means to personal control over a conventional social situation. Both Sir Sedley and Mrs. Arlbery use dress as a disguise, a consciously set decoy that distracts attention from their real capacities or motives. When Camilla first sees Sir Sedley, he is "dressed so completely in the extreme of fashion, as more than to border upon foppery." His clothes and manner serve as "a deep and wilful veil of conceit and affectation" under which lurks "a secret disposition to deride the very follies he was practicing" (64). The dress of a dandy serves as a "veil" for the sensible, intelligent social critic who sees others' "follies"— and his own—at a clarifying distance. His eccentricities bespeak more than detachment, however; Sir Sedley is a remarkably clear instance of contradiction in male power in that his self-protective veil hints at a psychological vulnerability within the empowered position of the male in courtship—a chronic condition, as Burney sees it, of masculinity. Disguising himself as a fool allows Sir Sedley to protect himself from the vulnerability of being taken seriously by young women like Camilla: his misleading attire is an extension of his frivolous and shallow manner, a mode of behavior that allows him to hide any real feeling for a woman in affectation. His lack of regard for social customs of dress—as when he appears at a public breakfast in dirty boots and a powdery coat the morning after his gorgeous appearance at the ball—is a ploy for asserting his autonomy, his immunity from others' opinions of him, just as his apparently heartless disavowal of his affection for Camilla is a way to slip out of the role of rejected suitor when it becomes clear she does not return his love.

Mrs. Arlbery similarly uses a disregard for conventions of formality in attire as a means of asserting her autonomy and denying her dependence on the approval and admiration of others. When Camilla first sees her at the ball where she also meets Sir Sedley, Mrs. Arlbery appears in a "complete but becoming undress, with a work-bag hanging on her arm, whence she was carelessly knotting." Her manner, as well as her clothes, aggressively asserts "a decided superiority to all she saw, and a perfect indifference to what opinion she incurred in return." And, as in Sir Sedley's case, this affectation of nonchalant nonconformity is a decoy to distract attention away from her need to be noticed, to dominate others with her eccentricity:

She was immediately joined by all the officers, and several other gentlemen, whose eagerness to shew themselves of her acquaintance marked her for a woman of some consequence; though she took little other notice of them, than that of giving to each some frivolous commission; telling one to hold her work-bag; bidding another fetch her a chair; a third, ask for a glass of water; and a fourth, take care of her cloak. She then planted herself just without the folding-doors, declaring there could be no breathing in the smaller apartment, and sent about the gentlemen for various refreshments; all which she rejected when they arrived, with extreme contempt, and a thousand fantastic grimaces.[p. 73]

Even Mrs. Arlbery's physical position—"just without the folding-doors"—suggests that her nonconformity is not a complete rejection of a restrictive set of social conventions (in which there is "no breathing") but an attempt to dominate others through the deliberate manipulation of behavioral norms.

The liability in this deployment of sartorial codes to personal advantage is the tendency to become trapped by one's own manipulations, to play the game of eccentricity so well as to exclude the possibility of being taken seriously within the conventional rules that Sir Sedley's and Mrs. Arlbery's rule-floutings are, in fact, slavish reactions against. Sir Sedley's affectation protects him from the psychological vulnerability of the lover, but it also means that he cannot fall in love with the credibility of the romantic hero—and there are no other roles in which he can care about a woman. His courtship of Camilla develops almost against his own will—even the tender-hearted Camilla has trouble taking it seriously—and he must foppishly and affectedly deny his feelings for her in order to save himself from the undignified position of the rejected suitor. Mrs. Albery is as inept in promoting the courtship between Camilla and Edgar as Sir Sedley is in promoting his own suit, and her advice to Camilla to play hard to get only serves to prolong the period of misunderstandings between the heroine and her lover. Both manipulators of the rules—both of clothes and of courtship—find themselves drawn in some capacity into the game of romance with an inexorability that suggests that it is, in the confines of the novel at least, the only game in town. And both manipulators find themselves, despite their intelligent detachment, pointedly impotent within the game that they attempt to turn to their own purposes. The power to deploy social custom to individual advantage is delimited for both by the ideology of romantic love. The autonomy they gain through their deliberate manipulation of social convention is hedged in by an ideology of romance that gives them no credibility, no power. Like Elinor, who finds no way to love off the beaten path, Mrs. Arlbery and Sir Sedley find no empowering ways to use their considerable skills as manipulators of form within the game of romance.

And this game seems, as we have seen in earlier chapters, the only possible—though highly ambivalent—means to power for the Burney heroine. Even Sir Sedley's and Mrs. Arlbery's limited options—outside of romance—at shaping social forms to their own desires are not open to Camilla. Sir Sedley is a rich, upper-class, single male with a far greater range of choices in behavior than the middle-class, economically dependent heroine. Mrs. Arlbery has the special license of a well-bred widow with an independent income. Both characters have access to socially sanctioned or at least tolerated powers that are unavailable to Camilla as a dependent single woman. Indeed, their power is antithetical to the only cultural definition that gives her value—the role of courted object in the paradigm of romantic love. Sir Sedley's and Mrs. Arlbery's successes and failures at social sub-version illustrate romance's function as a fault line for class and gender boundaries, the point beyond which individual subver-sion of social form cannot go. The heroine's ostensible means to power excludes any other ideological mode of transforming social roles to her own advantage. Romance, finally, delimits all methods of subversion, within and without its own boundaries.

Mr. Dubster and Mrs. Mittin dress up or dress down, like Sir Sedley and Mrs. Arlbery, in order to gain a personal advantage within a class- and gender-defined social system. While the latter two manipulate gender-linked conventions within their class, Mittin and Dubster use—or attempt to use—conventions of dress to slip through class boundaries that would delimit the range of their behavior. Clothes, the signifiers of socially defined roles, may also be used to subvert those roles. But this subversive possibility, as Mr. Dubster deploys it, is contained, as in the case of Sir Sedley and Mrs. Arlbery, by the ideology of romance. Camilla meets Mr. Dubster, a successful businessman who has set up as a gentleman of fortune, at the same ball where she first sees the foppish Sir Sedley and Mrs. Arlbery in her "undress." Whereas the two aristocrats play on conventional dress codes within their class as a means to autonomy, Mr. Dubster seems more controlled by his new gentleman's clothes than in control of them, as Camilla's brother Lionel suggests: "If there's not that delightful creature again, with his bran-new clothes? and they sit upon him so tight, he can't turn round his vastly droll figure, except like a puppet with one jerk for the whole body" (69). Mr. Dubster's clothes are a part of charade that enables him to cross class lines, to attend a ball with the gentry, to ask young ladies like Camilla to dance with him. But he is not fully in control of his sartorial "tools," as is comically evidenced by his struggle with gloves. Lionel mischieviously prompts Dubster to ask Camilla to dance. Miss Margland, her cousin Indiana's governess, manages to repulse his most unwelcome invitation by insisting that no young lady such as Camilla could, in propriety, dance with a man who has lost one of his gloves. Managing the proprieties of dress becomes a comically convoluted effort as Dubster tries, unsuccessfully, to negotiate the task of obtaining another pair, first through his friend, the head waiter, and then by sending a "boy" to buy a new pair: "I happened of the misfortune of losing one of my gloves, and not being able to find Tom Hicks, I've been waiting all this while for a boy as has promised to get me a pair; though, I suppose he's fell down in the dark and broke his skull, by his not coming" (72). Dubster's ambiguous position as a newly self-made gentleman is marked by the fine line between the two means he uses to obtain new gloves—through the favor of a lower-class friend and through an order to a subordinate; the ambiguity of his class position is not, however, empowering, but rather leaves him helplessly struggling to manage conventions— and clothes—that he does not understand. His awkwardness in dress underscores the difficulty of shifting class-linked roles, of course, and it does so in the specific context of asking a young lady to dance at her first ball, making Dubster a sort of Prince Charming *manqué*, a hilarious failure in the realm of romantic courtship. Mrs. Albery emphasizes this context for Dubster's ineptitude by asking, in play, if Camilla knew that she was socializing with a "tinker," a joke probably alluding to Plato's tinker who tries to court an aristocratic young woman. Whatever liberating slippage Dubster's clumsy manipulation of class-linked convention may effect, it is, like the more sophisticated manipulations of Sir Sedley and Mrs. Arlbery, clearly ineffectual in the realm of romance.

Mrs. Mittin, on the other hand (so to speak), understands the female conventions of dress, the trappings of romantic courtship, all too well, as is evidenced by her part as clothes-procurer in Camilla's economically disastrous attempts to stay in fashion. Like Mr. Dubster, Mrs. Mittin has moved up to the class of "gentle": "Mrs. Mittin had begun life as the apprentice to a small country milliner; but had rendered herself so useful to a sick elderly gentlewoman, who lodged in the house, that she left her a legacy, which, by sinking into an annuity, enabled her to quit her business, and set up, in her own conception, for a gentlewoman herself" (688). Unlike Mr. Dubster, Mrs. Mittin is a skillful manipulator of clothes, both her own dress and others', for her own ends. Her former profession stands her in good stead: as Camilla discovers, Mrs. Mittin, who augments her skimpy income by being "useful" to better-off gentlewomen, turns Camilla's need for proper clothes into a small-scale industry by which she always makes some profit. Whereas clothes are the awkward extensions of Dubster's economic success, they function as the means by which Mrs. Mittin scrapes up a subsistence. Mrs. Mittin's skill with clothes also extends to a facility for disguise. When Camilla first meets her, she has dressed down in class in order to gain more freedom of movement and action. She explains that while dressing as a gentlewoman gains her entrance and a free ride to the theater and other public amusements, her upper-class dress becomes a liability when she goes home by herself. To avoid the notice that a gentlewoman might draw walking by herself at times, Mrs. Mittin keeps handy a disguise: " 'But I go my own way,' continued she, 'and nobody knows a word of the matter: for I keep a large bonnet, and cloak, and a checked apron, and a pair of clogs, or pattens, always at this friend's; and then when I have put them on, people take me for a mere common person, and I walk on, ever so late, and nobody speaks to me; and so by that means I get my pleasure, and save my money; and yet always appear like a gentlewoman when I'm known' " (424). Mrs. Mittin uses clothes both as a means of economic survival—as a sort of amateur-status milliner—and as a means to slip past those who would prey in public on her class and gender.

Mrs. Mittin buys her greater range of freedom dearly, however, at the cost of economic independence, even physical comfort. Whereas Dubster's attempts to deploy class-linked sartorial convention are frustrated by assumptions about the rituals of romance, Mittin's are confined within economic rather than ideological limits. Unlike Mr. Dubster, whose attempts to dress up in class are simply inept, Mrs. Mittin is skillful at turning conventions of dress to her own advantage. Her skill—at dressing up, dressing down, and dressing others—is limited in its effectiveness, however, by a clear, hard economic reality. Her officious assistance in procuring Camilla clothes is premised on the false idea that Camilla is a rich heiress: Camilla's poverty is the hidden contradiction within the class- and gender-determined conventions of dress that are Mrs. Mittin's business. Similarly, economic necessity contradicts her own game of playing the gentlewoman. Her social status is based on "so very small an income, that to sustain her new post, she was frequently reduced to far greater dependence and hardships than she experienced in her old one" (688). Mrs. Mittin situates herself uncomfortably within an ideology of class-linked power—the supposedly greater freedom of the upper classes—that is contradicted by an economic reality that renders her less, not more powerful. The role of "gentlewoman" gives her a kind of social power, only to make her economically more vulnerable. Mrs. Mittin's active attempts to capitalize on the class- and gender-determined customs of dress explore a range of behavior beyond Camilla's innocent acceptance of the sartorial conventions appropriate to a marriageable young gentlewoman: they suggest possibilities for active manipulation of social forms and customs, for female control over the conventions that Camilla accepts because she sees no other options. But when this manipulative skill is employed in the service of the female role in courtship, it leads to economic disaster. As in the cases of Sir Sedley, Mrs. Arlbery, and Mr. Dubster, Mrs. Mittin fails as a manipulator of appearances in the realm of romantic love. The contradictions in her own situation as a newly self-made gentlewoman without adequate means to sustain her position also suggest a parallel with Camilla's near-disastrous acceptance of the role of courted object: both women implicitly buy into an ideology of class- and gender-based power that is in contradiction to economic reality. If Camilla functions as an economically grounded version of Cinderella, Mrs. Mittin plays a petit bourgeois fairy godmother who runs up bills every time she waves her wand.

In *Camilla,* clothing becomes a locus in the text for the management of social conventions, the means by which characters assume, attempt to assume, or manipulate the roles determined by class and gender ideology. The material nature of clothing as a commodity item to be bought and sold, combined with its ideological value as the coded representation of gender and class roles, makes it a probable and creditable expression of contradiction between economic and ideological reality. As a symbol of class or gender status, clothes can be manipulated and transformed; as material things, clothes must be bought and sold within a far less malleable economic structure. Hence, they serve to illustrate the extent—and limits—of the individual's ability to manipulate identity within the specific social and economic system depicted in the novel. *The Wanderer* situates the possibilities and limitations of the individual's manipulation of social roles in the behavior of the heroine herself. Juliet, like Mrs. Mittin, uses disguise as a means to escape from the specific limitations imposed on the actions of a "gentlewoman." Political necessity—not Mrs. Mittin's "simple egotism" (689)—motivates Juliet's manipulation of class- and gender-determined appearances: her victimization as an imperiled aristocrat during the Reign of Terror justifies her use of disguise as a means of escape from what amounts to legalized rape in a forced marriage. But her experience as a female manipulator of social appearances, a "wanderer" through a series of socially and economically defined roles as well as a traveler through physical space, exposes the same debilitating contradictions between ideology and economics that impinge on Camilla and Mrs. Mittin.

Juliet initially must depend on a deliberate confusion of the appearances that define her social role in the eyes of others. She manipulates appearances, quite literally, through physical disguise, and verbally, through an evasive and obfuscating discourse. These two modes of transformation—clothing and language—are obsessively linked in *The Wanderer*: words and clothes both signify class- and gender-based roles and obfuscate them. Terry Castle points out the cultural basis for analogies between clothing and language in the eighteenth century, the status of clothing as a "kind of discourse" and language's metaphorical status as the "dress" of thought. She also suggests the signifying and subversive potential of both.[4] *The Wanderer* deploys a sort of running analogy between Juliet's bodily and her verbal disguises as parallel means to female survival. Juliet's safety and the safety of those whom she loves depend on her not being accurately identified. Even names are a means to confusing, not defining, identity: for much of the first volume of the novel the heroine is known even to the reader only as the "Incognita," and then as "Ellis." When she first appears she has artificially darkened her complexion and dressed down, like Mrs. Mittin. It is not, however, the disguise itself that puzzles her viewers as to how to categorize her, but the shifts in her appearance, the elusiveness of her real identity. The masks that Juliet assumes are usually accepted at face value by her incurious viewers, but her changes in appearance both fascinate and frustrate the novel's other characters. Juliet's face and body signify, in their transformations, a mystery that simultaneously teases the other characters' curiosity and keeps them at a distance from who she "really" is. When she appears in her natural fair complexion, her transformation into a conventional English beauty puzzles far more than the enigma of her darkened face. Juliet's manipulations of her physical appearance parallel her verbal attempts to confuse the issue of her identity, as when Elinor asks her what it was that she "flung into the sea" at their first meeting. Juliet cannot tell her without revealing the secret of her marriage: the object in question is the wedding ring she rejects with horror and loathing. She decoys Elinor away from the truth with the story of her dealings with Mrs. Ireton, a rich and irascible old woman whose cruelty to Juliet is surpassed only by her curiosity to know her victim's true identity: "The recital that ensued of the disasters, difficulties, and choler of that lady, proved so entertaining to Elinor, that she soon not only renewed her engagement of taking her unknown guest free to Lewes, but joined the warmest assurances of protection" (1:102). Juliet uses story-telling—and her interlocutor's desire for narrative—to disguise her own situation and to gain herself a measure of economic protection.

Juliet's manipulative ability to excite curiosity by confusing appearances and then to evade satisfying it carries with it a certain epistemological power, the ability to keep her audience's attention. This ability provides her a tenuous survival through various forms of dependence. She gains Elinor's protection and support through the latter's good-natured curiosity, her eager enthusiasm at the prospect of a good tale: " 'O charming! charming!' cried Elinor, clapping her hands, 'you are going, at last, to relate your adventures!' " (1:93). Later in the novel and less happily, Juliet serves as a companion to Mrs. Ireton, who mistreats her and only supports her because of the mystery of her identity. When Mrs. Ireton asks Juliet who had given her permission to leave the room, Juliet replies, "A person, Madam, who has not the honour to be known to you—myself!" (3: 350). Enraged by the untouchability and defiance of her unidentified subordinate, Mrs. Ireton is tempted to turn Juliet out of doors, "but for the still sharpened curiosity with which her pretentions to penetration became piqued, from the general cry of 'How very extraordinary that Mrs. Ireton has never been able to discover who she is!' " (3: 352). Juliet is able to turn the shifting appearances of her identity to some practical account, but, in doing so, she risks uncharitable interpretations and exposure to the psychic violence of characters such as Ireton. If one appears black and then white, others may assume that the false appearance is the reality: Mrs. Ireton wonders "how many coats of white and red you were obliged to lay on, before you could cover over all that black" (1: 80-81.) Elinor's good-natured eagerness to hear the Incognita's tale is counterbalanced by her aunt's "So here's just the second edition of the history of that frenchified swindler!" (1: 114). Even those disposed to think well of the Incognita are limited in giving their aid by their ignorance. When Juliet asks Elinor for supportive confirmation of the latter's knowledge of her—"Will you not, Madam, have the goodness to explain who I am?"—Elinor understandably replies, "How can I,...when I don't know it myself?" (1:113). The Incognita herself realizes this liability but is helpless to remedy it; how, she reasons, when others place the worst possible interpretations on her situation, are people to do otherwise while she remains unknown and unexplained? (1: 151).

The mystery the heroine creates by transformation, by shifting, indeterminant appearances, holds for its creator a kind of advantage in that it gives her a limited means to other's protection. But it also constitutes a dangerous form of control for Juliet. The danger arises in part from the unpredictability and variance of human interpretation, but also, as *The Wanderer* makes clear, the danger of misinterpretation arises, not from Juliet's mysteriousness itself, but from her one characteristic that is clearly in evidence: her economic helplessness. Bereft of the protection the family traditionally affords to women, Juliet must make a living, and this need is painfully clear however mysterious her other circumstances may be. Mrs. Ireton's "insatiable passion" to know who Juliet is does not need to extend to her economic situation: "it was clear that the young woman was in want, whatever else might be doubtful" (1: 88). As in Mrs. Mittin's case, the economic reality of this vulnerability constantly impinges on the heroine's power to manipulate appearances to her own advantage. Juliet's considerable talents (we learn that she is a fine musician, a capable actress, a good story-teller, and an extraordinary seamstress) are inadequate to making even a minimal income for a single, unprotected woman. As Rose Marie Cutting has pointed out, *The Wanderer* reads, in part, like a catalogue of ways in which women *cannot* make a living at the end of the eighteenth century.[5] Juliet's economic misadventures also reveal that for women, economic vulnerability is, automatically, sexual vulnerability, a lesson that Burney's heroines from Evelina on had inculcated. In Juliet's case, the heroine's attempts at disguise and transformation take place within this context of female economic/sexual victimization. Juliet finally runs from the upper-class society in which she has been trying to make her living and begins a *Tess of the D'Urbervilles*–like tramp across the English countryside dressed in peasant clothes. Like Mrs. Mittin, Juliet finds that this garb releases her from the harassment and notice that would be directed at an unprotected middle-class woman, but she also discovers that it makes her vulnerable to another brand of class-defined harassment. On at least two occasions she finds that her disguise, meant to protect her from one form of notice, makes her the sexual prey of another segment of society (4: 278, 341). Shifting class, moreover, means more than changing clothes, as Juliet discovers; it brings real want. Hunger and fatigue, economic necessity's impact on her body, retransform her transformed appearance into a veritable enticement to sexual predators: "In losing the elasticity of her motions, she lost, to the vulgar observer, her appearance of innocence. Her eye, eagerly cast around in search of an asylum, appeared to be courting attention; her langour seemed but loitering; and her slow unequal pace, wore the air of inviting a companion" (4: 258). However clever Juliet may be as a manipulator of disguise, economic reality, with its power over the human body, is a more powerful transformer of appearances. Juliet's willed and deliberate transformations give her a power—however fraught with the danger of unsympathetic interpretations—but the unwilled transformations effected by economic necessity render her vulnerable and exposed.

Given the use that Burney makes of clothing in *Camilla,* it is not surprising that the making of clothing—literally, in a milliner's shop—becomes *The Wanderer's* locus of contradiction between the ideology of middle-class femininity and women's economic powerlessness. Juliet seeks to make an independent living, after various unhappy trials at being a dependent friend and companion to the better-off, by working in a milliner's shop. Aside from the exacting and unremunerative work, Juliet also discovers that the middle-class expectations and codes for female sexual behavior have little weight in a social system governed by the rules of commodity exchange. In this dehumanized and morally alienating system based solely on self-interest, the working-class woman that Juliet seeks to transform herself into is herself an object of exchange, not a subject with moral and social values. The marketplace of the shop and the self-interested negotiations between buyer and seller are antithetical to the middle-class moral standards that Juliet embodies: "In viewing conflicts such as these, between selfish vanity and cringing cunning, it soon became difficult to decide, which was least congenial to the upright mind and morality of Juliet, the insolent, vain, unfeeling buyer, or the subtle, plausible, over-reaching seller" (3: 110). Adam Smith's economy of free exchange is not only "uncongenial" to the middle-class woman's morality; it actually reduces her to a commodity item herself, an object on a sexual market controlled by male buyers. Juliet finds that working in an open shop exposes her to the sexual predation of men such as Sir Lyell, a nobleman who assumes that the obscurity of her social position and identity makes Juliet his to exploit, if he can. The defense of a disinterested male protector, without the socially sanctioned authority of a recognized relation to Juliet, is a frail barrier to Sir Lyell's aggression against her, as he suggests: "Melbury, in fact, knows no more of her than we do. He had nobody's word but her own for all her fine sentiments; so that he and his platonics would have kept me at bay no longer, if I had not believed her decamped" (3: 150-51). Physically leaving the marketplace of sexual and material commerce is the only way, Sir Lyell suggests, for a woman to avoid commodification. Without the conventional means of social defense, the family and friends that (in theory at least) support and protect women, Juliet finds herself economically trapped in the position of sexual commodity, to be connived for or seized: "But how avoid [Sir Lyell] while she had no other means of subsistence than working in an open shop?" (3: 159). The milliner's shop, ostensibly the site of Juliet's attempts at economic independence, is revealed as the locus of her economic entrapment as a sexual commodity. *The Wanderer* uses the public and social terms of the marketplace to inscribe, on a more explicitly political scale, the economically based oppression of women that *Camilla* expresses in the privatized, personal terms of the heroine's clothes. Both the women who make and the women who wear clothes are prey to sexual victimization and economic defeat. In both novels, the middle-class customs and institutions of female dress serve to expose contradiction between women's experience as it is defined by economic necessity and women's experience as defined by the received ideology of feminine moral and sexual behavior.

The available means to female power are, then, always defined, by Burney's fiction, within the context of a social economy that privileges men over women. Male authority is not, however, left uncriticized and unexamined as a sort of impassive structure within which the female heroine—and artist—must alternately rage or nestle; rather, it is often exposed as a cultural construct of power that masks an essential impotence. Luce Irigaray suggests that the Freudian assumption of women's castration is actually a means of asserting, through "an old dream of symmetry," the stability and supremacy of male power;[6] Burney did not, evidently, buy any possibly existent pre-Freudian version of the "old dream," and *Camilla,* in particular, reverses the process of constructing male domination on the premise of female weakness by revealing the contradictions within male control, the masculine incapacity that contradicts the socially sanctioned and economically reinforced authority of men over women. The problem, in Burney's fiction, is not that men are inherently all-powerful and women are inherently weak, but rather that women often end up acting in a power vacuum created by male impotence without having the economic and social sanction to fill the empty space of an ostensible rather than actual male authority.

The failure of Burney's heroes, after *Evelina*'s Lord Orville, to understand and reward the worth of the Burney heroine is the most obvious manifestation of male incapacity in her fiction; from Delvile through Harleigh, the doubts, uncertainties, and weaknesses of the male role in Burney's romance plots suggest a structural weakness within the system that relegates female happiness to male protection. Men, in Burney's fiction, simply have far more power over women than they know how to handle adequately. Aside from the ineptitude of Burney's romantic male leads, fathers or father figures are distant, like Villars; deceived, like Sir John Belmont; foolish, like Mr. Delville; or lacking in understanding or information, like Tyrold. Flawed male lovers and fathers provide the problematic context of male power and male impotence in which Burney's heroines attempt to act, to arrange their lives. *Camilla* provides an especially clear expression of the heroine's frustrating position vis-à-vis an economically and socially grounded male authority that is, in fact, inept, unable to sustain the protective control of the male role in the patriarchal family. The action of the novel begins with Sir Hugh, Camilla's rich, unmarried uncle, sustaining an injury that prohibits him from engaging in the active, outdoor pursuits of the country squire that had hitherto been his only recreation and employment: "Health failed him in the meridian of his life, from the consequences of a wound in his side, occasioned by a fall from his horse; exercise, therefore, and active diversions, were of necessity relinquished, and...he found himself at once deprived of all employment, and destitute of all comfort" (10). The economically powerful male who takes on the role of benefactor to the Tyrold children begins his career as their financial protector through a wound that forces him to quit the masculine sports that had formerly preoccupied him. Sir Hugh assumes the position of Camilla's protector through his own symbolic castration, the "wound" that alienates him from his prior male endeavours.

As an economically and socially powerful male cut off from his own socially constructed masculinity, Sir Hugh seeks to fill the void of his own "castration" by taking on Camilla as a surrogate daughter, an object that can take the place of his lost male occupations:

> He found in Camilla a variety that was captivation. Her form and her mind were of equal elasticity. Her playful countenance rekindled his spirits, the cheerfulness of her animated voice awakened him to its own joy. He doated upon detaining her by his side, or delighted to gratify her if she wished to be absent. She exhilarated him with pleasure, she supplied him with ideas, and from the morning's first dawn to the evening's latest close, his eye followed her light-springing figure, or his ear vibrated with her sportive sounds; catching, as it listened in successive rotation, the spontaneous laugh, the unconscious bound, the genuine glee of childhood's fearless happiness, uncurbed by severity, untamed by misfortune. [15]

In terms of Lacanian psychoanalysis, the father fetishizes the daughter in order to fill the gap left by his own castration; in more common discourse, Camilla supplies a lack that is occasioned by Sir Hugh's lost access to masculine pursuits. Whichever terms one uses to describe this action in the novel, it suggests a socially and economically grounded male authority figure who solaces his own sense of lack by objectifying the young female who falls, by social and familial convention, under his rule. Sir

Hugh embodies an essential contradiction in male authority over women as a form of control that is, in fact, a cover for lack, for impotence. Camilla's relation to her uncle is, then, a sort of paradigm for women's relations to men throughout Burney's fiction: it spells out the contradictory power and weakness of her romantic heroes and her good and bad fathers and father-figures, and it articulates their problematic objectifications of Burney's heroines as the reflections of their own desires and fears. Like Sir Hugh, Burney's heroes fall in love with—and love watching—the heroine, but rarely understand what they see. And like Sir Hugh's clumsy dealings with Camilla, their misunderstandings inevitably cause themselves and their female beloveds much suffering.

That heroines are not simply objectifications of what men want or fear is, as I among others have argued, one of the main principles of Burney's fiction. And repositioning the female objects of the male spectatorial gaze as acting subjects is one of the main techniques that Burney uses to expose contradictions in male authority and the flaws in a social system that sustains male power over women. Burney counters Sir Hugh's objectification of Camilla with Camilla's objectification of Sir Hugh in a crucial birthday party scene, set early in the novel, which initiates the events that make up the shape of the novel's plot. Sir Hugh has taken the young Camilla as his heir and proposes to indulge her and her childish friends by allowing them control over an entire day's diversions. In this carnivalesque celebration, disguise not surprisingly forms one of the first of the children's amusements, as Camilla turns Sir Hugh into a doll-like object who submits to her transformative powers as the little mistress of misrule: "She made him whiskers of cork, powdered his brown bob, and covered a thread paper with black ribbon to hang to it for a queue. She metamorphosed him into a female, accoutring him with her fine new cap, while she enveloped her own small head in his wig; and then, tying the maid's apron around his waist, put a rattle into his hand, and Eugenia's doll upon his lap, which she told him was a baby that he must nurse and amuse" (18). Terry Castle identifies the figure of the "she-male" in eighteenth-century English masquerade, a figure "often linked with sexuality or parodic motherhood" whose cultural precedents could be traced at least as far back as medieval ritual. Castle, following Mikhail Bakhtin's work on European carnivalesque modes, associates this grotesque maternal figure with both socially subversive and conservative tendencies,[7] but as Mary Russo points out in her discussion of "Lady Skimmington" rituals, its effect on gender roles, when "put on" by a man, usually "perpetuates the dominant (and in this case misogynistic) representation of women by men."[8] I would argue, however, that this scene works somewhat differently from the instances of male cross-dressing cited by Castle and Russo. The subversive potential of Sir Hugh dressed as a female grotesque lies in the fact that a little girl stages the masquerade and, in effect, creates the she-male, not with her own body, but through a playful objectification and subjection of the male body. In this game, the female object—Camilla—claims the power of controlling subject by scrambling gender-linked roles and positioning her uncle as the feminized object while she takes on the masculine authority suggested by his wig. The feminine articles that she uses to form his queue and, finally, the feminine role in which she casts her uncle momentarily transform culturally constructed gender roles. The child's play reveals that she is not, in fact, to be contained by or defined as the fetishistic object of masculine desire into which her uncle wishes to make her. The female subject becomes, in this scene, the actor/ manipulator of gender-based roles and appearances.

The problem with this repositioning of woman as the manipulator of social appearances—instead of the objectified embodiment of those appearances in the eyes of male viewers such as Sir Hugh or Edgar—is that it is, of course, a game sanctioned and tolerated by a male whose real weakness does not keep him from determining, finally, how far the game can be continued. Indeed, Sir Hugh reasserts control and ends the gender-masquerade *be-*

cause of his weakness: "He grew weary, however, first; and stretching himself his full length, with a prodigious yawn, 'Heigh ho!' he cried, 'Camilla, my dear, do take away poor Doll, for fear I should let it slip' " (18). Sir Hugh's ending of the game that Camilla controls dramatizes the contradictory weakness within his positioning as a socially and economically empowered male whose very failings have enormous power over women: his fear of letting Eugenia's doll slip ironically foreshadows the two occasions on which he lets Eugenia herself "slip," first by exposing her to a disfiguring case of smallpox and second by literally dropping her off a seesaw, an accident that permanently cripples and deforms her. Characteristically, Sir Hugh tries to make up for the damage he has done to Eugenia by making her his heiress; money seems the most reliable aspect of his power. Male authority sanctioned by economic and social right bounds and defines the action of female subjectivity, often limiting and even harming the female subjects within its control through the misworkings of its own impotent, castrated power. The potential transformative energy of Camilla's play with gender-linked disguise is reduced to and contained at the level of a child's game by the contradictory workings of her uncle's authority and impotence.

It seems important to note, however, that Camilla's game of cross-dressing with her uncle remains uncriticized in the context of the novel. The children meet misfortune, certainly, but not because of Camilla's childish game. Indeed, Sir Hugh's prerogative in ending the game and taking the children out for an airing in his coach, combined with his chronic bad judgment, does the mischief—Eugenia's exposure to smallpox—that has such far-reaching consequences in the plot of the novel. Camilla is disinherited and set upon her nearly self-defeating courtship with Edgar, Eugenia is maimed for life and made an heiress and a scholar when Sir Hugh decides that her physical ugliness disqualifies her for traditionally feminine roles, and so forth. Camilla's assumption of her uncle's wig, her dressing him up as a woman, and her placing him in a feminine role go unpunished and, indeed, unremarked. One thinks, by way of comparison, of Charlotte Charke's autobiographical account of parading around, as a child, in her father's wig and clothes, an act of cross-dressing for which she was certainly punished by her irate father, whose attitude towards such masquerades was considerably less accepting than Sir Hugh's—or, apparently, Fanny Burney's.[9] The cause of disorder and destructive chaos in Burney's novel is not the playful confusion of gender-linked appearances by the childish female subject, but the contradiction between power and weakness that is implicit in male authority. Female play with gender appearance is not the source of social disruption but the means by which this contradiction in male authority—and the moral economy that is structured around it—are exposed.

Camilla's brother Lionel illustrates the principle of male power as contradicted by its own weakness, in general, through his irresponsible economic exploitation of Camilla—he forces her to go into debt herself in order to pay the debts that result from his own weakness—and, specifically, in a cross-dressing scene that parallels and glosses Camilla's birthday games with her uncle. Again, cross-dressing exposes the dangerous weakness implicit in male power. Searching Mrs. Albery's attic with Miss Dennel and the hot-tempered Ensign Macdersey for costumes to be used in amateur theatricals, Lionel seizes the occasion for one of his practical jokes: "Having all paraded into various garrets, in search of adventures, Lionel, after attiring himself in the maid's gown, cap, and apron, had suddenly deposited upon Miss Dennel's head the Ensign's cocked hat, replacing it with the coachman's best wig upon the toupee of Macdersey; whose resentment was so violent at this liberty, that it was still some minutes before he could give it articulation" (264). The incident escalates as Macdersey, furious at the affront to his dignity, verges on challenging Lionel to a duel. Lionel, in turn, refuses to remove the wig from Macdersey's head, "holding this too imperious a command to be obeyed" (264). Miss Dennel is "pale with fright," and Mrs.

Arlbery is "alarmed at the serious consequences now threatening this folly" (264–65). As Russo suggests, "femininity as mask, for a man, is a take-it-or-leave-it proposition," one that ironically alludes to his own male power.[10] Lionel's self-feminization is, therefore, an assertion rather than a renunciation of his male privilege. But this scene also exposes the contradiction between the weakness and absurdity of male "folly" and the "serious consequences" that may result from it. Lionel and Macdersey are both ridiculous and dangerous, just as Sir Hugh, in the earlier scene, is both the object of the children's amusement and a very real danger to them. But whereas Camilla's orchestration of cross-dressing is itself subsumed, uncritically, into the contradictory male weakness and authority that it exposes, Lionel's is itself a part of the economy structured around the contradiction that it also exposes. Burney locates the destructive potential that is precipitated by shifting gender appearances in male authority, not in women's attempts to expose contradictions within that authority.

Camilla takes control away from Lionel, finally, in this scene, to avert the male violence that it threatens: "Camilla, picking [the wig] up, to render the affair merely burlesque, pulled off the maid's cap from her brother's head, and put on the wig in its place, saying—'There, Lionel, you have played the part of *Lady Wrong Head* long enough; be so good now as to perform that of *Sir Francis'* " (265). The allusion to Colley Cibber's *The Provoked Husband* glosses Camilla's role in helping to contain the male violence that Lionel's aborted theatricals threaten to bring to the surface. Sir Francis and Lady Wronghead are two of the comic, country characters in a play that is basically a dramatic argument for women's subordinate relation to men in the institution of marriage, a relation in the play that is—or should be—economically reinforced by women's financial dependence on their husbands. Lady Wronghead, whose rage for the expensive, fashionable life of London illustrates what a husband should *not* allow his wife to do, spends her husband dry—Burney's wry reflection on

Lionel's exploitation of Camilla; Sir Francis is the weak-minded male fool whose political ambitions are made ridiculous by his real inadequacy, summed up in his basic inability to control his own wife—again a reflection on Lionel, this time on his weakness in giving in to expensive fashions, including a manipulative mistress. Camilla's allusion and action restore order and avert violence by styling Lionel's disruptive behavior as comedy, literally, "merely burlesque," while also commenting on Lionel's abuse of his own power as a man, son, and brother. Her verbal and physical gesture points to the weakness and impotence in socially sanctioned male authority while simultaneously containing the violence created by it within the realm of comedy. Male dominance may pervade eighteenth-century life and art, but the interchange between Lionel and Camilla suggests that the socially intelligent woman will not accept this rule without a large grain of salt. The social system that privileges male authority is both burlesque and dangerous, however, and exposing the contradictions within it requires both tact and courage—and, perhaps, the careful duplicity of the woman speaking as a member of the society that discouraged her from using her voice.

Cibber's play again provides a sexual/political context for the heroine's actions in *The Wanderer.* Early in the novel, when Juliet's real name and story are still unknown to the other characters, Elinor promotes amateur theatricals that function, much like those of *Mansfield Park,* as a sort of litmus test for characters' social and moral qualities. Elinor initiates the social rituals of disguise and theatrical role-playing partially out of a desire to show off her abilities and partially out of hope for a romance with Harleigh, who participates in the game more out of acquiescence than desire. The amateur performance of Cibber's play about woman's submission to and economic dependence on her husband exposes the contradiction between performance—narcissistic feminine and reluctant masculine—in romance and the script of economically and socially sanctioned male supremacy. As in Austen's novel, amateur theatricals position characters within the novel's moral economy in relation to the romantic text they perform. Juliet plays a Fanny Price–like role as a subordinate party in the theatricals: she prompts, "goes for," and is called to stand in for other actresses during rehearsals. Her role is, literally, selfless in that she is not licensed to act out her desires, but rather serves others' needs. Her "go-for" role suggests her relation to the social games of self-display that are a part of the politics of romantic love: removed from them herself, she is nonetheless forced, by economic necessity and social custom, to serve them. The other characters act out their narcissistic blindness to the social relations that entertain some at the expense of others'— particularly Juliet's—victimization. Putting on the play becomes a paradigm for social relations that lead to the alienation and oppression of some members of the group rather than facilitating mutual knowledge and recognition among individuals. The players become so narcissistically involved with their individual performances that nobody knows or even notices what anyone else is doing, and, significantly, Elinor forgets her intention to help Juliet solve her real economic problems in her absorption in acting out the play's fiction. The theatricals reveal, especially through Elinor's behavior, the contradiction between the wo-man's narcissistic involvement in acting out a role that she hopes will empower her in the game of romance and the actual under-cutting of her power by a text that encodes her submission to male authority. Elinor's blind absorption in her acting also sug-gests, like the male-centered behavior of *Evelina*'s Mrs. Selwyn, the missed opportunity to refocus feminine energies on helping other women.

Juliet, on the other hand, is a knowledgeable victim of the theatricals—and the sexual politics they represent. As the prompter, she is one of only two characters who know all the parts and can therefore see any relation between them. Her knowledge of the fiction reflects her knowledge of the sexual relations it represents: unlike Elinor, who falsely sees herself as empowered by feminine self-display in the game of courtship,

Juliet understands, through firsthand experience, the powerlessness of women in marriage. When Juliet is asked to step into the
part of Lady Townley—opposite Harleigh's Lord Townley—her
superior knowledge does not, understandably, immediately
translate into superior performance. Not surprisingly, she is too
terrified to speak audibly. But she goes on to excel, as the narrator
tells us: "This...was nature, which would not be repressed; not
art, that strove to be displayed" (1: 206). The narrator dissociates
Juliet's performance from the self-displaying, unthinking artificiality that marks other characters' socially unselfconscious
performances. Juliet understands the whole and acts the part of a
wife who learns to submit to her husband's will with all too
much understanding. Her duplicity toward her part—she is, at
the moment of her performance, running away from, not sub-
mitting to a husband—is, like Fanny Burney's, grounded in an
acute understanding of the sexual/social system that renders her
powerless to refuse to play her role. The text of the play the
amateur actors have chosen itself comically reiterates the dominant authority of men in marriage, an authority that Juliet both
accepts and has reason to fear in her own reality. Just as the
heroine's comprehensive knowledge of the play contrasts with
the other characters' superficiality, her personal understanding of
the play's dominant theme is opposed to the light comedy of the
play itself. Juliet's understanding and the integrity, the reality of
her performance, in contrast to the socially unselfconscious nar-
cissism of most of the other players, gesture toward her real
understanding of and integrity within the sexual politic that the
play represents; she lives out, in fact, what is mindlessly acted out
by the others. She accepts the role—of feminine submission to
male authority—out of lack of choice, but her real victimization
within that role exposes the solipsism and moral emptiness of the
other players as well as the real danger of the sexual politics they
act out.

Juliet's performance goes unnoticed by Elinor, who is too
involved in her own acting to perceive either the other woman's

performance or the knowledge that informs it. This failure of one woman to see another, like Mrs. Selwyn's failure to support Evelina, suggests that the experience of female victimization may not be communicated. What good is accomplished if the woman screws up her courage for a performance that passes unnoticed by another woman who herself goes on—as Elinor does—to perpetuate the cycle of female victimization? Reading Burney's fiction entails the danger of not noticing, of being so caught up in one's performance as a critic in a male-dominated profession that the force of Burney's fictional acting-out of the painful contradictions implicit in eighteenth-century constructs of femininity goes unperceived. Burney's fiction suggests her awareness of that possibility, but it also suggests her sense of possibilities for more attentive readings—possibilities invested in *her* audience, if not in Juliet's—that this book is part of a growing attempt to fulfill.

NOTES

1. CRITICAL METHODS AND HISTORICAL CONTEXTS

1. Anthea Zeman, *Presumptuous Girls: Women and Their World in the Serious Women's Novel* (London: Weidenfeld and Nicolson, 1977); Patricia Meyer Spacks, *Imagining a Self: Autobiography and Novel in Eighteenth-Century England* (Cambridge: Harvard U.P., 1976), 158-92; Judith Lowder Newton, *Women, Power and Subversion: Social Strategies in British Fiction, 1778-1860* (Athens: U. Georgia P., 1981), 23-28.

2. Mary Jacobus, "The Difference of View," in *Women Writing and Writing About Women* (New York: Barnes & Noble, 1979), 16.

3. Leslie W. Rabine, *Reading the Romantic Heroine: Text, History, Ideology* (Ann Arbor: U. Michigan P., 1985), 8, Jane P. Tompkins, *Sensational Designs: The Cultural Work of American Fiction 1790-1860* (New York: Oxford U.P., 1985), 186-201.

4. Raymond Williams, *Marxism and Literature* (Oxford: Oxford U.P., 1977), 128-35.

5. Sandra Gilbert and Susan Gubar, *The Madwoman in the Attic: the Woman Writer and the Nineteenth-Century Literary Imagination* (New Haven: Yale U.P., 1979).

6. Mary Poovey, *The Proper Lady and the Woman Writer: Ideology as Style in the Works of Mary Wollstonecraft, Mary Shelley, and Jane Austen* (Chicago: U. Chicago P., 1984), 3-47.

7. Newton, *Women,* 39.

8. Frances Burney, *Diary and Letters of Madame D'Arblay (1778-1840),* ed. Austin Dobson, 6 Vols. (London: Macmillan, 1904), 1: 56. Subsequent references are to this edition and are indicated parenthetically in the text with the abbreviation *DL.*

9. George Saville, Marquis of Halifax, "The Lady's New-Year's Gift: or, Advice to a Daughter," *Miscellanies by the Right Noble Lord, the Late Lord Marquess of Halifax* (London, 1700; rpt. New York: Kelly, 1970), 8; Mary Hays, *Appeal to the Men of Great Britain in Behalf of Women* (London, 1798; rpt. New York: Garland, 1974), 118-19; Maria Edgeworth, *Letters for Literary Ladies to*

which is added, An Essay on the Noble Science of Self-Justification (London, 1795; rpt. New York: Garland, 1974), 47.

10. Halifax, *Miscellanies*, 33; William Kendrick, *The Whole Duty of Woman* (Boston: Fowle and Draper, 1761), 26. Kendrick admonishes his female readers to "boast not therefore" of the chastity so tenuously in their keeping.

11. Kendrick, *Whole Duty*, 14–15, for example, and Thomas Gisborne, *An Enquiry into the Duties of the Female Sex* (London, 1797; rpt. New York: Garland, 1974), 85.

12. Halifax, *Miscellanies*, 42; Hays, *Appeal*, 29; Gisborne, *Enquiry*, 201–02; Jonathan Swift, *Poetical Works*, ed. Herbert Davis (London: Oxford U.P., 1967), pp. 547-50.

13. See Aubrey Williams's classic analysis of this image in Pope's poem and Burney's novel: "The 'Fall' of China and *The Rape of the Lock*," *Philological Quarterly*, 41 (1962): 412-25. Mr. Villars' words are as follows: "nothing is so delicate as the reputation of a woman: it is, at once, the most beautiful and most brittle of all human things." Frances Burney, *Evelina; or, the History of a Young Lady's Entrance into the World*, ed. Edward A. Bloom and Lillian D. Bloom (Oxford: Oxford U.P., 1982), 164. Subsequent references are to this edition and are indicated parenthetically in the text.

14. Alexander Pope, *The Rape of the Lock and Other Poems*, ed. Geoffrey Tillotson (London: Methuen, 1954), 149.

15. J. Paul Hunter, "Fielding and the Disappearance of Heroes," *The English Hero 1660-1800*, ed. Robert Folkenflik (Newark: U. Delaware P., 1982), 116-42.

16. Pope, *Rape of the Lock*, 155.

17. Pope, *Rape of the Lock*, 196.

18. Swift, *Poetical Works*, 586.

19. Swift, *Poetical Works*, 115.

20. James Fordyce, *Sermons to Young Women*, 2 vols. (London: A. Millar & T. Cadell, 1766) 1: 69. (First edition: London: 1765).

21. Alexander Pope, *Epistles to Several Persons (Moral Essays)*, ed. F.W. Bateson (London: Methuen, 1951), 58.

22. Cynthia Stodola Pomerleau, "Resigning the Needle for the Pen: A Study of Autobiographical Writings of British Women Before 1800," Diss. U. Pennsylvania 1974.

23. Lawrence Stone, *The Family, Sex and Marriage in England 1500-1800* (New York: Harper and Row, 1977), 350.

24. Lois G. Schwoerer, "Lawrence Stone and the Women of Late-seventeenth Century England: Evaluation and Critique," delivered at a meeting of the Midwestern Society for Eighteenth-Century Studies, Normal, Illinois, 16 Oct. 1981, 10. See also Schwoerer's "Seventeenth-Century English Women Engraved in Stone?," *Albion* 16 (1984): 389-403.

25. Stone, *The Family*, 350.

26. Virginia Woolf, "Fanny Burney's Half-Sister," *Times Literary Supplement*, 28 Aug. 1930, 674.

27. Jane Austen, *Persuasion*, ed. D.W. Harding (Baltimore: Penguin, 1975), 237.

28. See Alice Clark's *Working Life of Women in the Seventeenth Century* (London, 1919; rpt. London: Routledge & Kegan Paul, 1982).

29. Reeve and Wakefield focus on the problem of the farmer's or tradesman's unmarried daughters who receive a "genteel" education, which does not prepare them to maintain themselves. Reeve sees them "with little or no fortune, unable or unwilling to work for themselves...they go on practicing the airs and graces of a fine lady till youth is past, and then discover, in after life, that they have been acting a part above them, without means to support it." Clara Reeve, *Plans of Education, with Remarks on the Systems of Other Writers in a Series of Letters Between Mrs. Damford and Her Friends* (London, 1792; rpt. New York: Garland, 1974), 61-62. Wakefield discusses the economic plight of a "woman genteely educated, whether single or married, who is deprived, by an unfortunate accident of the protection and support of male relatives," and champions the cause of giving women economically useful skills. Priscilla Wakefield, *Reflections on the Present Condition of the Female Sex: With Suggestions for its Improvement* (London, 1798; rpt. New York: Garland, 1974), 66-67. Hays and Radcliffe rather more bluntly point out that women have few professions outside of prostitution to turn to for support. Mary Ann Radcliffe, *The Female Advocate; or, An Attempt to Recover the Rights of Women from Male Usurpation* (Edinburgh, 1810; rpt. New York: Garland, 1974), pp. 409-10, and Mary Hays, *Letters and Essays, Moral and Miscellaneous* (London, 1793); rpt. New York: Garland, 1974), 84-85.

30. Arnaud Berquin, *The Looking-Glass for the Mind: or Intellectual Mirror* (London: J. Crowder, for E. Newbery, 1796), pp. 252-53.

31. Rose Marie Cutting explores the issue of female economic entrapment in Burney's last novel in "A Wreath for Fanny Burney's last Novel: *The Wanderer*'s Contribution to Women's Studies," *CLA Journal*, 20(1976): 57-67.

2. *EVELINA:* GULPHS, PITS, AND PRECIPICES

1. Gilbert and Gubar, *Madwoman.*

2. Pierre Macherey, *A Theory of Literary Production*, trans. Geoffrey Wall (London: Routledge & Kegan Paul, 1978), 79.

3. Macherey, *Theory*, 94.

4. Newton, *Women, Power and Subversion*, pp. 23-28.

5. Halifax prepares his daughters for husbands who will not be as subject

to their wives' wishes as their father had been. Halifax, *Miscellanies*, 8-17; Hays, *Appeal*, 260, 111, 97, 259; Kendrick, *Whole Duty*, 10.

6. John Bennett, *Letters to a Young Lady on Useful and Interesting Subjects: Calculated to Improve the Heart, to Form the Manners, and Enlighten the Understanding*, 2 vols. (Dublin: J. Jones, 1789) 2: 93.

7. Samuel Johnson, *The Rambler*, ed. W.J. Bate and Albrecht B. Strauss, 3 vols. (New Haven; Yale UP, 1969) 3: 366; 2: 211.

8. Bennett, *Letters* 2: 93. Hestor Chapone, *Letters on the Improvement of the Mind Addressed to a Young Lady*. 2 vols. (London: J. Walter and E. and C. Dilly, 1778) 2: 22, warns of the "teazing, mean, and fretful disposition" that she sees as an occupational hazard in female life (138-39). Johnson satirizes the old woman become splenetic and irascible with paying too much attention, for too long, to "nice" details in "Tetricia" (4: 25-27). Maria and Richard Lovell Edgeworth agree with Bennett's warnings against boredom as a common and dangerous malady of women's maturity and later years; see *Practical Education*, 2 vols. (London, 1798; rpt. New York: Garland, 1974) 2: 522. John Gregory tells his daughters, "Your whole life is often a life of suffering ... You must bear your sorrows in silence, unknown and unpitied," in *A Father's Legacy to His Daughters* (London, 1774; rpt. New York: Garland, 1974), 50. Richard Polwhele, "The Unsex'd Females: A Poem Addressed to the Author of the Pursuits of Literature," printed in Mary Ann Radcliffe, *The Female Advocate; or, An Attempt to Recover the Rights of Women from Male Usurpation* (Edinburgh, 1810; rpt. New York: Garland, 1974).

9. Hannah More, *Strictures on the Modern System of Female Education with a View of the Principle and Conduct Prevalent Among Women of Rank and Fortune*, 2 vols. (London, 1799; rpt. New York: Garland, 1974) 1: 59-60, and James Fordyce's *Sermons to Young Women*, 2: 31; Priscilla Wakefield's *Reflections on the Present Condition of the Female Sex: with Suggestions for its Improvement* (London, 1798; rpt. New York: Garland, 1974) also comments that women are trained to be courted, not for pleasing themselves or their husbands in maturity (29-31), and a century earlier Mary Astell makes a similar complaint in her *A Serious Proposal to the Ladies for the Advancement of Their True and Greatest Interest* (London, 1701; rpt. New York: Source Book, 1970), 10.

10. Gisborne, *Enquiry*, 411; Charlotte Smith, *Rural Walks: In Dialogues Intended for the Use of Young Persons* (Philadelphia: Thomas Stephens, 1795), 109; Bennett, *Letters* 1: 6 and Chapone, *Letters* 1: 114-15.

11. Frances Burney, *The Early Diary of Frances Burney 1768-1778*, ed. Annie Raine Ellis, 2 vols. (New York: Books for Libraries, 1971) 1: 46, 52. Subsequent references are to this edition and are indicated parenthetically in the text with the abbreviation *ED*.

12. James Boswell, *London Journal, 1762-1763*, (New York, McGraw-Hill, 1950), 43-46, 61-62.

13. James Fordyce, *Addresses to Young Men*. 2 vol. (London: T. Cadell, 1777), 1: 11-12 and Philip Dormer Stanhope, *The Letters of Philip Dormer Stanhope Earl of Chesterfield with the Characters*, ed. John Bradshaw (London: Allen and Unwin, 1926).

14. Hugh Blair urges young men to "come forward to that field of action where they are to mix in all the stir and bustle of the world; where all the human powers are brought forth into full exercise; where all that is conceived to be important in human affairs is incessently going on around them. The time of youth was the preparation for future action. In old age our active part is supposed to be finished, and rest is permitted. Middle age is the season when we are expected to display the fruits which education hath prepared and ripened." See *Sermons* 5 vols. (London: W. Sharpe and Sons, J. Maynard, E. Wilson, T. Mason, J. Robins and Co., and W. Harwood, 1819), 3: 65.

15. See Chesterfield, *Letters* 1: 122—"Deserve a great deal, and you shall have a great deal; deserve a little, you shall have but a little"—and Fordyce's *Addresses* 1: 116: "though you are never knowingly to aim at what is beyond your strength ... that should not hinder your embracing and improving any singular opportunity . . . to display an elevation of worth, or of wisdom, above the ordinary standard." Edgeworth, *Practical Education* 2: 528.

16. Williams, *Marxism and Literature*, 128-35.

17. Pope, *Epistles*, 17-18.

18. Pope, *Epistles*, 52.

19. Her expectations seem to become dimmer in direct proportion to the amount of praise she received: "I quite sigh beneath the weight of such praise from such persons—sighs mixed with gratitude for the present, and fear for the future" (*DL* 1: 120).

20. See *ED* 1: 269: "As to that rogue your father, if I did not know him to be incorrigible, I should say something of the regular course of irregularity he persists in—two, three, four, five o-clock in the morning, sups at twelve!—is it impossible for him to get the better of his constitution? has he forgot the condition he was in the winter after his first return to England?... Certain it is, that he uses his thin carcass most abominably, and if it takes it at his hands, it is the most passive, submissive slave of a carcass in Europe."

21. See *ED* 1: 271: "The death of Dr. Hawkesworth is most sincerely lamented by us all, the more so as we do really attribute it to the abuse he has of late met with from the newspapers." See also the *Early Diary*, 1: 66 for comments on Smart: "The Critical Reviewers, ever eager to catch at every opportunity of lessening and degrading the merit of this unfortunate man (who has been twice confined in a mad house), would think all the most rancourous observations on his declining powers fully justified, and perhaps pronounce him to be in a state of mind that rendered him a proper object to return to Bedlam, if they heard that he had descended to flatter and praise *me*!"

22. See *ED* 2: 327 for an excerpt from a letter from Crisp in which he tells Burney, "I have been a sufferer" at the hands of criticism.

23. Louise Bernikow, *Among Women* (New York: Harper & Row, 1980), 18-19.

24. Earl R. Anderson, "Footnotes more Pedestrian Than Sublime: A Historical Background for the Foot-Races in *Evelina* and *Humphry Clinker*," *Eighteenth Century Studies* 14 (Fall 1980): 56-68.

3. *EVELINA:* MARRIAGE AS THE DANGEROUS DIE

1. Newton, *Women, Power and Subversion*, 23-28.

2. See Joyce Hemlow's classic study of Burney's incorporation of "courtesy literature" into novel form: "Fanny Burney and the Courtesy Books," *PMLA* 65 (1950): 732-61.

3. Halifax, *Miscellanies*, 19, 10-17.

4. Fordyce, *Sermons* 1: 167; Sarah Pennington, *An Unfortunate Mother's Advice to her Absent Daughters; in a letter to Miss Pennington.* London: S. Chandler, 1761. 49-50.

5. Hays, *Appeal*, warns that "after the charm of novelty and the first frenzy of love are over with the other sex," women will "find, that those soft and heavenly graces, and etc.... are not only quite insufficient to disarm authority and dispel rage; but are even quite insufficient to procure them common justice" (120). John Bennett advises women to depend on religion for personal strength and stability, since the love of a man can drastically dwindle when the "angel of courtship" becomes but a woman (*Letters* 1: 6). See also Edward Moore's grim little fable, "The Wolf, the Sheep, and the Lamb," *Fables for the Female Sex* (London: R. Francklin, 1744), 31-38 for a parable of how male desire, sated in marriage, devours and destroys its object.

6. Johnson, *Rambler* 1: 213.

7. Hays, *Letters*, 81, 83.

8. *The Spectator*, ed. Donald F Bond (Oxford: Clarendon, 1965) 1: 377, 379.

9. Johnson sees women as incapable of making this decision for themselves: "they see the world without gaining experience, and at last regulate their choice by motives trifling as those of a girl, or mercenary as those of a miser" (*Rambler* 1: 214) Co-opting the role of making decisions is, of course, an excellent way of ensuring incompetence to make them.

10. See Thomas Gisborne's diatribe against a woman "in the decline of life... clinging to the leveties of a world which she is about to leave forever" (411) or his caustic portrait of a woman's futile efforts to efface time's effects on her beauty (397-98) in *Enquiry*. Halifax warns his daughters about becoming

like an "Old *Butterfly*" who affects youth in old age. Johnson responds to a "Miss Maypole's" complaint of her mother (a widow) who sees her daughter as a rival: such women "may refuse to grow wise, but they must inevitably grow old" (1: 299). Burney's Madame Duval, with her interest in clothes, cosmetics, and M. Du Bois is, of course, an example of the type commonly ridiculed.

11. In her *Serious Proposal*, Mary Astell proposes the scheme of a "protestant nunnery" to alleviate the financial hardships of single women, an idea that Richardson puts in the mouth of his hero in *The History of Sir Charles Grandison* (New York: AMS, 1970), 4: 203. Johnson is also sympathetic to the position of unmarried, impecunious young women. See *The Idler and The Adventurer*, ed. W.J. Bate, John M. Bullit, and L.F Powell (New Haven and London: Yale UP, 1963) 2: 300-302, for a letter from "Sophia Headful," a young lady left without resources after the death of her guardian.

12. See Mary Ann Radcliffe, *The Female Advocate* and Hays, *Letters and Essays*.

13. See *DL* 361-67 for the letters revealing Burney's conflicting feelings over the court appointment.

14. Johnson exposes the plight of a daughter "tricked out for sale" by a mercenary father (*Idler*, 2: 131-34) and lampoons the young women who themselves participate in the "prostitution of the modern marriage market" (*Rambler* 1: 192). Chapone writes: "The calamities of an unhappy marriage are so much greater than can befal a single person, that, the unmarried woman may find abundant argument to be contented with her condition, when pointed out to her by Providence" (*Letters* 1: 200).

15. Gregory, *Father's Legacy*, 105; Bennett, *Letters* 2: 96 (see also 2: 94-95: a "*single* woman is, particularly, defenceless. She cannot move beyond the pre-cincts of her house without apprehensions... She is surrounded with many, real dangers, and fancy conjures up *more* spectres of its own... As she goes down the *hill* of life, her friends *gradually* drop away from her, like the leaves in the autumn, and leave her a pining, *solitary* creature... she wanders through a wide, bustling world, uncomfortable in herself, uninteresting to others, *frequently* the sport of wanton ridicule, or a proverb of reproach."); Moore, *Fables*, 79; Kendrick, *Whole Duty*, 38.

16. Reeve, *Plans of Education*, 122-23, 125.

17. See Frances Burney, *The Journals and Letters of Fanny Burney (Madame D'Arblay)*, ed. Joyce Hemlow, 10 vols. (Oxford: Clarendon, 1973), vol. 4 for the record of Burney's last correspondence with her sister, and her attempts to promote Susan's return to England and to gain information about her failing health without provoking the wrath of Molesworth Phillips, her sister's some-times brutal, philandering husband. Susan's death was, perhaps, the severest blow that Burney sustained in her long life, and it cast a shadow over subse-

quent years as she regularly mourned the anniversary of Susan Burney Phillips' last day alive. In January of 1800, she wrote to Frederica Locke, "She was the soul of my soul—& tis wonderful to me my dearest Fredy that the first shock did not join them immediately by the flight of mine—but that over—that dreadful—harrowing—never to be forgotten moment of horrour that made me wish to be mad—over—the ties that after that first endearing period have shared with her my Heart came to my aid—Yet I was long incredulous—& still sometimes I think it is not—& that she will come—" (4: 386). Unable to cry at the first news of Susan's death, Burney could only vent her pain by screaming (4: 387). Subsequent references are indicated parenthetically in the text with the abbreviation *JL*.

18. Burney wrote to Susan Phillips: "Mrs. Rishton's history is long; but it's catastrophe is brief & briefly therefore I will relate it. When I was with her at Thornham, after quitting my Court service, she first opened to me her heart, & her misery; relating that she had never known real happiness with Mr. Rishton for more than a few weeks, though occasionally, & even frequently, she had had gleams of sunshine upon her discontent. Nevertheless, she had found his character austere, haughty, irascible, & impracticable...she conceived a hope of effecting a total separation from Mr. Rishton, & obtaining from my Father an honourable asylum under his roof, with such an allowance from her husband as her own fortune gave her a right to claim...she wrote to me almost incessantly, & came to me twice, to consult & counsel. I was always clearly of opinion that whatever were her wishes she had forfeited, by her marriage vow, the right of positively quitting him, if she could not obtain consent" (*Journals and Letters*, 4: 75). Maria's letters to Burney recounting her marital difficulties can be read in the Barrett Collection of the British Museum, and Virginia Woolf writes an account of Maria Rishton's story in "Fanny Burney's Half-Sister."

19. Burney wrote to Susan Phillips of d'Arblay, "except in my beloved Father and Mr. Lock, I have never seen such a man in this world, though I have drawn such in my imagination" (*JL* 1: 42).

20. Dolores Peters, "The Pregnant Pamela: Characterization and Popular Medical Attitudes in the Eighteenth Century," *Eighteenth Century Studies*, 14 (Spring, 1981), 432-51.

4. *EVELINA*: TRIVIAL PURSUITS

1. Swift, *Poetical Works*, 189-90.

2. Mary Wollstonecraft, *A Vindication of the Rights of Women* in *Mary Wollstonecraft: The Rights of Women and John Stuart Mill: The Subjection of Women*, ed. Pamela Frankau (London: Dent, 1955), 34: "Surely she has not an immortal soul who can loiter life away merely employed to adorn her person, that she may amuse the languid hours, and soften the cares of a fellow-creature who is

willing to be enlivened by her smiles and tricks, when the serious business of life is over."

3. Stone, *The Family*, 350.

4. See Mary Poovey's useful discussion of Wollstonecraft's internal conflicts as a "Proper Lady" and as a woman who saw the social inequities in women's roles: *The Proper Lady*, 48-113.

5. Astell, *Serious Proposal*, 27.

6. More, *Strictures*, 1: 100.

7. Wollstonecraft, *Vindication*, 34.

8. Pope, *Epistles*, 64-65.

9. Wollstonecraft, *Vindication*, 50; Gisborne, *Enquiry*, 142. Catherine Macaulay Graham, *Letters on Education with Observations on Religious and Metaphysical Subjects* (London, 1790; rpt. New York: Garland, 1974), 207.

10. Wakefield (*Reflections*, 39-54, 100) argues for the dignity of female labor appropriate to class standing. She sees the popular trend of educating lower class women like their upper class sisters as a dangerous trivialization of women's work and time. See also Halifax, *Miscellanies*. Mary Hays (*Appeal*, 240-50) sees domestic labor as potentially fulfilling but actually dehumanizing, perhaps providing us with a clue as to why writers so often approve it in theory and despise it in practice.

11. Chapone, *Letters* 2: 22.

12. Johnson, *Rambler* 2: 273-79, 4: 364-69.

13. Hays, *Letters and Essays*, 27.

14. Swift, *Poetical Works*, 564.

15. Fordyce, *Sermons*, 1: 204.

16. Edgeworth, *Practical Education* 2: 522, 530; Bennett, *Letters* 2: 9; Gregory, *Father's Legacy*, 51.

17. Reeve, *Plans of Education*, 114; Pennington, *Unfortunate Mother*, 40-42; Wakefield, *Reflections*, 114-145; Johnson, *Idler and Adventurer*, 43-44; Graham, *Letters on Education*, 64-65.

18. Edgeworth, *Practical Education* 2: 522, 528.

19. *The Spectator* 4: 270-72.

20. See C. Willett and Phillis Cunnington, *Handbook of English Costume in the Eighteenth Century* (Boston: Plays, 1972) and Inis Brooke, *Dress and Undress: The Restoration and Eighteenth Century* (London: Methuen, 1958).

21. Astell, *Serious Proposal*, 11-12; Wollstonecraft, *Vindication*, 47.

22. Jean-Jacques Rousseau, *Emile or Treatise on Education*, abr. and trans. William H. Payne (London: Appleton, 1906), 260, 290; James Fordyce, *The Character and Conduct of the Female Sex, and the Advantages to be derived by Young Men From the Society of Virtuous Women, a Discourse in Three Parts* (Boston: John Gill, 1781), 28-29.

23. Gisborne (*Enquiry*) advises women to accept a "reasonable and becom-

ing" conformity to the demands of dress but warns that too much attention to the matter is dangerous and must be discouraged (83, 120, 124-34); see also Graham, *Letters on Education*, 173-205, and Gregory, *Father's Legacy*, 55-57; Kendrick, *Whole Duty*, 37; Wollstonecraft, *Vindication*, 47.

24. Felicity A. Nussbaum notes that in the eighteenth-century popular tradition received by Pope, "Women provoke fear because their tenuous natures may more easily dissolve into thorough moral decay." *The Brink of All We Hate: English Satires on Women 1660-1750* Lexington: UP Kentucky, 1984), 146; Paul Fussell, *The Rhetorical World of Augustan Humanism: Ethics and Imagery From Swift to Burke* (Oxford: Clarendon, 1965), 213. Astell and Wollstonecraft are perhaps clearer than Swift in attributing women's "soullessness" (Wollstonecraft's term) to poor education and having little important or useful work to do. See Astell, *Serious Proposal*, 11-12, and Wollstonecraft, *Vindication*, 47.

25. *Spectator*, 2: 596; 2: 7. For other examples, see 1: 46, 66-69, 346-49, 413-16, 426-29, 432-35; 2: 4-8, 327, 530-33.

26. Johnson, *Rambler*, 4: 250; Bennett, *Letters*, 1: 139 and Fordyce, *Sermons* 1: 69, 77.

27. Joyce Hemlow's painstaking editing of Burney's papers has disclosed that many of the inked-out passages concern dress. Although certainly not obsessed with the subject, Burney seems to have given it a considerable amount of attention in her personal writings. In 1770, she relishes describing her masquerade costume—"a close pink Persian vest,...covered with gauze, in loose pleats" (*ED* 1: 71). It seems possible that Burney's perspective on dress is thoroughly conventional, if mixed: contempt for the demands that dress made on women's time mingles with acceptance of the sartorial and cosmetic arts in the sermons of Fordyce, the essays of Catherine Macaulay Graham, and the educational theories of Rousseau, for example.

28. Swift, *Poetical Works*, 173.

29. Hélène Cixous, "The Laugh of the Medusa," in *New French Feminisms: An Anthology*, ed. Elaine Marks and Isabelle de Courtivron, (Amherst: U Massachusetts P, 1980), 245-64.

30. See Mary Ann Radcliffe, *The Female Advocate*. See also Wakefield, *Reflections*, 164, and Reeve, *Plans of Education*, 119-20. Rose Marie Cutting explores the issue of female economic entrapment in Burney's last novel in "A Wreath for Fanny Burney's last Novel: *The Wanderer's* Contribution to Women's Studies," 57-67.

31. Judith Lowder Newton's fine discussion of *Evelina* in *Women, Power, and Subversion* makes the point that Burney's position as "a genteel unmarried woman could force her to credit and give value to ideologies about her experience which at some level she understood to be untrue" (39).

5. CECILIA: LOVE AND WORK

1. For the history of *Cecilia*'s publication, see Joyce Hemlow's *The History of Fanny Burney* (Oxford: Clarendon, 1958), 139-69.

2. Frances Burney, *Cecilia: or Memoirs of an Heiress* (New York: Penguin/ Virago, 1986), xv. I have chosen to use the Virago edition of *Cecilia* for reasons of its accessibility. Subsequent references to *Cecilia* are to this edition and will be noted parenthetically in the text by book and page number.

3. I owe the ability to make this point to a paper given by Margaret Doody at the annual meeting of the Midwest American Society for Eighteenth-Century Studies at Northwestern University, Evanston, Illinois, Oct. 23-25, 1986: "Pictures of Youth, Women-Haters, and Good Advice: Fanny Burney's Subversive Writings."

4. For this point as well as for a more comprehensive reading of the masquerade scene in *Cecilia* than I have given here, see Terry Castle's *Masquerade and Civilization: The Carnivalesque in Eighteenth-Century English Culture and Fiction* (Stanford: Stanford UP, 1986), 253-89.

5. Castle, *Masquerade*, 5-7.

6. Castle, *Masquerade*, 5.

7. Castle, *Masquerade*, 59.

8. Mary Russo, "Female Grotesques: Carnival and Theory," *Feminist Studies/Critical Studies*, ed. Teresa de Lauretis (Bloomington: Indiana UP, 1986), 216.

9. I owe the idea of doubling to Ellen Pollak's suggestive reading of Aphra Behn's *Oroonoko* in a paper given at the South Central Modern Language Association Meeting in New Orleans, 1986: "Gender, Doubling, and Incest in Aphra Behn's *Oroonoko*."

6. THE RECEPTIVE READER

1. Lillian D. Bloom and Edward A. Bloom suggest that *Evelina*'s fairy-tale plot results from Burney's early sanguine fantasies about her own destiny, fantasies that progressively darkened and, in turn, darkened the novels after *Evelina*. "Fanny Burney's Novels: The Retreat from Wonder," *Novel* 12 (Spring, 1979); 215-35.

2. Patricia Meyer Spacks' work in *Imagining a Self*, 158-92, suggests that writing was, for Burney, a means of psychological defense.

3. See Annie Raine Ellis's summary of Burney's conflict with Crisp over sharing her "Tingmouth Journal" with his sisters in *ED* 1: 228-29.

4. Newton's discussion of *Evelina* in *Women, Power, and Subversion* makes the parallel point that Burney's position as "a genteel unmarried woman could

force her to credit and give value to ideologies about her experience which at some level she understood to be untrue" (39).

5. Poovey theorizes that the role of a "proper lady"—the retiring and submissive attitudes appropriate to the female denizens of the domestic and private sphere—cut women off from direct uses of power, reserving their energies for a strictly supportive relationship with the public, male world. *Proper Lady* 3-47.

6. See Hemlow, *History*, 53-77, for an account of Burney's introduction into the Thrale household by her gregarious father.

7. See *ED* 1: 222-23 for Susan Burney's breathless account to Fanny of their father reading *Evelina*, and *DL* 1: 35-37 for Burney's agitated response to her father's praise.

8. Hemlow, *History*, 105-38.

9. See Hemlow, *History*, 135-36 and *DL* 1: 166-72 for an account of Burney's distress.

10. Hemlow, *History*, 137.

11. Frances Burney, *Camilla; or, a Picture of Youth*, ed. Edward A. Bloom and Lillian D. Bloom (London: Oxford UP, 1972), 877-78. References to *Camilla* are to this edition and are indicated in the text.

12. Frances Burney, *The Wanderer; or, Female Difficulties* (London: Long-man, Hurst, Ress, Orme, and Brown, 1814) 5: 47-48.

13. Julia L. Epstein, "Fanny Burney's Epistolary Voices," *The Eighteenth Century: Theory and Interpretation* 27 (1986): 162-79.

7. *Camilla* and *The Wanderer*

1. Margaret Doody and Julia Epstein are both currently completing book-length studies that promise to do far greater justice to Burney's last two novels than the scope of this book allows.

2. I owe this point to Margaret Doody, "Pictures of Youth."

3. Adrienne Rich, "Jane Eyre: The Temptations of a Motherless Woman" in *On Lies, Secrets, and Silence: Selected Prose, 1966-1978* (New York: Norton, 1979), 92-93.

4. Castle, *Masquerade*, 55-56.

5. Cutting, "A Wreath," 57-67.

6. Luce Irigaray, *The Speculum of the Other Woman*, trans. Gillian C. Gill (Ithaca: Cornell UP, 1985), 46-55.

7. Castle, *Masquerade*, 22.

8. Russo, "Female Grotesques," 216.

9. Charlotte Charke, *A Narrative of the Life of Mrs. Charlotte Charke* (London, 1755; rpt. Gainesville: Scholar's Facsimiles & Reprints, 1969), 17-20.

10. Russo, "Female Grotesques," 216.

INDEX